# AAP
# AND
# KEJRIWAL

## GREAT EXPECTATIONS OR IRRATIONAL EXPECTATIONS

Rajnikant Puranik

ATLANTIC

PUBLISHERS & DISTRIBUTORS (P) LTD

Published by
**ATLANTIC**
**PUBLISHERS & DISTRIBUTORS (P) LTD**
7/22, Ansari Road, Darya Ganj, New Delhi-110002
Phones : +91-11-40775252, 23273880, 23275880, 23280451
Fax : +91-11-23285873
Web : www.atlanticbooks.com
E-mail : orders@atlanticbooks.com

Branch Office
5, Nallathambi Street, Wallajah Road, Chennai-600002
Phones : +91-44-64611085, 32413319
E-mail : chennai@atlanticbooks.com



Printed in India at Nice Printing Press, A-33/3A, Site-IV, Industrial Area, Sahibabad, Ghaziabad, U.P.

**Future generations are not going to ask us what political party were you in. They are going to ask what did you do about it, when you knew the glaciers were melting.**

*—Martin Sheen*

*To the fond memory of my late parents*

Shrimati Shakuntala

and

Shri Laxminarayan Puranik

# Preface

Emerging from the all-round support and the high of the Team Anna Agitation, the Aam Aadmi Party (AAP) had raised great expectations.

Its main planks were honesty, rooting-out of corruption, anti-VIP culture and participative democracy. The agenda was non-partisan, and was above and beyond caste, creed, region and religion. It was non-complex and easy to understand. It steered clear of all "isms". It appealed to all sections.

It particularly enthused the Delhiites. Delhi is a city of babus, nurtured on the debilitating bureaucratic socialism of the Nehru-Indira tint. Being a citadel of babudom, it is also a capital of the corrupt. Delhiites are witness to all-pervasive corruption and the flashy lifestyles of the corrupt. They are also victims of the red-beacon VIP culture flaunted shamelessly in their face—day in and day out—inconveniencing them, insulting them, and reminding them at each turn that they are lesser human beings.

The Congress having brandished its brazen corrupt hand in Delhi by the scams such as the CWG, and at the Centre through the record-breaking and mind-boggling 2G and coal-scam; and the BJP having painted itself in a corner through its years of corrupt and inept governance of the Municipal Corporation of Delhi (MCD), was ripe for the taking by the AAP, and it did not fail to pluck the low hanging fruit.

Circumstances apart, it goes to the credit of the AAP that they employed innovative fund-collection techniques, effectively leveraged social media, conducted intensive house-to-house campaign, came up with promises and manifesto that appealed to the public, and won the mandate, despite intensive mud-slinging and negative campaign against them by the opposition, which had far more resources.

But, would the AAP measure up? Would they come good on their promises? Would the great expectations of the public from them be fulfilled? It is one thing to ride to election-victory on top of the tall promises and assurances of "being different", and quite another to actually come good on the promises and prove through your actual conduct that you are indeed "different".

So, how does AAP look as of now: 11 May 2015. Things have been so fluid that what holds for now may not hold for future. There is much that the AAP has to prove and to demonstrate in practice in the next one year for anyone to give a judgement on it. As of now, one can only comment on what has already happened so far, what might happen, and what one hopes ought to happen in future.

First, the positives. The AAP has indeed fulfilled some of its promises. It is demonstrating innovative thinking to tackle several areas. You can't accuse it of corruption or dishonesty—a major asset in the Indian political scenario.

While several prominent members of the AAP have resigned, some including Prashant Bhushan (PB) and Yogendra Yadav (YY) have been thrown out. However, one would prefer to judge the party on what it does for the people, rather than on these internal issues. And, in any case, throwing out of PB-YY and their allies could be a case of good riddance, not because they are "bad" people, but because the poverty-perpetuating and the misery-multiplying globally-failed socialist-marxist-communist ideas they espouse and with which they wished to dominate the AAP are not in the national interest.

While the young people the AAP fortunately abounds in do have forward-looking ideas, sadly, despite the exit of

PB-YY, there is no dearth of stale leftists-socialists-JNU-types in it who would stick to populist nonsense to fool people and get votes à la Congress, SP, TMC, CPM. Only time will tell who triumphs. Would AAP be another Congress (perhaps "rather-clean" Congress) or would it be a party that genuinely works in national interest?

## Postscript

As mentioned in this book, it was hoped that with the passage of time the Indian public would witness increasingly better results from the two new governments: the Modi government at the Centre and the Kejriwal's state government in Delhi. However, during the interval between the completion of this book and its actual date of publication, that hope has been unfortunately belied to some extent. While the Modi government has taken a number of good steps, and it is certainly far, far superior to the previous UPA, it has failed to measure up to the expectations and its own promises. On the other hand, much was expected from the new experiment: the AAP. With a heavy heart one has to admit Kejriwal's government, while it has taken several commendable steps, has been a bit of a disappointment. Both have still several years in power. Let's hope they would rise to the challenge.

**Rajnikant Puranik**

# Table of Contents-I: Outline

# Table of Contents-II: Detailed

# 1

# PRELUDE: TEAM ANNA AGITATION

*To oppose corruption in government is the highest obligation of patriotism.*

—G. Edward Griffin

*Team Anna agitation against corruption and for Jan Lokpal Bill was like a festival of democracy.*

There would have been no Aam Aadmi Party (AAP) or Arvind Kejriwal, as we know him now, had there been no Anna's agitation against corruption and for the Jan Lokpal Bill. So, let's first get an overview of that landmark event.

## Background

Nehru, unfortunately illiterate on what makes a nation rich and prosperous, had laid concrete foundations of India's misery by thoughtlessly imitating the Russian model and adopting poverty-perpetuating and misery-multiplying socialistic economic system that has been successful in NO country in the world. His populism-driven daughter, rather than reversing Nehru's disastrous policies, indulged in much-much-more of the same, thereby converting India into a License-Permit-Quota Raj ruled at the mercy of the corrupt, incompetent Babudom and dishonest, venal politicians. In the geometric progression of generation-to-generation falling standards of the Nehru-Dynasty, Rajiv Gandhi scaled new heights, rather new depths.

The cumulative effect has been mass hunger, poverty, wretchedness and untold misery. The periods of Narsimha Rao and Vajpayee were like silver linings in the dark clouds that had engulfed the nation, but the lengths of their rules were limited, truncating the many goods they could have delivered.

Regrettably, the people of India unwisely brought back the Nehru Dynasty in 2004 for a decade-long drag. As mentioned above, the geometric progression of generation-to-generation falling standards of the Nehru-Dynasty became even pronounced in the decade of Sonia-Rahul dominated UPA-rule beginning 2004. Corruption and scams became endemic.

While the progress and economic development took a plunge, huge corruption scandals and scams involving top UPA politicians and bureaucrats began to emerge one after the other in a never ending sequence, each bigger and more brazen than the previous, with mind-boggling figures. Adarsh Housing Society Scam, Radia Tapes, CWG Scam, 2G-Spectrum Scam, Tatra Truck Scam, Coal Scam, Agusta Westland Chopper Scam, and so on. Going by the money earned by the Modi-government in the recent coal auctions, the *UPA Coal Scam* was worth lakhs of crores!

All this infuriated the general public and it had to find a channel to vent its anger. That channel was the anti-corruption *Jan Lokpal Agitation of Anna Hazare and Indian Against Corruption* (IAC).

## 1st Phase: Anna's Hunger Strike, April 2011

*It is the duty of youths to war against indiscipline and corruption because they are the leaders of tomorrow.*

—Ifeanyi Enoch Onuoha

Anna Hazare had demanded formation of a joint-committee comprising government and civil society representatives to draft a suitable Lokpal (ombudsmen for the Centre) and Lokayuktas (ombudsmen in the states) Bill. Upon rejection of the request by Prime Minister Manmohan Singh, Anna began his hunger strike on 5 April 2011 at Jantar Mantar in New Delhi.

About 150 persons joined Anna in fasting. Anna wanted the agitation to remain apolitical, and disallowed politicians who wanted to share stage with him. Protests quickly spread to other metros and state capitals—even abroad in the US, the UK, France and Germany. Protests and public pressure began to have its effect.

Cabinet Minister Sharad Pawar was made part of the GoM (Group of Ministers) responsible for reviewing the draft Lokpal Bill. However, succumbing to the public pressure and a snide remark from Anna on Sharad Pawar (those alleged to be corrupt drafting an anti-corruption bill!), Pawar withdrew from the GoM on 6 April 2011. The government promised on 8 April 2011 that it would table the Lokpal Bill in the upcoming Monsoon session of the Parliament.

On 9 April 2011, the government agreed to establish a joint Lokpal drafting committee; and the same was later formed with five representatives of civil society, namely Anna Hazare, Shanti Bhushan (co-chairperson), Prashant Bhushan, retired Supreme Court Judge Santosh Hegde and Arvind Kejriwal; and five ministers, namely the then Finance Minister Pranab Mukherjee (chairperson of the Joint Drafting Committee), Telecom Minister Kapil Sibal, Law Minister Veerappa Moily, Water Resources Minister Salman Khursheed and Home Minister P. Chidambaram.

The first meeting of the joint Lokpal drafting committee was held on 16 April 2011. Hazare demanded that its proceedings be televised live but the government refused.

Incidentally, the government, which was dragging its feet in since 2010, finally ratified the *UN Convention against Corruption* on 13 May 2011, thanks to the side-effect of Anna's agitation.

Looking at the tardy pace of drafting of the Lokpal bill, Anna demanded more frequent meetings. Anna also said that the government had been postponing discussions on even simple issues; and that given such a state of affairs, the drafting would go on indefinitely. As expected, the government kept fooling around and placing many roadblocks, ultimately ensuring there was no joint draft—broadly, the government disagreed on almost everything.

Ultimately, nothing came of the joint Lokpal drafting committee; and the government declared it would come out with its own bill.

Hazare gave an ultimatum setting 15 August 2011 as the last date for passage of a strong Jan Lokpal Bill, threatening otherwise to intensify his anti-corruption agitation which he called as the "*Second Freedom Struggle*" and commencing next fast from 16 August 2011.

## 2nd Phase: August 2011 Agitation

Rather than doing something tangible against corruption and in favour of the Jan Lokpal Bill, the Central government through the Delhi Police, that comes under it, issued Prohibitory Orders under section 144 on 16 August 2011 to abort Anna's scheduled protest. On the pretext that Hazare and his group "intended to defy the Prohibitory Orders", they arrested them all, including Anna, Kiran Bedi, Arvind Kejriwal, Manish Sisodia and Kumar Vishwas, and sent them to Tihar Jail. The arrests set off protest all across India. To stem the spreading protests and the unanticipated bad publicity, the Delhi Police decided to release them all from Tihar Jail.

Hazare, however, refused to leave Tihar until the government agreed for unconditional permission for protests at Jai Prakash Narayan National Park, and permission to him to fast for 15 days at Ramlila Maidan against corruption. On 19 August 2011, Hazare left Tihar and headed in a huge procession to Ramlila Maidan.

The agitation forced a debate on the Jan Lokpal Bill in the Parliament. Both houses of the Parliament agreed, in principle, on the agitationists' demand for provision in the Lokpal Bill (1) for a Citizen charter, (2) for inclusion of lower bureaucracy under the Lokpal and (3) for establishment of Lok Ayuktas in the states.

Following the above, on 28 August 2011, Hazare announced suspension of his fast, hoping for passage of a strong Lokpal Bill by the Parliament, that would also include the above provisions.

## 3rd Phase: December 2011 Agitation

Adept at its deception game, the Parliamentary Standing Committee came up with a draft of the bill that Anna and group found highly unsatisfactory and contrary to the solemn promises made which had persuaded Anna to end his fast on 28 August 2011. Hazare, therefore, sat on a day-long fast at Jantar Mantar on 11 December 2011 protesting the unsatisfactory anti-graft proposals of the Parliamentary Standing Committee. Leaders from many opposition parties (BJP, CPI, CPM, SAD, TDP, BJD, etc.) shared the stage with Anna and spoke on the Lokpal Bill, hoping to remain in the good books of the public, though none of them was genuinely sincere about it.

Expectedly, nothing satisfactory transpired in the Lok Sabha in December 2011 forcing Anna to announce a hunger strike on 27-29 December 2011 at the Bandra-Kurla Complex in Mumbai.

The turnout of people at Mumbai was unfortunately underwhelming, and the protest at Mumbai fizzled-out. One of the reasons was also the feeble health of Anna.

Lok Sabha passed the Government Lokpal Bill (not the one suggested by Team Anna) on 27 December 2011. Team Anna claimed it was too weak to make a difference to the prevailing corruption. Even that weak Lokpal Bill could not be passed in the Rajya Sabha for want of time for voting! The Chairman of the Rajya Sabha abruptly ended the proceedings at 12:00 midnight on last day of the Winter session.

It was becoming increasingly obvious that neither the ruling party nor the opposition parties were really interested in an effective Lokpal legislation. They were only indulging in political manoeuvres to stall what might hit them.

## 4th Phase: March-June 2012

The Lokpal Bill that had been passed in the Lok Sabha in December 2011, but was stalled in the Rajya Sabha, was reintroduced in the Rajya Sabha in February 2012. However, that Rajya Sabha session too ended without the bill being passed! Why? The bill could not be timetabled for debate! The gross insincerity of the government was obvious.

Team Anna alleged that the ruling party had cheated them by introducing a useless, watered-down anti-corruption bill. Hazare declared that the protest movement would recommence and as a mark of protest he sat on hunger strike of a day on 25 March 2012.

Along with Baba Ramdev, Hazare undertook another one-day fast at Jantar Mantar on 3 June 2012 in protest.

### 5th Phase: July-August 2012

The fifth and final phase of the agitation began on 25 July 2012 at Jantar Mantar where fast was undertaken by various members of Team Anna, including Arvind Kejriwal. Being unwell, Hazare initially did not fast, but got involved four days later.

This phase included an additional agenda: protest against the government's refusal of an inquiry against the prime minister and 14 cabinet ministers, whom Team Anna had accused of corruption, for which they had prepared dossiers.

*We hang the petty thieves and appoint the great ones to public office.* —Aesop

The fast ended on 3 August 2012. Hazare later announced cessation of talks with the government looking to their indifference. Anna also declared end of protests under the name Team Anna.

Team Anna movement thus ended without, unfortunately, achieving anything tangible.

Political parties had been chiding Team Anna that in case they wanted a legislation like they desired (their Jan Lokpal Bill) they must fight elections, get elected, and then pass the bill. Arvind Kejriwal and team, having by then exhausted all avenues to get an effective Lokpal Bill passed, decided to call the bluff of the arrogant politicians and declared they would form a political party to teach them a lesson. Ultimately, the

Aam Aadmi Party (AAP) was floated on 26 November 2012. Anna Hazare dissociated himself from Kejriwal's team as he, in his words, "abhorred political quagmire".

### The Grand Atmosphere of TAA

The atmosphere of the TAA—Team Anna Agitation—was grand and carnival-like. It was festive and full of hope. The energy was infectious. Those who attended it described in superlatives how great it felt.

Unlike the Congress election rallies, the people came on their own, spending their own money. There were people from all walks of life. Rich and poor and middle-class. Literate and illiterate. Metro, urban, and rural. Males, females and children. Elderly and young. Hindus, Muslims, Christians, and others. People cutting across castes—Dalits included.

It was a committed crowd out to change the system. "I am Anna" caps were a great hit, what with even children donning them. It was a great way of bringing about a feeling of unity of beliefs.

"Doesn't your company or your boss have a problem your participating like this for days on end?" a young IT-techie was asked. "My boss is himself participating!" came the enthusiastic response.

Another young financial executive narrated later: "My boss was so happy about my participation, he later—after the agitation was over—invited me home for drinks and dinner. To hear all that happened there. An eye-witness account, rather, a participant's account. He and his wife were deriving vicarious pleasure from it. 'How I wish I too had joined! Only the pressing work held me down. But, next time I am going to be there, come what may. About time we took our destiny in our hands,' he remarked grandly."

A young professional was heard saying: "I now feel I ought to look beyond my job and professional ambition and do my bit for the country."

Said another: "Talking about Annagiri, well, we can't be talking all those things about what ails India, the blunders of the Nehruvian era and the greater blunders of Indira and the Nehru-Indira dynasty, and then just sit at home or attend office and go on with life as usual."

Said a person who had come from the interiors of Haryana: "Anna provided us with an opportunity to participate in the nation's cause at least in a small way. We could not have frittered away that chance without feeling guilty. I am so happy I came all the way and participated."

"This participation has made me feeling very good. It has greatly helped reduce my cynicism," remarked an elderly Delhiite.

"I too used to feel nothing would come of these. Nothing would change. But, now I feel there is some hope that things can change, provided we all are supportive," remarked his colleague.

That TAA had inspired people from all sections of the society and particularly the educated-young into political activism was a huge plus.

How dramatically the methodology of the public movement had changed—social networking sites were the new fora. Facebook, blogs, twitter—all were harnessed for the cause. The way TAA had harnessed technology and social networking tools to mobilise people was really admirable.

### TAA a Success?

If the success of the TAA (Team Anna Agitation) is to be evaluated on the passage or otherwise of the JLB (Jan Lokpal Bill), then it was only a partial success, because although a Lokpal Bill was ultimately passed by the Parliament, it differed in many significant ways from the JLB, and even that watered-down bill was not passed by the end of the agitation in August 2012, but much, much later on 18 December 2013: 16 months after the TAA had folded up, and a whopping 52 years after it was first introduced in the Parliament! Although, as a consolation it can be said that even that belated passage would not have happened but for TAA.

However, if the success of TAA is evaluated on criteria other than the JLB, then it was a great success.

It fired up the imagination of the young, it lifted many out of their cynicism and feeling of hopelessness, it brought many honest and committed people into politics, and it led to formation of the Aam Aadmi Party (AAP), which in a record time after its formation is now ruling Delhi, and is endeavouring to follow the path of alternate politics, free, or largely free, from corruption, casteism and communalism.

### Success: How and Why?

Well, one main reason is this: *Quantitative changes lead to qualitative change.*

You keep heating water, it continues to remain a liquid—the form does not change—but heating it to 100 degree centigrade and beyond suddenly changes its form: turns it into steam. Gradual quantitative increase in temperature results in the qualitative change of liquid turning into gas.

You had been having corruption, but for over one year you had watched helpless as big, bigger, and even more big scams surfaced. And all you heard were falsehoods from the lawyers turned politicians turned party spokespersons. You watched in disgust the callous, corrupt, irresponsible politicians defending their positions or accusing those from the other political parties, in a reciprocal blame-game. How long could one watch such a dysfunctional parliamentary system. Even as the people at large were being ground down by ever-rising prices and finding it difficult to make the two ends meet, you had the disgusting spectacle of corrupt politicians, rather than being apologetic, turning even more combative and confrontational, and a PM, brandishing his personal honesty at the drop of a hat, defending the corrupt!

How long could people tolerate that blatant dishonesty. The sins had crossed the threshold, their quantitative aggregation had transformed into a qualitative uplifting call for action in the form of TAA.

The second reason was the issue raised. Corruption cuts across. All are affected by it in one way or the other. It is caste, class, region and religion neutral.

The third was the personality of Anna. He had been in the selfless service of the public for over two decades. He had a clean, honest image. His sacrifices were there for anyone to see. He owns nothing. He lives and sleeps in a mandir. The senior mischief-makers of the Congress tried to tar him, but their attempt backfired.

You had rogues like Digvijay Singh (Diggi) of the Congress mudding waters and criticising Anna; and the MSM (Main Stream Media) allowing him unlimited sound bites, without enlightening the audience on his dubious record. The fellow irresponsibly and callously wasted ten long years of the poor people of Madhya Pradesh (MP) as Chief Minister doing nothing constructive, and just playing dirty politics to cow down his detractors, that included Congressmen. Even as the Chief Minister, he mischievously supported Medha Patkar's *Narmada Bachao Andolan* (NBA). Why? Just to ensure the opposition-ruled Gujarat did not get water for its farmers and for its thirsty public. In the process, he even harmed his own state's interests. The rapid agricultural progress made in MP and Gujarat after the completion of Sardar Sarovar itself proves how anti-development, anti-farmer and anti-poor NBA's and Digvijay's policies had been. NBA and Digvijay, by delaying the project, managed to add several thousand crores to the expenditure. It is significant that after Diggi and the Congress lost power in MP, the NBA fizzled out.

Digvijay tried to take the blame away from Pakistan for the *26/11 Mumbai Terror Attacks* calling it the work of the RSS! And, such persons are given free run by the MSM!! A book named "*26/11: RSS ki Sazish*" (RSS Conspiracy) written by Aziz Burney, Editor-in-Chief of Urdu Sahara newspaper, was released by the Congress General Secretary Digvijay Singh on 6 December 2010 in Delhi, where Diggi heaped further rubbish on the organisation. Later, in January 2011, the writer of the book himself apologised for part of the stuff and the title of the book! Among other things, Burney said, "...Circumstantial evidence procured by the investigating agencies proves that my stand was wrong." Commented Maulana Mahmood Daryabadi of the All-India Ulema Council: "*If he was not sure who were behind the 26/11, he should not have opposed the view of the investigating agencies. He misled his readers.*"

Despite court's verdict, Diggi claimed: "*I stick to stand that Batla House encounter was fake.*"

Diggi's cultural upbringing got exposed when he called a woman Congress member of Parliament from Mandsaur in MP, Meenakshi Natrajan, a "100% *tunch maal*!"

On 17 December 2015, while he called Narendra Modi a Hitler, he addressed pro-Pakistani separatist Masarat Alam, who has been creating trouble in Kashmir valley, as "sahib"! Enough of Diggi! There is no limit to his mischief and his antics.

Coming back to Anna, his work speaks far louder than words. Anna has transformed his village, Ralegan Siddhi. He has also implemented alcohol prohibition, grain banking and water management successfully. People of his village and those of surrounding villages adore him.

Majority perceives the State as corrupt, unhelpful, insensitive, exploitative and often oppressive. Across caste, class and community, the politicians are disliked, distrusted and perceived as selfish, self-serving, promoting their own clan, and getting rich at the cost of the nation. Given that scenario, an agitation directed against the political class, and led by a group with a clean image, was bound to evoke support.

The most critical factor was the numbers. Had so many people cutting across age, sex, class, caste, region and religion not come out on the streets in such numbers nothing worthwhile would have happened.

### Positives of TAA

Summarised below are some of the positives of *TAA—Team Anna Agitation*. First the **JLB** (***Jan Lokpal Bill***) positives. (***P1, P2***, *...for positives.*)

- **JLB-P1:** A positive and active action by the public to tackle the menace of all-pervasive corroding corruption.
- **JLB-P2:** A Bill drafted not by the self-seeking, indifferent bureaucrats, but by members of the public, after a wide-ranging discussions—truly democratic.

- **JLB-P3:** An attempt at a strong and effective law to curb corruption.
- **JLB-P4:** Flexibility and Open-mindedness. JLB was not touted as a last word on what the law should be. TA was open for further improvement—but only improvement, not deterioration into an ineffective, toothless bill like the one that had been presented by the government.
- **JLB-P5:** Government and their spokespersons had got away with hiding, covering-up, misleading, fooling and lying for a very long time, but at a very heavy cost—they had lost people's trust. That situation had been brought about by lawyers—professionally used to lying—doubling as spokespersons. A good, strong and effective Lokpal Bill would have helped bring people's trust back in the government. Viewed from that angle, actually the government needed a bill like JLB more than the public which was demanding it.

Let's look at the **Other Positives (OP)**:

- **OP1.** Only for a short period leading up to the election time, the political class pretends to be accountable and humble, and soon after the same are over it comes into its true colours—indifferent, arrogant, and selfish. TAA was a way to force them to be accountable and humble all through. The message to the political class was resoundingly clear—deliver accountability and drop arrogance and complacency.
- **OP2.** TAA was a positive development and it was hoped it would lead to further demands—electoral reforms, legal reforms, police reforms, administrative reforms, and so on.
- **OP3.** Anna had also commenced the process of inculcating good values in Indians. Many of us may not be strongly principled in practice, but even then, a part of us yearns to be good—that part had received inspiration and a cause to fight for. TAA had injected that mass booster shot of morality.

- **OP4.** For the first time since independence one saw youth take to streets not to destroy property or hurt others or take up a partisan regional or religious or caste issue, or to jostle for leadership and promoting self in the process, but to fight for a selfless cause of making Indians more honest and India a more honest nation.
- **OP5.** Hopefully, the people at large would have realised that it was their duty to participate in the electoral process and vote in the elections to select a right candidate, rather than sitting at home or going on an outing, regarding election day as a paid holiday.
- **OP6.** Not only that they would have realised that they needed to rise above caste, region and religious considerations and vote for an honest candidate.
- **OP7.** TAA demonstrated that mass action is also a part of the parliamentary process; and that general public can give inputs for law-making and raise relevant questions. People's participation strengthens democracy.

## Anti-Anna FAQs: How an MSM Section Stood Exposed!

One more positive of TAA was that it exposed many politicians and also a section of the MSM.

It was interesting and revealing to notice a plethora of questions against the Jan Lokpal Bill, TAA and Annagiri posed by the politicians, select editors, and by the wise essayists on the editorial page, or the op-ed page, or the *Think! Reflections* page, or the *All That Matters* page, or the *Opinion* page or in "*National Interest*". Also, those by the chronic debaters on the TV; by the veteran anchors pushing their words into the interviewee's mouth; and by the lawyer-spokespersons from the political parties busy doing their professional duty of projecting right as wrong and wrong as right.

Let's examine their pleas one-by-one. Let's take it category-wise to avoid, to the extent feasible, repetition and mixing-up.

Let us take the first category of FAQs.

Incidentally FAQ in this context also expands to *Frivolous, Arrogant Questions* manufactured by a class of intellectuals who think they have the monopoly on truth and who "really" know what is in the "national interest". They are also the persons cheesed off on "how can anything important happen in the country without our approval".

## FAQ-Category-1: Find fault with the Jan Lokpal Bill (JLB) itself

*FAQ-1.1: JLB is draconian.*

What was meant by that term "draconian". Were punishments advocated draconian? No, they were reasonable. Did those critics want it to be soft on the white collar?

*FAQ-1.2: JLB is too all-encompassing.*

That was because corruption too is all-encompassing. Did they want some to be left out? Why?

*FAQ-1.3: JLB would make the Lokpal institution too unwieldy.*

You have courts spread all across: big or small appropriate to the place. You have police stations spread all across. By this definition, they are therefore unwieldy and undesirable. How would Lokpal be unwieldy? It would not be one single office in the nation's capital handling corruption-related matters of the whole country. There would be a Lokpal at the Centre, Lokayukt office in the capital of each state, and also district offices. If there is more work—more corruption—to handle, there would be that many more Lokpal resources to handle them. Does one say that Infosys or Tatas are unwieldy, and therefore undesirable, as they have too many staff and too many offices to handle?

*FAQ-1.4: JLB would make the Lokpal a Super Authority—more powerful than even the PM.*

Justices of even lower courts can pass order against a minister. Does that make justices of even lower courts more powerful than ministers? Police can move against a PM for wrong doing. Does it make police more powerful? Similarly, in matters of corruption, Lokpal can move against a PM. What is wrong with that? Should PM be exempt from action against her or him for corruption?

*FAQ-1.5: Why not NAC and other drafts on Lokpal Bill? Why only Anna's?*

Team Anna had no objection to considering as many alternatives as were proposed by various groups. Only, they could not be a pretext to delay the bill. The Parliamentary Standing Committee could have worked hard—worked sixteen hours a day—and considered all aspects. Having delayed the bill by four decades, a time limit, a target had to be fixed. If the Parliamentary Standing Committee members were sincere and hard-working, they could have done the needful in one month. Another aspect was that it could not merely be a mix of the drafts of JLB, NAC, Sarkari, and so on. It was not a give-and-take affair, a *baniagiri*. Parliamentary Standing Committee had to spell out with reason why a given point of JLB stood rejected and replaced with an alternative or why certain additions, modifications and deletions were proposed—and the same must have been subjected to a public debate too. What was required was a Lokpal Bill that could effectively tackle corruption, and not some comprise between contending factions.

*FAQ-1.6: Why should Parliament pass only JLB? That's an absurd demand from Team Anna.*

Despite Team Anna having repeatedly made it clear that they were open to JLB being modified, strengthened and made better, their only concern being that it should not be diluted and made ineffective; you still had the *wise-critics* obstinately putting words in their mouth and writing things like: "...I'm disturbed by his repeated insistence that Parliament pass his Jan Lokpal Bill and none other. It's a defiance of the Parliament's right to pass whatever bill it thinks fit. Whilst each one of us can protest and complain about what Parliament does or doesn't do, to insist that it follow our dictates is another matter. It's subordinating Parliament to our personal preference. Remember

Parliament represents the collective will of the country. By definition that's greater than any individual." Unnecessary and unwarranted words—may be as wise-critics they had to fill-in their mandatory weekly columns!

*FAQ-1.7: What if the Lokpal itself becomes corrupt?*

What if CVC chief or CAG chief or judges of the Supreme Court themselves becomes corrupt? Should we then not have those institutions? There is a way to deal with them if they become corrupt. Similarly, JLB provided for dealing with corrupt functionaries of the Lokpal institution.

*FAQ-1.8: But, can JLB remove corruption 100%?*

Were those *wise-critics* contending that not unless JLB removed corruption 100% was it of any use? Well, if JLB brought down corruption by even 40% it was good enough. There were so many other steps that needed to be taken to remove corruption in a big way. JLB was only one of those steps. Nobody was contending that JLB was by itself enough to root out corruption. But, just because JLB was not a complete solution, did it mean it should have been thrown out?

Who had said JLB would wipe out corruption? Even Team Anna claimed it would help reduce corruption, not wipe it out. Other measures too were required, but one had to take them up one-by-one. Tackling corruption was certainly not a one-bill affair. It was not that simple. Team Anna also knew it. They did not need to learn it from those *wise-critics*. But, one had to start somewhere. Let JLB at least be done. Then take up other measures.

To give a parallel, there are so many steps that are required to be taken to remove poverty. There is no one single solution. Are we then to argue that unless a given poverty-removal proposal helps remove poverty 100%, it is not worth implementing?

Those *wise-critics* had not only questioned Hazare's credentials but also resorted to sophistry that while TAA would not wipe out corruption, it would surely harm democracy!

Now let us look at the second category of FAQs.

### *FAQ-Category-2: Anna's methods are undemocratic and inappropriate*

*FAQ-2.1: How can Anna & Co appropriate the parliamentary function of making laws?*

Did anyone, including *Anna & Co*, prevent parliament from carrying out its function, among other things, of passing a Lokpal Bill? They had been fiddling with it for the last four decades. If they failed to do their job, someone has to nudge them into doing it. They had been in no hurry about it, because it affected them and the babus adversely. *Aaa bail seeng maar*—why invite problems on oneself? Babus were the biggest beneficiaries, apart from the netas, of not bringing in a strong Lokpal.

Further, was Team Anna passing the bill? No. They had no authority. The bill had to be passed by the parliament only—nobody else could pass it. So how was it a case of appropriating parliamentary function? Team Anna was merely prodding them to do their work.

Did those *wise-critics* object to Team Anna providing the draft of the bill, on the pretext that it was not their job? If those whose job actually it was to frame the law failed in their duty, and deliberately came up with a very weak law, only to fulfil a formality, what was to be done? Somebody had to tell them what the law should be.

Besides, it was a suggestion. Team Anna had never been rigid that the bill had to be what they had drafted. All they said was that they had put in their best and sincere efforts to come up with a bill that could prove effective in curbing corruption. They had never said theirs was the last word on it. If it could be improved upon, they were certainly open to it. What—with good reason—they were worried about was that in the name of accommodating other views the bill should not have been watered-down and made ineffective: that was a legitimate concern, given the ways of the government and the bureaucracy.

Perhaps the *wise-critics* came out with those points for they felt cheesed off their 'wise' counsel was not taken. The general opinion of the public was let that class of *intellectuals-who-*

*know-better* keep cribbing TAA was a threat to democracy, let them entertain the false notions that what they say was sane and wise and carried weight—although no one bothered about them anyway. The overwhelming majority correctly believed that TAA was one of the defining moments in our post-independence political history.

Perhaps those *wise-critics* were not aware of what the US Supreme Court Justice Felix Frankfurter had remarked: "In a democracy, the highest office is the office of the citizen."

One interesting aspect was that although the ruling-class politicians and those *wise-critics* had been crying hoarse about the parliamentary function having been usurped by Team Anna, the fact, which they also knew, was that the parliamentarians had never really exerted themselves on any law or bill, what to talk of JLB. It must actually have come to them as a shock that so many people in the street were talking about the law and dissecting it, something they had themselves never done. Mostly bureaucrats and some experts frame the laws, which without much discussions get passed in the parliament. Here was general public—civil society—being accused of trying to do things which they, the politicians, were supposed to do, but had never done!

*FAQ-2.2: Did not Anna's agitation amount to blackmail? Was it not coercive?*

Was Anna or any member of his team trying to extract something personal for himself or herself? Did they stand to gain materially? No. How was it a blackmail then? Were these *wise-critics* alleging that Mahatma's methods were methods of blackmail?

Did Anna resort to fast without first having exhausted all other avenues of talks and dialogues and debate? No. It was when he realised that nobody in the government was prompted into doing anything through mere talks and dialogues that he had to resort to a more effective way to make the government do the needful.

*FAQ-2.3: Anna's agitation was undemocratic. Was it not a threat to democracy?*

It may have been "undemocratic" as per some private definition of "what is democratic or otherwise" manufactured by the *wise-critics*. In truncated version of democracy for the *wise-critics*, the citizens' role was only to vote once every five years!

Were Gandhiji's fasts undemocratic? Was JP's agitation undemocratic? Was agitating against corruption undemocratic? In case it was, so be it.

One of the biggest threats to democracy is corruption, and any move to root it out can't be undemocratic. It would be necessarily pro-democracy. TAA was indeed an *utsav* (a festival) of democracy, as somebody had remarked. Democracy is strengthened when people, who are otherwise passive, take time off to fight for their country.

Anna's agitation could have been a threat to the corrupt and to the vested interests, but certainly not to democracy.

It were the politicians—alarmed by the slipping away of the ground beneath their feet—who were creating a spectre of crisis. Prime Minister Manmohan Singh's alarmist claim that the path that Anna Hazare "has chosen to impose his draft upon parliament is totally misconceived and fraught with grave consequences for our parliamentary democracy" was sheer bunkum. How Manmohan Singh discharged his responsibility as a prime minister and what he did to the nation and to the parliamentary democracy is now in everyone's knowledge. How could a peaceful civil society action demanding enactment of effective laws in the interest of the nation could ever be a threat to democracy? It was the dragging of feet over them and their non-enactment that was a threat to democracy. The real threat to democracy comes from the misdeeds of the politicians themselves and, of course, from the *wise-critics* who run-down such agitations without any rationale.

All those pompous talks of supremacy of Parliament and the majesty of our institutions was pulling wool over our eyes. Those institutions had long since been hollowed out and eaten up by corruption thanks to the very people who had been accusing Team Anna of disrespecting them. Where was their respect when they were destroying them. TAA could have ultimately restored respect to those institutions, because thanks to JLB of Team Anna and many other additional measures, they could have become corruption-free, or at least, less corrupt.

*FAQ-2.4: Was not fasting and forcing things on democratically-elected government undemocratic?*

Was Anna trying to force government into doing something sinister? There had been persons who had fasted for other causes, but they had failed to attract as much public support, and they could not bring the government to agree to them. Anna's cause had universal sympathy, that is why government had no alternative but to listen. Had Anna raised some inane or partisan or regionalist or communal or casteist or controversial issue there would have been little public support.

*FAQ-2.5: Was not Anna's agitation harming our democracy and denting our Constitution?*

Team Anna was actually contributing to strengthening of the democracy and the constitution by suggesting a strong law to curb corruption.

*FAQ-2.6: Was it not obvious that Team Anna had no respect for procedures?*

Since when those *wise-critics* had also become *wise-babus*—sticklers for procedures—and clever upholders of a rotten status quo. Why let a good thing get bogged down by procedures. Those same *wise-critics* would howl against red-tape in another context, but in the context of the bill they wanted to be fastidious with procedures! But, was Team Anna against procedures. All they said was do what was required, but don't postpone further, having already wasted four decades.

*FAQ-2.7: Parliament is supreme. How could Team Anna dictate to them?*

Who said Parliament is supreme. People are supreme and Constitution is supreme. Not Parliament. Parliament is one wing of governance voted by people.

*FAQ-2.8: Team Anna have no respect for parliament.*

Respect has to be commanded, not demanded. Respect should be a by-product of your good work and behaviour. You can't dictate, "*Respect me*!" It is like trust. Trust has to be earned and not demanded. It is for the parliamentarians to ponder why they are not respected and why the parliament has lost the trust of the people.

*FAQ-2.9: If Anna & Co wish to bring in their legislation, why don't they fight elections, win, and bring-in what they want? Why don't they follow the democratic, election-based parliamentary route?*

Were the government and the wise-critics telling us that fighting elections once in five years, getting elected, obtaining a majority, and then getting promises and demands fulfilled is the ONLY democratic way; and that there is no other democratic way through which public can have its demands met? That's crazy! And, what if the promises on the basis of which a party got the majority are not fulfilled by that party? Wait for another five years, elect another party, and hope it would fulfil the promises? Non-violent agitational methods, including fasting, are legitimate constitutional and democratic methods for the public to make the powers that be listen.

Electoral politics is not the only way for working for public good in a democracy.

*FAQ-2.10: How can there be any agreement with Team Anna? Whom do they represent? Certainly not the whole of Civil Society.*

Why did Indira Gandhi negotiate with Sheikh Abdullah? He didn't represent all of J&K. Why did Rajiv Gandhi have an accord with Sant Longowal? He didn't represent all Punjabis. Why was there an agreement with AASU, All *Assam Students Union*. They didn't represent the whole of Assam. They were not a political party either. All these were cases of dealings with unelected representatives. In these cases even the parliamentary approval was taken subsequently.

*FAQ-2.11: Wise-critics and the ruling party politicians also raised questions on constitutional propriety of dealing with Team Anna.*

Was it constitutionally proper to make Rajiv Gandhi the prime minister upon the death of Indira Gandhi? No meeting of Congress Parliamentary Party was held. Constitutional precedent dictated that the senior most cabinet minister should have become the interim PM, pending final election, like it had happened when Gulzarilal Nanda became PM. Rajiv was not even a minister. Breaking all traditions, Giani Zail Singh swore him as PM—only to show his loyalty to the Dynasty, ignoring what was appropriate, what was the constitutional precedent and tradition. One wonders if Zail Singh regretted his action later judging by what happened to the Sikhs in the anti-Sikh attacks upon the death of Indira and the beginning of the term of Rajiv as PM—Zail Singh's own car was attacked. Now, even if Rajiv can't be held responsible for the anti-Sikh attacks, surely he can be held accountable on several counts:

(a) for having failed to quickly bring the situation under control, at least in Delhi;
(b) for having failed to save precious lives and property of Sikhs;
(c) for not bringing the guilty to book;
(d) for the complicity of the government in scuttling all probes; and
(e) for his government giving good positions to many of those whose role was suspected in the carnage.

*FAQ-2.12: Wasn't Team Anna unnecessarily too rigid? How could they force things like that? It was not fair.*

Well, the reality was actually the reverse. Team Anna had never been intransigent. It was deliberately portrayed to be irrationally rigid by the ruling party politicians and the pliant section of the media and *wise-critics*. TA never claimed JLB was the last word. But, certainly they insisted on 'rationale' for changes to JLB. They needed to make sure that changes were for the good, and not to make the bill weak. It was the government which had stuck to its unbending position.

Team Anna has been flexible, but firm. Without that firmness and the obduracy of Anna nothing could be extracted from that shameless, lethargic, corrupt and status-quoist system.

The third category of FAQs.

### *FAQ-Category-3: Anna's agitation is superficial, rightist and regressive*

Unable to provide any solid reasoning for criticising the Anna agitation, the purpose of this category of questionings was to somehow discredit the agitation. The *Nehruvian-Marxist-Socialist-"Liberal"-Left*, thanks to whom India has gone to dogs and is a corrupt nation that forced TAA, sneeringly mouthed many of these questions, curling their lips and raising their eyebrows—exposing their trademark limited (Marxism does that) cerebral landscape.

They came from the same band of intellectual mercenaries who used to most fiercely endorse the Nehruvian and then the Indira's elusive search for socialism, even as both father and then the daughter, given their frighteningly wafer-thin understanding of economics and "what really makes a country prosperous", went in for populist measures that helped them win elections and power, but sadly, to the misfortune of poor, wretched, hungry millions, laid the foundations of India's misery, and consigned the promising independent India into the dark ages.

Currently, they advocate various anti-causes: anti-capitalist, anti-multinational, anti-globalization, anti-development, anti-fascist, anti-this, anti-that,...

Here are the FAQs under this category.

#### *FAQ-3.1: Anna's agitation was a superficial, urban middle-class affair.*

Why then were rural masses also with it. A contestant had come from a village in MP on the KBC TV show. He was a poor person of extremely modest means. He complained of absence of any pukka road to his village, and informed that on paper the road had been built and repaired many times. He said he had gone to Delhi to participate in Anna agitation, spending his hard-earned money, because he felt it was his duty to show such solidarity. What is the use of complaining, without doing anything about it—he argued.

Those *wise-critics* who claimed Anna's agitation was superficial and urban middle-class were actually themselves superficial and belonged to those sections of upwardly-mobile upper urban middle-class who volunteer as mercenaries for the establishment, expecting a suitable accommodation and reward.

Till then, those same people have been pillorying the middle classes for their poor voting record, for being too full of themselves—preoccupied with their jobs, families, cricket, consumerism and Bollywood—and for being too pre-occupied to take any interest in the civic and the political life. But, after they had voluntarily and enthusiastically come out on the streets for TAA to challenge the *chalta-hai* corruption and the rotten status quo, those same *wise-critics* were accusing them of impetuosity and lack of respect for the system!

### *FAQ-3.2: Wasn't the flag-waving enthusiasm of young people in the Anna agitation nothing but World Cup boisterousness?*

What's wrong with being as enthusiastic in the anti-corruption crusade? Is it not a positive sign? If the youth is waking up to the real issues, is it not something to rejoice about? Or, is it something to ridicule—as the *wise-critics* were doing!

### *FAQ-3.3: Anna's agitation was regressive, rightist and potentially fascist.*

That was the jargon of the irrelevant left-history has put them globally on the dung-heap of history, but in India, the jokers continue to fool people and mouth those inanities. Anything which does not fit-in with their hackneyed thinking is regressive and rightist. Leftists feel that only they are entitled to really represent the suffering masses, even though the masses have rejected them globally.

*FAQ-3.4: Where would agreeing to Anna's demand on Lokpal lead to? What if they demand scrapping of reservations subsequently? What if they came up with something anti-minority later? If Anna had his way he would set a precedent for Hindu fanatics to demand a theocratic State tomorrow or....*

Anna's agitation, unlike many agitations in the past, was becoming successful for several reasons. One, Anna carried credibility for fighting for the right and just causes. Two, Anna was himself an honest and upright person. Three, Team Anna comprised dedicated, honest and reasonable persons. Four, the specific issue of corruption raised by them had a universal appeal—it was non-partisan, and above caste or religion or politics. Five, the Jan Lokpal Bill was for a long time on the web and had been widely discussed and agreed as a good base. Six, the agitation had wide public support in view of the five previous factors.

There was no question of Team Anna coming up with demands like scrapping of reservations or something that was anti-minority? Team Anna comprised reasonable, liberal people. They were also very democratic. Even JLB was put up on the web and they went in for a wide-ranging discussions on it. They were prepared for a public debate on the JLB with the government and with those who differed from it.

If they were to come up with additional items in the future, they would obviously first go in for discussions with the public. In the worst case scenario, had they came up with the regressive demands as stated, they were never likely to receive public support. Those supporting Anna were not blind followers or fools, quite unlike say the Congress crowd and the Congress leaders who blindly kowtow to the Dynasty.

Going by the logic of the *wise-critics*, the lesson would have been "*do not allow a good thing, because if a good thing was allowed to happen, a bad thing might also follow!*"

*FAQ-3.5: Did Anna & Co really represent the Civil Society? How could a crowd of just several thousand represent the will of the people? Was not the agitation of Anna & Co mere media-driven?*

Those who had said so should have done some ground-level research in metro, urban, semi-urban and rural areas. They would have got the answer. The support for Anna's cause was much more widespread than was made out through the media.

That is why Team Anna had even thrown a challenge: "Conduct a nation-wide referendum!"

*FAQ-3.6: Communal forces were behind Anna's agitation.*

Just because certain so-called communal groups had supported Anna's agitation, the agitation did not become communal. Supposing certain thing proposed by Maoists is accepted by the Congress, does that make Congress communist or Maoist?

How could an agitation against corruption be communal? Did corruption affect only the Hindus?

*FAQ-3.7: Were not anti-Dalit and anti-Minority forces behind Anna's agitation?*

The worst sufferers of high-handedness, injustice and corruption have been the Dalits. How could the agitation be against them. Just because many active participants in the agitation may not have been Dalits, it did not mean the agitation was anti-Dalit. In fact, the agitation was religion-neutral and caste-neutral.

Such comments were actually an attempt to derail the agitation by stoking imaginary fears among Muslims, OBCs and Dalits—the old divide-and-rule colonial formula copied from the British by the Congress, which had paid them rich dividends in the past.

*FAQ-3.8: Were not the US, IMF and World Bank forces behind Anna's agitation?*

High time one discounted and ignored the leftists.

*FAQ-3.9: Were not anti-national forces behind the agitation?*

Were the Congress or the *wise-critics* redefining patriotism? Those against corruption were anti-national, and those for it were patriotic!

*FAQ-3.10: Did not waving of national flag, and chanting of "Vande Mataram", "Bharat Mata ki Jai" and "Ram Dhun" reflect domination of reactionary forces of the extreme right?*

Only the lunatic left and the sick secularists could mouth those idiocies. It was the national cause that had brought them together, hence the national symbols.

*FAQ-3.11: There was a nefarious design, and a hidden agenda behind Anna's agitation.*

True. Viewed from the angle of the corrupt babus and netas, the nefarious design was to root out corruption. And the hidden agenda was to come up with further agendas that might hurt the vested interests.

The fourth category of FAQs.

### *FAQ-Category-4: FAQs on Lokpal and Govt-NAC-Sonia-Rahul*

*FAQ-4.1: Wasn't Lokpal idea actually of Sonia that had been hijacked by Anna & Co?*

The Dynasty has been in the habit of taking or rather usurping credits due to others. Who brought independence to India?—Gandhi and Nehru. Others were insignificant, minor players. Who ushered economic freedom and liberalisation?—Not Narsimha Rao, it was Rajiv who started it. Finding that JLB had popular support, why not usurp the credit for it?

*FAQ-4.2: Isn't Rahul Gandhi's suggestion of Lokpal as a Constitutional Body a real "game-changer"? Wasn't Rahul Gandhi's speech in the Parliament on Lokpal and corruption highly significant and wise?*

Did Rahul say anything relevant in the debate? Did he say JLB should be accepted? And, if not, why? Or, what was acceptable and what was not, and why? He had nothing worthwhile to say. When the most important deliberations took place the next day in the Parliament, he was simply absent! That exposed his sincerity.

As for his suggestion being a game-changer, that was a term conveniently invented by the obsequious sycophants to accord him undeserved credit. When Anna sat for the initial fast, did Rahul propose the "game-changer"? In the many months leading up to the Government formulating its Lokpal Bill and tabling it in the Parliament, did Rahul make that suggestion? During the fast of Anna in August, 2011 did Rahul make that suggestion? No. Why didn't Rahul get his suggestion incorporated in the Government Lokpal Bill? Why was the Lokpal Bill presented by the government so toothless and ineffective? Why Rahul played no role then to improve it?

*FAQ-4.3: Many had questioned the impatience on the part of Team Anna. Why won't they let the due process happen?*

The actual problem was the trust-deficit in the government. They believed that once Anna broke his fast on mere "assurances" it would be back to the old ways. Don't do anything. Buy time. Find new excuses. Defame and discredit TAA in other ways. But, don't do the actual thing. Patience? Over four decades had passed for the bill to be in place!

There have been scores of cases of killing demands through delays and mere promises. Baba Ramdev's agitation was the most recent one. So many things were promised by the government in writing to stop Baba Ramdev from undertaking the fast and the agitation. Later, they beat up the people sleeping at Ramlila Maidan at 1 a.m. in the night and broke the agitation. But, what happened to the government's written promises? Nothing!

*FAQ-4.4: Team Anna was too demanding. You couldn't ride roughshod over the government like that. Anna should have known that fasts have their limits.*

Really funny such questions were raised. Was Anna demanding something for himself? Was he troubling the government to get a personal favour? If those *wise-critics* had a better way to achieve what Anna intends achieving, they should have spelt it out.

## WCs and the Belittling of TAA

*The person who has nothing for which he is willing to fight, nothing which is more important than his own personal safety, is a miserable creature and has no chance of being free unless made and kept so by the exertions of better men than himself.*

—John Stuart Mill

As has been mentioned before, one of the beneficial by-products of TAA was that it exposed many *WCs* (*wise-critics*), that included many politicians, media-persons and columnists, masquerading as wise-people out to defend national interests!

The *WCs* never missed a chance to belittle Anna and his cause. It was strange that these people with insight and foresight failed to grasp how Anna had made the government gasp for air in just five months. They failed to see that Anna even scored over JP in that he had managed to inspire and mobilise even the non-political class-people who had otherwise never came out on streets.

They even tried to divert the main issues of corruption, black-money and Lokpal to the indirect sycophancy of the Dynasty by debating and highlighting the "hard line" of Chidambaram and Sibal at the instance of Sonia and Rahul Gandhi in breaking Baba Ramdev's agitation, faulting the initial soft handling of Ramdev—as if the brutal treatment of the sleeping people at 1 a.m. in the night was something to be commended!

Any sensible and sincere government would have gracefully accepting the pathetic state of affairs, thanked Team Anna for highlighting the issue of corruption and coming with a good JLB, and would have promised to do the needful in the interest of the nation, and sought cooperation from Team Anna, the opposition parties and all others to root out the bane of corruption. This would have actually given credibility to them and would have strengthened their position. But, how the government and their *WCs* responded!

The first step of the Congress and the government and the *WCs* was to discredit the members of Team Anna. If they could make people believe that Anna and his team members were themselves not above board, where was the legitimacy of their anti-corruption agitation. Their mischief-monger-in-chief first came up with wild allegations. A CD was manufactured and circulated. A pro-Congress media-man got the CD conveniently authenticated from a government lab, and went to town with it. It was later proved to be bogus. A lawyer-spokesman dug out "proof" to nail Anna and heap abuse on him. It was very funny watching all that. Did those gentlemen think they had any credibility that people would listen to them.

With their smear-campaign not yielding the desired results, the Congress mobilised their overt and covert friends in the media and the academics and elsewhere to run-down JLB. This their mercenary army dutifully did. Articles upon articles by obliging editors and columnists and journalists and academics tried to take apart the JLB and TAA. As their pleas and arguments wore thin, there being no convincing reasons and logic behind them, they tried ridicule. Unfortunately for them, it were they who looked ridiculous, as their supposed jokes and ridicule fell flat, and cut absolutely no ice.

Then they tried bullying. "They would meet the same fate as Ramdev's!" they threatened. Those mad guys thought that would deter the activists. The government's penchant for subterfuge and low cunning was to be seen in practice to be believed. To what level could they fall!

Then they engaged their obliging editors and columnists and journalists and academics to talk about threat to democracy by such agitations. Issues were not discussed, proper reasoning was not advanced; instead a scare was created about takeover of governance, playing on people's fears over national security.

Then the government called upon their faithful NGOs and also the others—anyone who differed from Team Anna—to help muddy the water. Multiple alternate competing drafts of Lokpal bills appeared. One wondered what their originators were doing for so many months and years. As if the jholawalas in the NAC headed by Sonia had not done enough damage to the country, they obligingly came up advocating break-up of Lokpal into five different bills and not giving a single agency any power. People saw through the game.

Judging from how the government and the Congress and the *WCs* had reacted and handled the issue, there was one inescapable conclusion: the ruling class, that included *WCs*, had no genuine interest in disturbing a cosy, self-serving status quo.

Annoyed that they were forced into a corner, several parliamentarians promptly took the initiative to have the privilege notices issued against civil society members. Being too arrogant and drunk on power, it was not possible for them to do things gracefully. The culture of political haughtiness prevailed.

To illustrate the hostility of the *WCs* (*wise-critics*), a typical WC, in his column, noted with dismay the patriotic outpourings at Ramlila Maidan. He talked of pre-independence movements, of great leaders of the freedom and their comparative patriotic display in the context and so on to establish his intellectual credentials and his mastery of the past and the present, and then lambasted the patriotic tamasha on display at Ramlila Maidan. The concerned *WC*, of course, had a justified grouse. He complained that looking to the patriotic fervour of TAA, those who did not agree with them risked appearing unpatriotic-like him, his well-established *national interest* notwithstanding.

That particular *WC* normally writes English that jars and feels artificial and laboured. But, in the TAA context, eager to reassure his masters of his faithfulness and also his competence to be in their service with his "mastery" of both prose and poetry, he almost went lyrical running down what all others considered an inspiring sight of committed youth wholeheartedly participating in TAA-flags waving! He came up with a number of adjectives, metaphors, and contrived filmi lines. Like "*Bollywood-style hyper-nationalism*", "*mere paas tiranga hai, tumhare paas kya hai*?", and so on.

The fellow must have been feeling he was being very funny. But, in a wrong context, things don't sound funny, they jar! The words seemed to be coming from a guy spurned: whose wisdom everyone had ignored.

The fellow also posed: "*In any case, how can you use the Tricolour to fight your own constitutionally elected Parliament?*" So, don't ever wave a national flag while agitating. Because, the agitation would mostly be against those who rule. Such a wise counsel! Or, maybe he could have elaborated to what extent one could wave a flag. Because, earlier he had written that there had been too much of waving of national flag. May be once every five minutes might have been his idea of tolerable waving! And, not just the frequency, but the wavelength too. Perhaps he wanted to limit the sweep of the flag.

He also ridiculed the prominent among the agitators as "*those in their fancy dresses*"—they were wearing regional/ethnic outfits. What if they, whom he accused, viewed his attire as a fancy dress? Not having any worthwhile logic to his criticism, he endeavoured to engage in ridicule, but miserably failed. One found new dimensions in the *journalism of courage*!

What one found very odd, strange, frustrating and highly disappointing was that those intellectuals should have engaged in such hostility towards TAA.

Did they not know that corruption was a very big menace? Did they not realise that some way had to be found to curb it? Did they not recognise that even if Lokpal was not a complete solution, it was one among the several critical steps forward? Were they not aware that the governments and the political parties had been dragging their feet on it for many decades, and did not really favour a strong Lokpal? Did they not understand that but for agitations like that of Anna, the ruling class would not care?

If they did, then why rather than being supportive, they engaged in criticism and ridicule and belittling of the agitation and its members? Why were they supportive of the ruling dispension? Why were they coming to the rescue of the government? Were they no longer genuine journalists and true to their job as part of the fourth state?

If that was not so, then did they have a better alternative? Not something on paper—which they have been writing for decades—which changes nothing. If they could do it, let the *WCs* lead a movement or do whatever they deemed fit and deliver the results for the public. On one hand, they do nothing, except writing their hackneyed suggestions repeatedly on opinion-pages under different headings and with different turns of phrases, which no one bothers about. In other words, nothing that they do has any positive effect. On the other hand, when people like Anna and his team take the trouble, make so many selfless sacrifices, and try to achieve the desired result, those *WCs* simple engage in opposing them.

Really sad. The actions of those *WCs* amounted to this: We are incapable of delivering anything positive to the public, but we would try and see that you too fail in your mission. In the process, if the government of the day feels pleased, rewards can be expected.

## Mere Words, Inane Reasons and No Action

*You cannot legislate intelligence.*

Government kept saying corruption needed to be rooted out, but did little. The PM talked of coalition compromises. What compromise? Allowing corruption? Hard to believe a PM who kept brandishing his honesty could say that in the same breath! Or, did he have some private definition of honesty?

Had the government or the ruling party shown even a modicum of regret at such huge scams? Did we hear from the honest Prime Minister even a word of apology? Rather than acknowledging the governance deficit, expressing regret and concern about it and taking appropriate action to reassure the nation, the PM dismissively told us that there was no *magic wand* to fight corruption.

It was interesting to watch the government's response to 'expose' on corruption and scams, along with Sonia-Rahul who controlled them. You didn't find them ashamed or apologetic. You didn't hear them promising action and rectification. You didn't see them take any expeditious action against the culprits. What you saw and watched were a bunch of lawyers turned politicians turned spokespersons aggressively attacking whoever dared to find fault with the government, accusing instead the whistle-blowers and messengers of wrong-doing.

*Politicians were mostly people who'd had too little morals and ethics to stay lawyers.*

—George R.R. Martin

Any action that the government took was the action forced on them by the Supreme Court. And, even then they dragged their feet as much as possible to delay or obfuscate the issue. All that from a government whose PM brandished his personal honesty at the drop of a hat!

To thc honest PM and to the Congress headed by Sonia-Rahul went the credit of presided over and, in certain cases, actively engineering the collapse of every single democratic institution. Rather than taking action against the corrupt following the recommendations of its own institution, the CAG, the central government had been fielding its own senior ministers to attack and discredit the CAG. If PAC brought to light the wrong-doings, attack the PAC. If Ramdev dared to agitate against black-money (please see below), teach him a lesson. If Team Anna talked against corruption, start defaming the members and the agitation.

## Crushing of Baba Ramdev's Protest

Another notable event of 2011 was Baba Ramdev's agitation. Baba Ramdev began his hunger strike on 4 June 2011 at Ramlila Maidan where about 60,000 of his followers had gathered demanding action to bring back black money from foreign tax havens.

At midnight, police suddenly, without any provocation, raided Ramlila Maidan, lobbed tear gas shells, lathi-charged the sleeping gathering of men, women and children, and partially burned the place.

The then Prime Minister Manmohan Singh shamelessly claimed there was no alternative but to take the action that was taken. He brazenly avoided explaining why force was used on a peaceful gathering and why the sleeping public was attacked in the dead of the night at 1 a.m.! So much for our democracy!! It demonstrated how a government which is shamelessly corrupt can also be crassly brutal.

Sonia-Rahul, who (purely and pretentiously for getting votes) keep hyperventilating their empathy for the poor and tom-tom their pro-poor stand, remained silent on the barbarity perpetrated on the poor, peaceful, sleeping men, women and children in the dead of the night; and their prime minister and ministers even defended the act!

# 2

# THE DAWN OF AAP

*One of the penalties for refusing to participate in politics is that you end up being governed by your inferiors.*

—Plato, *The Republic*

*One of the key problems today is that politics is such a disgrace, and good people don't go into government.*

—Donald Trump

### Background

As detailed in the previous chapter, *Team Anna Agitation* (TAA) lead by *India Against Corruption* (IAC) for the *Jan Lokpal Bill* (JLB) reached a dead end by August 2012, thanks to the deviousness of the political parties across the spectrum: the intransigent, corrupt and scam-ridden ruling political party, the *Indian National Congress* (INC), and the wily opposition, that included the *Bhartiya Janata Party* (BJP), which wanted to run with the hare and hunt with the hounds, even as it blissfully but wrongly and foolishly thought it was too clever to be found out by the general public.

During the agitation, many politicians and *wise-critics* had chided Team Anna that if they desired a Lokpal Bill to their liking to be passed by the parliament, they should fight and win elections and then do so. With agitation not having yielded the fruit, many members of Team Anna and their supporters felt they ought to take up the challenge thrown by the corrupt, devious and arrogant politicians and teach them a lesson.

One of the forte of the *India Against Corruption* (IAC) was net-mastery and social-media savviness. They quickly conducted a poll among members and supporters and found there was a good support to head the political way.

However, Anna Hazare and several prominent members of Team Anna like ex-judge Santosh Hegde and ex-IPS Kiran Bedi were not in favour of going political. Anna believed only in non-political agitational methods. He regarded politics as a quagmire, and he advised all against dirtying their feet by walking into it. In any case, where was the money and the resources to fight elections, he argued. And, if one were to garner money and augment resources, one would become like other politicians: corrupt and unprincipled!

Younger people found in Anna Hazare's arguments a genuine reflection of the unfortunate ground realities as had existed for decades; yet the acceptance of the essence of Anna's position amounted to giving up without a fight; of being fatalistic about the dirty reality—that not only would it not change, but that it can't be changed! For optimists and do-gooders, Anna's arguments therefore appeared presumptuous, fatalistic, cynical, unreasonable and unconvincing—and even contrary to the potentials of a democratic system of government. It was as if Anna and those who agreed with him had resigned themselves into believing that the democratic system of elections could not be leveraged for the nation's good by the honest and well-intentioned; and that only the dishonest, moneyed and crafty, who were up to no good, could leverage it.

*Freedom isn't free. It shouldn't be a bragging point that "Oh, I don't get involved in politics," as if that makes someone cleaner. No, that makes you derelict of duty in a republic. Liars and panderers in government would have a much harder time of it if so many people didn't insist on their right to remain ignorant and blindly agreeable.*

—Bill Maher

People's agitations had severe limitations as the TAA supporters had practically seen for themselves. Politics was certainly the strongest weapon to change the nation. If only dirty people dirtied their feet in politics, how would dirty politics ever become clean? Further, if only the dishonest, moneyed and corrupt could triumph in elections, were non-political agitationists like Anna condemned to agitate non-violently and plead with those dishonest, moneyed and corrupt to carry out the desired changes for the good?

Extrapolation of Anna's logic seemed to lead to situations that were comic and bizarre. The *good guys*, like Anna & Co, through their non-participation in elections, make way for the *bad guys*. The *bad guys* get elected and sit in position of authority to decide on good and bad proposals, acts and reforms. The *good guys* then agitate non-violently through fasts, rallies, dharnas and other means to get the good work extracted from the reluctant *bad guys*, including restricting them (*bad guys*) from doing *bad things*! It's a farcical *good guys* vs. *bad guys* struggle, made never-ending by the *good guys* themselves through their convoluted thinking on "why not to fight elections" that works to the advantage of the *bad guys*. Bizarre as it may seem, it is as if the *good guys* have facilitated the permanent rule of the *bad guys*! Who then is responsible for democracy turning into a farce? The *good guys*!

*Politics is too serious a matter to be left to the politicians.*

—Charles de Gaulle

Fortunately, a major section of *Team Anna* and *India Against Corruption* (IAC) and their supporters led by *Arvind Kejriwal* (AK) decided they would challenge the *bad guys*, while remaining *good guys*. They decided to break the vicious cycle. They yearned to show *good guys* could also win elections.

## AAP Formation

*Vision is the art of seeing things invisible.*

—Jonathan Swift

On 2 *October 2012*, the *Gandhi Jayanti Day*, Arvind Kejriwal announced their team would be forming a political party. The Party's constitution was adopted on *24 November 2012*. *A National Council* comprising 320 people and a *National*

*Executive* of 23 were formed. Both were expected to expand to cover all districts and all classes. The party was formally launched on *26 November 2012*. It was fittingly, appropriately and thoughtfully named as the "*Aam Aadmi Party*" (AAP): party of the common person. AAP certainly had brilliant people with brilliant ideas. It was registered as a political party by the Election Commission of India in March 2013.

## AAP Ideology

*Politics is more difficult than physics.*

—Albert Einstein

Unlike the prevailing political system after 15 August 1947 where an oppressive foreign power transferred power to an Indian political elite that continues to arrogantly rule and exploit the common people of India who remain unheard and unseen except during the elections; the AAP seeks to be directly accountable to the people, inspired by the Gandhian concept of *swaraj*, with stress on people-participation, self-governance, community building and decentralisation.

Although much of what Kejriwal & Co propagate is clearly populist, socialistic and leftist, given the ideology and background of some of the people that comprise the group, Kejriwal grandly proclaimed: "We are aam aadmis. If we find our solution in the left we are happy to borrow it from there. If we find our solution in the right, we are happy to borrow it from there." In other words, the AAP does not wish to be bracketed as either leftist or rightist or centrist or left-of-centre or right-of-centre or anything else. It wants to take up "whatever is good". Be pragmatic. Be populist, in the process? Be even opportunist? Only time will tell.

However, any party with socialist, left-leaning economic ideology can never deliver for any nation—this the AAP would have to realise and appreciate from the global experience in this regard, else it would ultimately turn out to be yet another ineffective (for the nation) party like the Congress, or the communists, or the socialists.

# 3

# DELHI ELECTIONS 2013 AND AAP'S FIRST STINT AT POWER

*Politics is war without bloodshed while war is politics with bloodshed.*

—Mao Zedong

## Build up to Elections

The AAP has to be lauded for its innovative and effective social media campaign, and for house-to-house publicity through thousands of dedicated part-time and full-time young volunteers, who took time off from their jobs or resigned from their well-paying jobs to work for the party. They took up the party work as a national mission to clean up the country from corruption and misgovernance. That Arvind Kejriwal and his team could enthuse and inspire so many to sacrifice their cosy life and selflessly dedicate themselves to the party work demonstrated how ideas can move people.

The AAP began a protest movement in Delhi against "inflated" water and electricity bills in March 2013, urged Delhi citizens not to pay the same, demanded an audit of power and electricity supply in Delhi by the CAG. Kejriwal began an indefinite fast on 23 March 2013 to mobilize public, and ended the same on 6 April 2013.

The AAP supported the agitation by Delhi auto rickshaw drivers on 10 June 2013 protesting the Delhi government's ban on advertisements on auto rickshaws.

It goes to the credit of Arvind Kejriwal and his team that they could convince a large section of the middle class, the urban poor and disadvantaged, and the young professionals and college-going youth so magically that most of them became AAP's committed supporters.

## Delhi Elections 2013

The AAP made its electoral debut in the 2013 Delhi legislative assembly election. The AAP published its election manifesto on 20 November 2013 promising, inter alia, to implement the Jan Lokpal Bill within 15 days of coming to power.

Attempts were made by the established political parties opposed to the emergence of the new, fledgling party to somehow tar them. Among those efforts was a sting operation conducted on the AAP by one *Media Sarkar* in November 2013. It sought to discredit two prominent leaders of the AAP, Kumar Vishwas and Shazia Ilmi, by trying to show that they had agreed to extend their support to some people seeking assistance with land deals and other financial arrangements in return for donations in cash to AAP. The charges, however, fell flat.

The Delhi legislative assembly elections were held on 4 December 2013, and the results were announced on 8 December 2013.

Hard work of the AAP leaders, members, volunteers and supporters bore fruit. Their clean image and sincerity impressed people. Voters reposed trust in them. Their debut into politics proved successful. They unexpectedly won 28 of the 70 seats, emerging as the second-largest party after the BJP, which won 31 seats. Their vote percentage was 29.49%.

With no party obtaining a majority, ways and means of forming a government were explored by the BJP and the AAP, the two parties with largest number of seats. Although the BJP with 31 seats had 3 seats more than the AAP, it could not get others to support it so as to cross the half-way mark of 35.

The only way then for Delhi to have a government was for the AAP to get others to support it. The Congress with 8 seats declared it would support the AAP. A few others also supported taking the AAP+ tally beyond 36.

However, it was a dilemma for the AAP. They had fought against the Congress calling it totally corrupt. Would it be proper to take their support? The Congress obliged. It promised them unconditional support. The AAP was in two minds. To resolve the dilemma, the AAP decided to conduct a referendum among its voters: "Should the AAP form a government?" The response to the referendum was an overwhelming "Yes". That settled the issue.

Arvind Kejriwal finally took oath as Chief Minister of Delhi on 28 December 2013 at the historic Ramlila Maidan, along with his six cabinet ministers, Manish Sisodia, Somnath Bharti, Saurabh Bhardwaj, Rakhi Birla, Girish Soni and Satyendra Jain.

## Post-Elections Work

Among the steps that the AAP took after assuming power were: announcement of subsidy-driven reduction in electricity bills for up to 400 units; ordering of an audit of power distribution companies; announcement of 20 kilolitres of free water per month for the homes with metered connections—however, payment of 10% more upon exceeding of that limit; scrapping of FDI in multi-brand retail in Delhi; establishment of an anti-graft helpline for citizens.

The plan of conducting Janata Durbars (public hearings with ministers) were abandoned following the initial setbacks and mismanagement.

## Controversies

Prashant Bhushan of AAP had publicly spoken against the *Armed Forces (Special Powers) Act* in Jammu & Kashmir, and had talked of a referendum in that state. In protest, the AAP's office in Ghaziabad was attacked.

AAP Law Minister Somnath Bharti had demanded action against the police officials who he claimed had failed to take appropriate action relating to allegations of wrong-doings in the neighbourhood popular with immigrants from Uganda and

Nigeria. Demanding action, Kejriwal and group staged protests and dharna at Rail Bhavan on 20 January 2014 against the Union Home Ministry, and also pressed for transfer of the direct control of the Delhi police from the Union Home Ministry to the Delhi government. However, such agitation by a person in power who was expected to deliver on his election promises did not go down well with the media and the people, and attracted heavy criticism from the opposition. Kejriwal somehow extricated himself from the embarrassing situation of his own creation after the Delhi Lieutenant Governor Najeeb Jung provided him a fig leaf to end his fast after two days.

On 11 February 2014, the AAP Chief Minister Arvind Kejriwal enacted another drama to impress people about his anti-corruption and anti-corporate credentials. He did something which was not really within his jurisdiction: he ordered the Delhi *Anti Corruption Branch* (ACB) to file an FIR against the chief of Reliance Industries Ltd., Mukesh Ambani, Union Petroleum Minister Veerappa Moily and former Union Petroleum Minister Murli Deora under the *Prevention of Corruption Act* for alleged collusion to raise prices of natural gas from the KG basin.

## Abandonment of the Mandate

The AAP introduced the Jan Lokpal Bill in the Delhi Legislative Assembly in February 2014, seeking to fulfil its promise in its election manifesto.

The Lieutenant Governor of Delhi Najeeb Jung advised the Assembly Speaker to table the bill as per the laid-down procedure of first obtaining his consent and that of the Centre—and that not doing so would be unconstitutional. The Congress and the BJP supported the view of the Lieutenant Governor; and even stated that they were not opposed to the bill, but wanted proper procedure to be followed. The AAP government, however, contended there was no need to obtain prior approval of the Centre or the Lt Governor, and tried tabling the bill. Being in minority, they were not successful.

On the pretext that the other parties were not supporting the legislation, the AAP government resigned on 14 February 2014, after it had been in power for mere 49 days.

## The Aftermath

The aftermath of the abandonment of power proved very costly for the AAP.

It disenchanted many of their supporters—not just their voters in Delhi, but many of their supporters all over India. Damning analysis and derisive comments flowed freely:

Arvind Kejriwal & Co are only agitators, they neither can, nor want to govern and deliver. Knowing they won't be able to deliver on their wild promises, they latched on to a convenient excuse of lack of support for their Jan Lokpal Bill and resigned. When it was a question of assuming power given their lack of majority, they made a lot of song and dance about first ascertaining the public opinion through a referendum and obtaining voters' approval; but when it was a question of relinquishing power, or rather, running away from responsibilities, they did not deem it fit to ascertain the opinion of the public. All their "swaraj" and "people-driven rule" is a deception and a self-serving drama. Arvind Kejriwal is actually over-ambitious. The Delhi-support led him to believe he had pan-India support. Why then be satisfied with being just a CM of a state that is not even a full state? Why not encash the surge in public support for the AAP to stake claim on the PM's chair? Why not expand the AAP all over India? Why get locked down governing Delhi? Why not instead use the precious time and resources to campaign for Lok Sabha all over India?

There were also sympathetic and defensive voices, and rationalising logic:

It wasn't worth continuing in power in Delhi on the Congress-provided crutches. The history of the Congress treachery is well-known. What had Rajiv Gandhi done to Chandrashekhar? They are untrustworthy. Come re-election and we would gain absolute majority—so why regret. Ours has been a very smart move. Now that we are free from the onerous administrative responsibilities of governing Delhi, we can properly focus on Lok Sabha elections. As for Delhi, we would anyway win it hands-down with full majority when elections are re-held, provided of course we explain to the people properly and do smart publicity.

Unfortunately for the AAP, the public refused to buy their arguments and didn't get convinced. The public showed them their place in the Lok Sabha elections.

# 4

# 2014 TROUGH, FOLLOWED BY THE CREST OF 2015 ELECTIONS

*The goal in the end is not to win elections.*
*The goal is to change society.*

—Paul Krugman

## Attempted Pole Vault: Lok Sabha Elections 2014

Blinded by its success in the Delhi Assembly elections, the AAP began dreaming big and fielded a massive number of candidates all over the country for the 2014 Lok Sabha elections—candidates in 434 seats out of the total all-India seats of 543. Many well-known personalities joined the AAP, and were given the tickets for fighting the elections.

The AAP and Kejriwal were so brimming with over-confidence that they boasted that whosoever contested from AAP ticket in Delhi would win. This led them to field strong candidates including Kejriwal from constituencies other than Delhi. In March 2014, Kejriwal had claimed the AAP would get at least 100 seats in the upcoming Lok Sabha polls and the next government would not be formed without AAP's support.

The outcome was dismal: the AAP drew a blank in its original *karmabhoomi* of Delhi and managed a grand all-India total of just four seats, all from Punjab. 430 of its 434 candidates faced crushing defeat—414 forfeited their deposit, failing to secure even one-sixth of the votes in their constituencies.

The AAP made a number of strategic mistakes in candidates selection. Among the major errors was the seat chosen by Arvind Kejriwal himself. It was foolhardy of Kejriwal to project himself against an immensely popular BJP prime ministerial candidate Narendra Modi from Varanasi in UP. Against Modi's well-known and unmatched record of development and good governance of Gujarat, and his plank of its pan-India replication, Kejriwal's anti-Modi rhetoric fell flat and cut no ice with the voters. If at all he had to select a constituency outside Delhi, he should have chosen Amethi. UPA's shine was totally off, and the blame largely fell on Sonia, Rahul and Manmohan Singh. Amethi's development was dismal under Rahul. Kejriwal, with his eloquence and charisma, could have easily drowned Rahul; and that would have been a master-kill that would have catapulted him further.

Given the poor showing, Arvind Kejriwal, the poster boy of new-age politics, had to go in for serious introspection as the party's relevance itself became a question.

Kejriwal realised he should not have jumped into the Lok Sabha polls dishonouring the sentiments of Delhi voters, who had catapulted his fledgling party into power in Delhi. He later mentioned he was not in favour of fighting too many Lok Sabha seats and wanted the AAP to focus on a limited winnable seats, but that under the persuasion of Prashant Bhushan and Yogendra Yadav he went along the way they desired.

## Delhi Elections 2015 and AAP's Second Stint at Power

### *Build-up to Elections*

2014 Lok Sabha elections were a big let-down for the AAP. In the greed for pan-India spread, Lok Sabha seats, and a decisive presence at the Centre, they had lost their only power-base: Delhi. They tried their best to revert to the old position by partnering with the Congress, but to no avail. They tried expediting holding of assembly elections, but the BJP foolishly refused to play ball. However, BJP acting difficult ultimately proved advantageous for the AAP. Had the Delhi assembly re-elections been held soon after the Lok Sabha elections, the BJP might have garnered a majority, given the wave in its favour. BJP's postponement of the same in the hope that it could manipulate to come into power without holding the re-elections gave the AAP that much more time to regain its ground.

It goes to the credit of the AAP's leadership and their devoted, selfless, hard-working cadres that despite being down in the dumps after the Lok Sabha elections, they rose like a phoenix from the ashes. Their persistence, their courage in the face of defeat, their moral strength, their ability to reinvent themselves, their strategy, and their skill and persuasive powers in convincing the voters have to be commended. No other political party in the Indian electoral history after independence has re-risen after a crushing defeat and abject rejection by the voters in so short a period, and with such blinding fury as to wipe out all opposition.

Following intense publicity and door-to-door campaign, the AAP released its *70-point Action Plan* of Delhi on 31 January 2015, a week before the election.

Like in the last assembly elections, in this election too, dirty media-tricks were played upon the AAP by a section to abort their coming to power. However, the sins of the Congress over its 15-year rule were so much, and the performance of the Municipal Corporation of Delhi (MCD) controlled by the BJP had been so pathetic that no amount of dirty tricks could dent the growing popularity of the resurgent AAP.

The election results were something no one—including the AAP leadership itself—had expected in their wildest dreams.

### *Unprecedented AAP Victory*

The AAP scored an unprecedented victory in the 2015 Delhi Legislative Assembly election held on 7 February 2015: it won 67 of the 70 seats!

Its main opponent, the BJP, which had won the highest number of 31 seats in December-2013 elections, and which had declared former IPS officer and *India Against Corruption* activist Kiran Bedi, a former colleague of Arvind Kejriwal in

TAA, as its chief ministerial candidate, was reduced to just 3 seats; while the Congress party, which had been ruling for 15 long years till 2013, was reduced to zero!

Vote share of the AAP was a massive 53.4%, against the almost unchanged or marginally reduced vote share of 32.2% of the BJP, and drastically reduced vote share of 9.7% of the Congress. While the BJP vote-share had remained almost unchanged compared to the previous election, there was en-bloc transfer of votes from the Congress to the AAP. In other words, the Congress loss was the AAP's gain.

### *BJP's Defeat*

Even those who were not AAP-supporters or those who didn't expect much from the AAP or even those who were otherwise Modi-supporters wanted BJP to bite the dust in Delhi! Why? MCD—Municipal Corporation of Delhi—a thoroughly corrupt organisation has been controlled most incompetently by the BJP for long. A party with such a dismal record in MCD surely didn't deserve to win in the legislative assembly elections. Had it won, it would have been a case of rewarding bad performers.

Induction of an honest and competent Kiran Bedi as BJP's chief ministerial candidate at the last moment or campaigning by Modi should not have been allowed to make a difference to the outcome. How could those stratagems wipe out BJP's sins of many years in the MCD.

The Congress and the BJP deserved to lose and lose badly, and they did. The AAP deserved a chance and they got it. Things happened as they should have. The people of Delhi need to be complemented for that. Also, the Delhi public was wise enough to accord the AAP such an overwhelming majority that they could never complain of lack of numbers to implement their promises.

# 5

# LOOKING AT CORRUPTION THE RIGHT WAY

**(Does AAP show this understanding?)**

*Corruption, embezzlement, fraud, these are all characteristics which exist everywhere. It is regrettably the way human nature functions, whether we like it or not. What successful economies do is keep it to a minimum. No one has ever eliminated any of that stuff.*

—Alan Greenspan

*Corruption is authority plus monopoly minus transparency.*

As the main plank of the Team Anna Agitation (TAA) was corruption and the Jan Lokpal Bill (JLB) to tackle it; and as the AAP emerged out of the TAA with corruption as the main issue, it would be in fitness of things to look at the various aspects of this issue.

## Ethical Considerations Apart, Why is Corruption Bad?

*Corruption is a true enemy to development.*

—Tsakhiagiin Elbegdorj, President of Mongolia

The necessity of curbing corruption goes beyond the purely ethical considerations of ensuring honesty and fair play, and beyond just monetary considerations of checking leakages.

Many critical benefits, including investments, economic growth, poverty-removal and India's demographic dividend, are dependent upon it. Corruption hurts economic growth because it allows crony capitalists get an upper hand over genuine ones. Graft discourages genuine Indian and foreign investors. Corruption affects investments, which affects growth and employment generation, which affects the millions of young coming into the labour market every year, leading to frustration and social instability. Can India afford a volatile political, economic and social environment?

Curbing of corruption would give a boost to the Indian economy: more foreign investments, more people opening new companies, ethical companies getting competitive, and so on. It would also help India realise a global leadership role.

## What is the Right Way to Tackle Corruption?

Corruption is not a one-dimensional problem and there is no one single way to root it out. A multi-pronged strategy incorporating preventive, detective and punitive measures is required, including, among other things, liberalisation and economic reforms that have been stopped half-way, much higher level of transparency, innovative automation and online delivery of services, systemic changes, and also independent Lokpal, with investigative powers.

TAA and AAP's one-point agenda of Lokpal was a very partial solution. The major, impactful solution is change of policies, liberalisation, and economic reforms. Unfortunately, these latter don't fit-in with the backward-looking, pink-to-red, socialistic claptrap policies that sought to dominate the AAP policies thanks to the dominance of people like Prashant Bhushan, Yogendra Yadav, and the communists-socialists-marxists-JNU-types like Prof. Anand Kumar, Kamal Mitra Chenoy and Medha Patkar. Hence, the AAP can never really be successful in removing big-time corruption. They can only talk, shout and be abusive about it, and slam corporates, to get votes. Would things change with the exit of Bhushan-Yogendra & Co?

## How does "Liberalisation" Reduces Corruption?

Even though all brands of *Socialist/Leftist Economics* have proved a dud both in theory and in practice, socialists-leftists-marxists keep concocting rationale for their defunct economics to somehow retain their relevance. The latest being that the increase in corruption is thanks to *Liberalisation* since the nineties. That it is the *neo-liberal* policies from the times of Narsimha Rao onwards that have led to increase in corruption.

Leftists do not seem to appreciate that a moribund, minuscule economy till 1991, thanks to the disastrous socialistic policies of Nehru-Indira-Rajiv, has grown to over a trillion dollar, precisely because of post-1991 reforms. To the extent the economy has grown many-fold, the corruption has also grown, because the necessary preventive, detective, regulatory and penal systems to control the corruption have not kept pace with the change in the post-1991 economic policies, thanks to the rapacious politician-babu combine, who have retained the pre-1991 socialistic-bureaucratic setup.

It is worth remembering that there was widespread corruption before 1991 also—right since Nehru's time, and even before in the British-India. It became much worse with Indira and her descendants! The Congress ministries elected in the various states of the British-India in the late thirties had turned so corrupt that Gandhi had called for disbanding of Congress after Independence!!

Although Indira's and Rajiv's times were much more corrupt and Sonia-MMS times had crossed all limits, even the Nehru period had many financial scandals: the Jeep scandal, the Mudgal case, Mundra deals, Malaviya Sirajuddin scandal, Pratap Singh Kairon case—to name a few.

Those who talk of "better, less-corrupt pre-liberalisation days" of Nehru-Indira-Rajiv are suffering from amnesia. In the "good" old days of Nehru-Indira-Rajiv socialism, if you wanted to bunk the long queues extending to several years for getting a gas-connection or telephone or scooter, you had to bribe. Contrast that with the position now. Each of these things are now for the asking—the concerned companies would come to your home to do the needful. It took India 110 years to reach 5 million phones by 1991. However, thanks to liberalisation, that number grew to a whopping 300 million by 2008! In the pre-1991 days, even if you were the lucky one to have a gas-connection, you still needed to bribe periodically to get the gas-cylinder in time. Not so now. Same for telephone—if you did not want your telephone to be dead, you had to grease palms. Now the poor and the rich all have telephones or mobiles, and they hardly go dead. Even items like cement and steel were on quota. If you were building your house, bribe the officials to get your quota. Same with the railway reservations—stand in long queues and try your luck, or bribe.

Those bad-old days are now gone. Thanks to the post-1991 reforms, common people have been freed from many hassles and humiliations, as many avenues of corruption have been done away with—but, not all. Much more needs to be done. What are needed are more reforms, not rollback of what has been done, more liberalisation, not going back to the command-and-control-license-permit-quota-raj economy.

In the pre-liberalisation days, if you travelled abroad, upon return, you stood as a suspect culprit in a long queue to be pounced upon by ill-mannered customs officials looking for their chance to make *moolah*. As an entrepreneur, if you wanted a license or a permission or an import licence or if you wanted to stop your competitor from getting one, you needed to bribe a set of officials—which continues even now, because reforms are incomplete. Many new firms like Infosys with no pedigree like Birlas and Tatas have sprung up in India from scratch thanks to liberalisation, and have massively contributed to GDP, exports-earnings and employment.

The current crop of mega-corruptions are not on account of liberalisation and economic-reforms, but on account of government's decision to stop halfway with reforms, massive discretion still exercised by politicians and babus, and lack of empowered, autonomous institutions to prevent, detect, and penalise corruption. What are needed are institutional reforms to eliminate or minimise corruption.

Leftists also need to note that without the massive revenues growth, thanks to liberalisation, there would have been no funds for MGNREGA, NRHM, FSB, RTE, and the like.

In a bureaucratic-socialistic culture, which still prevails, reforms being still an unfinished project, the culture is of easy money through corruption; and incentive to retain this system of graft and to run-down reforms is very high, because reforms are anti-easy money. Crony capitalism, thanks to bureaucratic-socialistic culture and half-baked reforms, has to give way to rule-based capitalism by undertaking reforms across the board. Only then would corruption be effectively curbed—not fully eliminated.

## Can a Socialistic Setup be Ever Corruption-free?

Doubtful. More the spread and hold of the state, more areas would likely be infected with corruption. Contrary to what the socialists-leftists and the new kid on the block, AAP, say, an unreformed, non-liberalised socialistic setup is likely to be much more corrupt.

# 6

# HONESTY AND COMPETENCE

**(What AAP & People should learn to differentiate.)**

*What matters is professional honesty and integrity, and not just personal honesty. And, of course, competence.*

While accusing most others as dishonest and corrupt, the AAP keeps harping day in and day out on its honesty and on it being free from corruption, as if that's a huge qualification. Manmohan Singh used to flaunt his personal honesty, even as he headed the most corrupt government of our times. So, let us examine these terms: personal honesty, professional honesty and competence.

## Is Honesty a Qualification?

No. Honesty is a basic requirement. It is a pre-requisite for a job or an assignment. That is, it is a pre-selection criteria. For persons deemed dishonest or "not of good moral character", the question of processing their application does not arise. Actual qualifications and experience and other requirements are evaluated for only those candidates who are deemed to be honest and "of good moral character".

## Is Honesty a Measure of Competence?

Certainly not. Honesty is but a basic requirement. It has nothing to do with a person's competence for a job or assignment. Out of say "x" applicants for a job, you may have x1 who are honest and certified as "of good moral character", but are found to be unfit or incompetent for the job; x2 who are fit and competent for the job but are reported to be of not "good moral character"; leaving the remaining x3 who are honest, "of good moral character" and also fit and competent for the job. You would select the best out of x3. You would not consider an honest person who is incompetent, nor a competent person who is dishonest. However, out of several honest persons you would select the one who is most competent. Therefore, honesty is a basic requirement, not a qualification. Competence is the qualification. However, a competent person who is dishonest fails to fulfil the basic requirement, and is therefore unfit.

Therefore, for the AAP or for any party or for Arvind Kejriwal or for any person to tom-tom honesty is to only talk of fulfilment of a fundamental or basic requirement. It is no measure of competence as a leader.

## Would You Employ an Honest, but Incompetent Person?

Certainly not. Can you employ a driver who is honest, but is rash and not quite skilled at the wheels? Can you employ a software coder who is honest, but whose coding is generally faulty and error-prone? Can you employ a teacher or a trainer who is honest, but whose speech is unintelligible and who can't really teach? Can you have a political leader who is honest, but has no understanding of administration or competence to manage or ability to lead? Can you have a player in a cricket team who is honest and upright, but can neither bowl, nor bat, nor field?

## Professional Honesty is the Real Test

*With integrity, you have nothing to fear, since you have nothing to hide. With integrity, you will do the right thing, so you will have no guilt.*

—Zig Ziglar

It is not enough to be only personally honest. Where others report to you, and you are responsible for their performance, professional honesty demands you ensure the conduct of those under you is also honest and above board, and that they are not indulging in any malpractices and corruption. In case it is found to be otherwise, you need to take action against them. Your professional duty demands that you ensure the whole area or department or ministry or ministries under you perform their duly in an honest and professional manner. Professional honesty requires that while you yourself don't do a dishonest or unprofessional act, you also don't ignore those acts in others under you.

*What is easier: personal honesty or professional honesty?*

Personal honesty, of course, because it concerns only yourself. If you are not a greedy person, or if you are already a well-provided person, or if you are by nature or upbringing upright, or if you are a self-respecting, principled person, or if you are a conscientious person, it is not difficult to be personally honest. So many are. In fact, you take pride in being so. It gives you a sense of self-worth. You feel good about yourself.

However, it is not easy to be professionally honest. Because, that requires competence to manage, evaluate, judge and control those under you.

*What is superior: personal honesty or professional honesty?*

Of course, professional honesty. Because, professional honesty includes personal honesty as a sub-set or a pre-condition.

Professional honesty is what Narendra Modi summarises in his dictum: "*Na khaunga, na khane dunga* (I won't take money, nor would I allow others to take money)!"

*What is better? To have honest people or to have competent people?*

You need people who are both honest and competent. It is not worth having in employment or on assignment people who are honest but incompetent, or people who are competent but dishonest.

*Examples*

Ex-Prime Minister Manmohan Singh was personally honest, but dishonest in the higher level of honesty—professional honesty. He couldn't measure up as a prime minister, hence was not competent. Ex-Defence Minister A.K. Anthony was personally honest, but incompetent.

Narendra Modi is professionally honest, which includes his being personally honest, and he is also competent on the job.

Arvind Kejriwal is also professionally honest, which includes his being personally honest. His competence for the job would take time to evaluate. He has been on the job for a very short time. But, so far, there is no reason to believe he is not competent.

# 7

# SOCIALISM AND INDIA'S SELF-INFLICTED POVERTY

**(What AAP has failed to appreciate.)**

*If you put the federal government in charge of the Sahara Desert, in 5 years there'd be a shortage of sand.*

—Milton Friedman

## "Scientific" Socialism: The Theory of Non-Affluent Society

Marxism and socialism were something Nehru was sold out on since the 1920s, wrote approvingly about in his books, advocated vigorously all through, and, unfortunately for India, implemented it post-independence in his own Nehruvian way.

*How do you tell a communist? Well, it's someone who reads Marx and Lenin. And how do you tell an anti-Communist? It's someone who understands Marx and Lenin.*

—Ronald Reagan

For the context of this book, we will use leftism, socialism, *scientific* socialism, communism, Marxism and socialistic state interchangeably to mean dominance of the state, pubic and state sector at the commanding heights of the economy, predominant state controls of the economy and means of production, over-regulated bureaucratic state, mai-baap Sarkar and lesser or marginal role for the private sector and individuals. We are NOT implying socialism or socialistic state to mean a welfare state or a state engaged in social justice and equality, because as per actual global experience such a socialistic state as just defined by us is neither capable of ensuring general welfare nor social justice nor equality.

Marxists call their socialism *scientific* socialism, as if the self-assigned, self-adulatory adjective *scientific* is sufficient to testify to it being *scientific*—correct; however preposterous it might be from a genuine scientific angle, where the litmus test is the real practical proof. Mere dialectics of self-serving arguments and logic does not result in truth! Marxism as a science or as an alternate economic thought for a nation to build on has failed—it has been proven wrong both in theory and in practice.

Those who do not genuinely understand science or scientific-methods are taken-in by mere allusion to something as *scientific*. Many became Marxists because being so implied being *scientific*-spirited, rational, progressive, pro-poor intellectual, aligned to the *forces of history*! Rather than being aligned to the forces of history or being on the right side of it, to the dismay of the Marxists, the unfolding history proved them to be on the wrong side; and their science—"scientific" socialism—turned out to be an alchemy!

The capitalist economic thought, the capitalist societies and the associated democratic system themselves evolved and adapted since the time of Marx in such a way that they not only brought unprecedented prosperity to the concerned nations, they also significantly uplifted the status of the masses—falsifying, in the process, many of the foundations and assumptions of Marx.

Of course, that doesn't lessen the genius of Marx. He contributed to the economic thought, the political thought, the social science and the knowledge of the evolution of societies and religion in a very major and a tremendously impactful way. Not just the converted, the others too were not left untouched by his thought. Writes John Kenneth Galbraith in *The Affluent Society*: "Marx profoundly affected those who did not accept his system." Perhaps, the evolution of capitalism itself was affected by his thought—becoming more inclusive. Writes Galbraith further: "In part this was the result of the breathtaking grandeur of Marx's achievement as an exercise in social theory. No one before, or for that matter since, had taken so many strands of human behaviour and woven them together...."

It doesn't matter if his theory or line of reasoning has proved to be partly or largely erroneous. Current capitalist economic thought is not exactly what Adam Smith propounded. That doesn't lessen Adam Smith's contribution. Certain conclusions of Ricardo and Malthus have proved to be wrong. But, they helped bring focus on important economic aspects. The current atomic model is not what Rutherford proposed. Newton's laws of motion have been superseded, or rather refined, by the Einstein's theory. But, that doesn't make them less of a scientist.

In science, society, economics and indeed all disciplines knowledge evolves, concepts change, new theories replace old ones in the light of new experiments, experiences and knowledge gained. To be scientific is to keep an open mind on things, to be willing to change, to be ready to jettison the old in the light of new evidence, and to go by actual practical results.

The quest for justice, the empathy for the poor and the deprived, and the idealism that drove Marx and Engels has to be acknowledged, respected and emulated. However, if Marxism was indeed "scientific", then to elevate it to a dogma or a religion, that can't be questioned, is itself unscientific. The proponents of "scientific" socialism have not been scientific enough to factor in the changes since the death of Marx, and stick to the dogma. Sadly, Marx himself, once he had built up his arguments and theory, chose to ignore many facts and statistics that had come to light during his own lifetime, for they interfered with his constructs. He clung to only those facts that fitted-in with his theory. His method itself was therefore unscientific.

Further, Marx didn't elaborate on the nature of society and organisation that would replace capitalism, and how it would be managed, except talking vaguely about the "dictatorship of the proletariat"—without allowing for the possibility of the Frankenstein it would unleash, and the surreal "1984" it would beget.

## Practice Proves the Theory Wrong

For anything to be scientifically correct, it has to be proved truly and convincingly in practice, without a shadow of doubt. Till the same is done, it remains merely a conjecture, a hypothesis, a theory. Has the so-called *scientific socialism* or Marxism proved successful anywhere in the world in practice? No.

Facts, figures, statistics and ground-level experiences of various countries prove that all brands of leftist politics—Communist, Socialist, Fabian, Nehruvian, and so on—are inherently incapable of delivering anything positive for any nation or for its poor. In fact, they have actually been at the root of poverty, want and stagnation.

Dismal fate of all nations that went socialist proves the point. Take USSR. It claimed to be following *scientific* socialism or Marxism. But, what were its practical results? It drew an iron-curtain so that no one got to see the disaster: the wide-spread poverty and famine and suppression of human rights. Had things been really good, why would USSR be so secretive about it, and not let those interested—journalists, writers, academicians, researchers, politicians, sociologists, and general public—have unrestricted access and see the state of affairs for themselves, especially when they wanted other nations to emulate them, and go communist! Why only guided tours, under strict supervision? Whom were they fooling? Perhaps people like Nehru. One guided tour in 1920s, and Nehru returned fully sold out, like school-boys taken on guided tours! Subsequent guided-tours of both Nehru and his daughter post-independence to the USSR, and both were re-sold!! Ultimately the USSR fell apart, and all its parts are still struggling to throw away the bad old days of communism.

One is not likely to come across a more hilarious indictment of communism than what the author Tim Harford says in *Adapt*. First, the background. We learn by understanding why and how a *thing works*. We also learn by understanding why a thing *does not work*. The normal method is the former, the latter being an add-on: understand the normal working, and as an additional learning, examine also the abnormal working. In the field of neuroscience, however, the study of the abnormal is the normal method of learning. Observe the abnormal behaviour and determine which part of the brain is responsible for it—that's the way to understand the brain. As V.S. Ramachandran, whom Richard Dawkins calls "the Marco Polo of neuroscience", says in his book, *The Tell-Tale Brain*: "My approach to these questions has been to study patients with damage or genetic quirks in different parts of their brains that produce bizarre effects on their minds or behaviour."

Reverting to Tim Harford in Adapt: "*The Soviet Union is to economics what Phineas Gage [a brain-injury victim] is to neuroscience. Neuroscientists study patients with damage to specific regions of the brain because their plight illuminates how the brain is ordinarily supposed to work. In much the same way, economists study dysfunctional economics when attempting to figure out the secrets of healthy ones. It is of course not a new insight that the Soviet system failed, but the unexpected details of why it failed are often glossed over—and they hold an important lesson....*"

Millions died from hunger and famine in Soviet Russia, yet the communist leadership did not have the heart to save them by seeking help from outside, lest the outside world became aware of the pathetic conditions. Same with China under Mao—about 40 million perished in famines! Country-wise unofficial estimates of the total number of persons who perished thanks to communism, through man-made famines and state-terror, as per *The Black Book of Communism* are: USSR–20 million, China–65 million, Combodia–2 million, North Korea–2 million; the world-total being around 100 million! Compare this with the estimate of Holocaust victims at about 6 million, and total World War II military deaths of all countries put together at about 25 million.

Take the case of East Germany: contrast it with the prosperity in West Germany. Why the Berlin Wall ultimately fell? See the fate of the East-European countries: Czechoslovakia, Yugoslavia, Poland, Bulgaria, Romania. Consider the case of

Albania under its *Mao*—Enver Hoxha. What of Cuba under the "great" revolutionary, Fidel Castro: it is now desperately trying to shed its socialistic past. Note the growing economy of Vietnam after the gradual shedding of its communist policies. The terrible fate of Cambodians under the Khmer Rouge and Pol Pot—brought out so chillingly in the movie, *The Killing Fields*! Appalling conditions in North Korea: George Orwell's "1984" continuing in the 21st century!

Take the example of the relatively recent red-hot socialist showman given to mega posturing on the world stage, Hugo Chavez, the president of Venezuela for the last 14 years, who succumbed to cancer on March 5, 2013. Called *Commandante* by his followers, he implemented several populist measures—which he could afford thanks to the country's oil-wealth—to remain popular. But, what is the legacy of his 14-year socialist revolution? Decline in oil-production, a severely dented economy, dysfunctional state institutions and administration, and Caracas, its capital, turning into one of the most dangerous cities in the world. An article by Rory Carroll in *The Economic Times*, Mumbai of 7 March 2013, reproduced from NYT, reads: "The once mighty factories of Ciudad Guayana, an industrial hub... are rusting and wheezing, some shut, others at half-capacity. Underinvestment and ineptitude hit hydropower stations and the electricity grid, causing weekly blackouts that continue to darken cities, fry electrical equipment, silence machinery and require de facto rationing.... Reckless money printing and fiscal policies triggered soaring inflation, so much so that the currency, the bolivar, lost 90 per cent of its value since Chavez took office, and was devalued five times over a decade. In another delusion, the currency had been renamed 'el bolivar fuerte', the strong bolivar—an Orwellian touch. Harassment of privately owned farms and chaotic administration of state-backed agricultural cooperatives hit food production, compelling extensive imports, which stacked up so fast thousands of tonnes rotted at ports.... Politicisation and neglect crippled the state-run oil company PDVSA's core task—drilling—so that production slumped. Populist subsidies reduced the cost of gasoline to $1 a tank, perhaps the world's lowest price of petrol, but cost the state untold billions in revenue while worsening traffic congestion and air pollution.... A new elite with government connections, the "boligarchs", manipulated government contracts and the web of price and currency controls to finance their lavish lifestyles.... As Venezuela atrophied, he found some refuge in blaming others, notably the "squealing pigs" of the private sector...." Of course, this is not to overlook the blatant exploitation of Venezuela by the West earlier—it is only to highlight that even if Chavez can be credited with fittingly rebuffing the West, socialist policies implemented by him proved to be no panacea.

There is not a single example of a country which prospered or whose poor were better off under communism or socialism. The democratic countries like the UK which were going downhill with their socialistic policies did course correction under Thatcher and prospered. Near home, see the unfortunate and the pathetic fate of India and its poor thanks to India's socialistic policies, which are only gradually getting dismantled.

It is also worth noting that terror has always been a dominant factor in communism. Besides, like the vandals of the olden times, they destroyed precious cultural treasures. Pol Pot dismantled the Phnom Penh cathedral and allowed the jungle to take over the Angkor Wat temples. In China priceless treasures were smashed or set on fire by the Red Guards.

We know how communists wrecked West Bengal during their 34-year rule! Those who still advocate socialistic policies do so not because they are innocent about these facts, but because it suits them politically, so what if those policies actually amount to being anti-progress and anti-poor. Sadly, Mamata Banerjee of the TMC, which is now in power in West Bengal replacing the CPM, is continuing those destructive socialistic tradition.

Why is Kerala which should have been a number one developed and prosperous state in India, given both its excellent natural resources and its excellent human resources, NOT so? Because, the communists of the CPM variety or the socialists of the Congress variety have alternately ruled it, misruled and misgoverned it.

Jayaprakash Narayan had remarked: "History will soon prove that Communism, instead of being the final flowering of human civilisation, was a temporary aberration of the human mind, a brief nightmare to be soon forgotten. Communism, as it grew up in Russia and is growing up in China now, represented the darkness of the soul and imprisonment of the mind, colossal violence and injustice. Whoever thinks of the future of the human race in these terms is condemning man to eternal perdition."

## India's Socialistic Suicide

*The inherent vice of capitalism is the unequal sharing of blessings; the inherent virtue of socialism is the equal sharing of miseries.*

—Winston Churchill

Nehru uncritically accepted socialism. It is strange that while Nehru's books approvingly talk of Marxism and socialism, there is no comparative analysis by him of much more proven competing economic thoughts. It was as if Adam Smith, Alfred Marshall, J.S. Mill, John Maynard Keynes and others did not exist for Nehru. Economics is a serious subject for its effects on the lives of millions, and for Nehru to take up a firm position on one trend of economics without critical appraisal of the alternatives was not only unwise in the academic sense, it proved disastrous to the nation in practice. Further, even if Nehru mistakenly believed that communism was doing good for one country, the USSR, how was it that he did not notice the many countries prospering under capitalism, like the US, the Western-European and the South-East Asian countries. Was Nehru—the *scientifically-minded* person—going more by personal bias than by facts!

As the Nehru years rolled by, the numbers started causing concern, state of the nation went from bad to worse, and famine conditions developed. *Scientific thinking*, of which Nehru was a passionate advocate, demands that you take facts and statistics seriously, analyse data, find the reason, check where you have gone wrong, find what other countries are doing and succeeding, and do a course correction. But, since you were never genuinely *scientific* in the first place, where was the question of any course correction? You and your socialism and your path could not be wrong. You cannot lose face. Persist. Invent excuses: *Public Sector is not supposed to make profit*!

Although one can't doubt Nehru's good intentions, one can't ignore the fact that the road to hell is paved with good intentions.

Post-independence, and till the early 1950s, India did command great respect and prestige around the world, and there were lots of expectations from democratic India as a beacon for other developing countries, particularly the erstwhile colonial ones, to follow. Unfortunately, Nehru's policies proved so disastrous on the ground that all hopes stood belied. Nehru's socialism delivered a monumental tragedy lacking not only in growth and poverty alleviation, but also in delivering social justice.

Nehru, through his anti-private-sector policies, throttled industrialisation. Although, in comparison with the deliberate neglect in the British period, the progress in industrialisation during the Nehru period was much better owing to significant public sector investments. British set up or allowed setting up of only those minimal things that helped them in their trade, business and greed—not what was required for a country like India.

Post-independence industrialisation was also helped by the very significant second world war sterling debt repayments by the UK, and aid by other countries like the US, the USSR and Germany. However, when the repayment of the sterling debt by the UK tapered off, and not much further foreign aid was forthcoming, and the public sector into which Nehru had sunk the investment was either in loss or not able to generate adequate surplus, the industrialisation momentum began to taper off, as there were no funds; and given Nehru's socialistic approach, the private sector was anyway shackled!

*The problem with socialism is that you eventually run out of other people's money.*

—Margaret Thatcher

Further, not learning anything from Japan and others, who had dramatically prospered with their outward-looking, export-led growth, India under Nehru went in for inward-looking, import-substitution model, denying itself a world-class, competitive culture, incentive for production of quality products, share in the world-trade, and the consequent prosperity. Instead, India invested heavily in the inefficient public sector, over-regulated and strangulated private enterprise, shunned foreign capital, and ignored better technology. India under Nehru also neglected the two vital sectors—agriculture and education.

Nehru and his team were seemingly innocent of the basics of economics: without a prosperous agriculture, you can't have agricultural surplus, and without that, you can't feed the growing urban population and sustain industrialisation. Yet, they neglected agriculture, which adversely affected industrialisation, and resulted in mass poverty, hunger and famines. India under Nehru became a land of the hungry millions, and was forced to go around the world with a begging bowl.

Congress also allowed the *working class* the pleasures of *not working* for the sake of votes and politics, lowering their productivity and spoiling the work-culture. There are so many examples. An engineer at Bhilai Steel Plant (BSP), a public sector unit, narrated that pending allotment of suitable quarters, he was given temporary accommodation in a sector, where his neighbour was a steel-plant worker staying in BSP-provided quarters. The worker went to the steel plant only three to four days a week. Rest of the time he used to be generally drunk. He would somehow have his attendance marked for the other days too. Not only that, he used to mark double-shifts too—having worked extra-eight hours, for which the payment was double! Nobody—his boss or senior officers—dared do anything, for he was an active member of the Workers Union. Nehru wanted India to advance industrially through the public sector peopled by such non-working working class, and a management, subservient to the politicians, that dare not question the non-workers! In due course, public sector management too became indifferent, incompetent and corrupt—like the IAS-IFS-IRS-IPS combine.

Gurcharan Das mentions in his book, *India Unbound*, that soon after Independence, Kasturbhai Lalbhai undertook the pioneering work of establishing a chemical plant in collaboration with American Cyanamid. It was in the wilds of Gujarat. He built a whole township for the plant and provided jobs to many tribals. He named it Atul—the incomparable. He invited Nehru in 1952 to inaugurate it. However, Nehru agreed after considerable reluctance. Why? Because, it was in the private sector!

By 1954, Nehru made Parliament accept as the aim of economic development the "socialist pattern of society". Socialism was enshrined in 1955 as the official policy of the Congress at its Avadi session. The 1956 version of the Industrial Policy Resolution made the state even more dominant—it allowed new ventures in textiles, automobiles and defence only to the state, and vested exclusive controls to it over many other sectors. All these inaugurated an era of stifling private enterprise, grievously hurting industrialisation and development, severely limiting employment opportunities, plunging the country in chronic poverty, and promoted babudom and corruption.

Democratic and liberal Nehru was able to manage dissent so effectively, through various subtle means, that whether it was the press or the opposition or even the opponents within the Congress, he was able to carry through his policies—that ultimately proved disastrous. The voices of dissent were muffled through various covert and overt methods, using carrot and stick. The initial opponents of socialism ended up defending nationalisation in order to remain in his good books.

Many industries were barred for the private sector. When entrepreneurs in the countries in Southeast Asia, like South Korea, were being encouraged to expand and set up industries and their government was offering them cheap credit, here in India we were doing the opposite: G.D. Birla was refused a license for setting up a steel plant; scores of business proposals of Tatas were rejected; Aditya Birla, looking to the hostile business environment in India, chose to set up industries outside India;...the list is endless. Krishna Menon [the right-hand man of

Nehru] had reportedly snubbed offers of the Japanese corporate representatives for collaboration saying it was out of question on account of the vast differences in the policies of the two countries.

Given license-permit-quota-raj, reluctance to give licenses to the so-called "monopolies", anti-business policies and extortionist taxes—maximum slab rate being over 80%—industrialisation had to suffer. Industrialisation and industries were sought to be controlled and managed by Nehru's IAS babus who knew next to nothing on how to run an industry. Nehru and the socialists had very simplistic notions on wealth creation: Nehru thought that all it took to have economic prosperity was to invest in industrialisation, especially in heavy industries, and to put babus in charge. Market, competition, entrepreneurship, quality, top-line, bottom-line—those funny words existed in the English dictionary in total contempt of the Nehruvians. No entrepreneurship was required. Sarkar was the entrepreneur. It would decide what to produce, what not to produce, and how much to produce, and at what rate to sell—the market itself would be controlled by Sarkar.

Nehru and the socialists never understood what it really took to create wealth and banish poverty, and persisted with their sterile, copycat methods. Socialists concerned themselves more with the distribution of wealth, than with its creation. They shunned understanding the complexity of wealth creation. Nations which understood this raced ahead, created wealth and also managed to distribute it, while India failed to create the wealth itself, what to speak of distributing it: India stagnated.

Being not a communist state, we cannot fully throttle private enterprise, but we can certainly keep them on a tight leash—thought the thrilled, socialist bureaucracy, sensing all power coming to them. It is the State which has to be dominant, and has to achieve *Commanding Heights. Still*, if anybody is foolish enough to still wish to set up private industries and businesses, they need to first take our permission, and we would make it so complex for them that most would give up even before they got permissions, and those who manage to get permissions—of course, after greasing palms—would face so many regulatory hurdles, in practice, that they would give up later; except, of course, those who continue to grease palms.

It would be wrong to call babus mere babus and not entrepreneurs. They have been running very efficient private enterprises of loot for themselves and their netas based on very skilful investment of their authority. It was Rajaji who had so rightly coined the term *licence-permit-quota raj, and alleged that to be the reason for the Congressmen and the officials getting rich.*

Socialism and leftism is something which benefits large sections of vested interests, but not the intended beneficiaries. Why do poor, who can ill-afford, prefer private schools to Government schools, private hospitals to Government hospitals? They know that this socialist claptrap is for the babus and politicians to make money, not to help them. Communism and socialism assume the State as a kind, empathetic *mai-baap*, meant to do good for the people; when the experience and the practical reality is that very often it is the State—through its agency of politicians, babus and police—that is the biggest *exploiter* and *mafia* around.

Investment in the public sector leviathan was a huge two-thirds of the country's investable funds during Nehru's time, but to little avail—the public sector churned out shoddy goods and remained in loss. Of the entire paid-up capital in India, the share of the public sector rose to a massive 70% by 1978, with little benefits accruing to the nation. Our extremely scarce resources were squandered and precious public money was literally burnt by the Dynasty in trying to do business; while the sectors for which a government is primarily responsible remained neglected, and were starved of funds.

Why did India fail? There are any number of convenient and false explanations: problem of national character; people not being hard-working; lack of discipline; colonial baggage; democracy, which is "soft"—what is needed is dictatorship, preferably military dictatorship. Those who advance such pleas should be asked: "Why is the economy doing relatively much better now after only partial liberalisation? Have the lazy of the old days suddenly become very hard-working? Has the national character changed for the better? Are people now more disciplined?" The real reason for the woes had nothing to do with those factors. It was a plain, bad, borrowed Nehruvian economic model of socialism that did us in.

## What They Said

*A government which engages itself in trading [read business] activities will come to grief.*

—Sardar Patel

Sardar Patel never believed socialism was a panacea like Nehru and many other socialists, including Jayaprakash Narayan and Rammanohar Lohia, believed. Sardar was liberal enough to even offer a deal to the socialists on these lines: "*Select a province and run it on socialist principles. If they did better than others, he would gladly hand over the country to them.*" (Quoted by Rajmohan Gandhi in *Patel—A Life.*) The offer was not taken, as JP and Lohia later recalled.

*While I usually came back from meeting Gandhiji elated and inspired but always a bit sceptical, and from talks with Jawaharlal fired with emotional zeal but often confused and unconvinced, meetings with Vallabhbhai were a joy from which I returned with renewed confidence in the future of our country. I have often thought that if fate had decreed that he, instead of Jawaharlal, would be younger of the two, India would have followed a very different path and would be in better economic shape than it is today.*

—J.R.D. Tata

*Raja Vyapari taya Praja Bhikhari.*

—Indian proverb

The Western-European countries devastated by the Second World War—particularly West Germany, which was reduced to rubble—recovered from the ashes, progressed and became highly prosperous. Japan was totally ravaged by the War and the Atomic Bomb. Remember that Raj Kapoor song of the fifties, "*Mera joota hai Japani...*" pointing to the torn shoes, representing the condition of Japan then. Japan recovered, quickly industrialised, and grew at over 9% for over twenty-three years, to become one of the largest economies of the world. India, in contrast, was untouched by the war and the devastation. Yet, India remained a poor third-rate third-world country.

In the pre-independence era, Nehru had stated: "If the future is full of hope it is largely because of Soviet Russia." Nehru was much impressed by George Bernard Shaw, and his concept of socialism and Fabianism. Mentions Stanley Wolpert in his book, *Nehru: A Tryst with Destiny*: "Mac [M.O. Mathai] recalled that Shaw told Nehru that he and Stalin were 'the only hope' for the world." Perhaps Nehru took Shaw too seriously! There were other accomplished people like Bertrand Russell: one wonders why Nehru did not listen to what Russell had to say about Bolshevism. This is what Churchill had to say of the Fabian socialist, Bernard Shaw: "*Shaw had always preached the ownership of all forms of wealth by the state; yet when Lloyd George budget imposed for the first time the slender beginning of the super tax, no one made a louder squawk than this already wealthy Fabian. He is at once an acquisitive capitalist and a sincere communist.*"

Rajaji rightly commented—as reproduced in *Rajaji: A Life* by Rajmohan Gandhi: "*Mr Jawaharlal Nehru returned from Cambridge with notions of how an all-governing interventionist state can force people into happiness and prosperity through socialism.... He sticks to this bias in spite of the demonstration of world experience against it.... I hate the present folly and arrogance as much as I hated the foreign arrogance of those [British] days.*" Rajaji considered statism as a menace.

In fact, Nehru's prejudice—which he picked up at Harrow and Cambridge—against capitalism had more to do with his cultivating himself as an upper-class Englishman, who had a bias against trade, than on understanding of economics or economic history; just as his socialism had more to do with upper-class English Fabians, than with any genuine experience of or revolt against poverty. Unfortunately for India, Nehru, as prime minister, institutionalised his personal, upper-class Englishman prejudice, plunging India into fruitless, dead-end socialism, shackling the masses and suppressing initiative and growth. Nehru's class or caste bias is apparent in his autobiography where he mentions that "*right through history the old Indian ideal...looked down upon money and the professional money-making class*" and that "*today*" it is "*fighting against a new and all-powerful opposition from the bania [Vaishya] civilization of the capitalist West*".

Stanley Wolpert writes: "*Nehru's inability to rise above his deep-rooted Marxist equation of Western capitalism with imperialism, and his almost paranoid, partly aristocratic, distrust of free enterprise in its most successful form as 'vulgar', cost India dearly in retarding its overall development for the remaining years of his rule, as well as for the even longer reign of his more narrowly doctrinaire daughter.*"

David Lloyd George, the British Prime Minister in 1920, had said: "*A young man who isn't a socialist hasn't got a heart; an old man who is a socialist hasn't got a head.*"

Said Winston Churchill: "*The vice of capitalism is that it stands for the unequal sharing of blessings; whereas the virtue of socialism is that it stands for the equal sharing of misery.... Socialism is the philosophy of failure, the creed of ignorance, and the gospel of envy.*"

Chester Bowles, who had also been the US Ambassador to India, had this to comment: "*He [Nehru] had no idea of economics. He talked of Socialism, but he did not know how to define it. He talked of social justice, but I told him he could have this only when there was an increase in production. He did not grasp that. So you need a leader who understands economic issues and will invigorate your economy.*"

Walter Crocker, who was the Australian ambassador during the Nehru era, made some very incisive remarks in his book, *Nehru: A Contemporary's Estimate*: "*There was not much inhibition about asking for aid; and, according to some critics, not much gratitude. A frequent note was: aid should be bigger.... The independence of the foodless or the heavily mortgaged debtor is normally precarious.... Prices nearly doubled during the time I was in India.... Further, the professional and the middle class, already ground down by taxation...as well as by inflation, sink lower in the economic scale.... State intervention, too, grew apace under Nehru's plans. Permits, licenses, controls, foreign exchange prohibitions were always increasing. With them the corruption increased too.... The parlous food position in India, including the low, and still falling, yield per acre was... dangerously concealed...through the millions of tons of free or dumped food from the Unites States.... It is hard to escape the fear that the main achievement of Nehru's economic and social policy will turn out to be social disruption.... And it is certain that over most of India the low standard of living in the villages has not risen; over much of India it has fallen, in the last ten years. Socialists governments, notoriously, run into difficulties over food production; as Communist China did in recent years, and as Soviet Russia has been doing even forty-odd years after the Revolution...."*

## Why Persist with the Failed Model?

Just because India, thanks to the lead given by Nehru-Indira, chose the disastrous economic model of socialism, it does not mean we need to persist with those defective and failed ideas of mankind. Sadly, Nehru's legacy lives on—his socialist way of thought still flourishes—and it remains a challenge to uproot it. Outlook wise and also materially, India is still largely feudal, and it appears that the feudal ways and the Marxist/socialistic ways gel well, as both are driven by paternalistic mai-baap mentality: Sarkar knows best.

As per the article "*World's Only RDC*" in *India Today's* issue of 12 August 2013, Japan, which had almost the same GDP as India in the early 1950s, grew so fast that by 1980, India's GDP was a mere 17% of Japan's. Japan grew at massive 18% annually during the 15-year period starting 1965 and took its GDP from 91 billion dollars to a mammoth 1.1 trillion dollars by 1980. In 1982, India's per capita income was 39% higher than China's; but, by 2012, it had become mere 24% of China's—during the period China's per capita income grew

30 times, while India's grew mere 5 times. South Korea's per capita income is currently 1400% that of India, although at the time of our Independence it was on par! While India is variously terms as a Developing Country or as LDC, Less Developed Country, or as UDC, Under Developed Country, the article finds India uniquely as an RDC—*Refusing-to-Develop-Country*.

That Japan achieved what it did, and so also South Korea, Taiwan and Singapore, was because their leaders refused to follow the politically convenient and self-serving populist socialistic path to nowhere. Thanks to the wisdom that dawned upon China, it junked its socialistic past, tremendously improved its governance, and is now a superpower both economically and militarily. That India remains an RDC is thanks solely to our politicians, economists and intellectuals of the socialistic and leftist variety.

The socialist monster unleashed by Nehru is worse than Frankenstein's. Frankenstein's monster voluntarily decided to disappear after its creator's death. Not so the socialist monster. It continues with its insidious ways. And so also India's Kaliyug fashioned by Nehru's socialistic dreams gone sour.

China bid good-bye to Marxism in 1979; Berlin wall came down in 1989; USSR fell apart in 1991; host of Eastern-European countries have given up the communist ghost; Cuba is lately struggling to liberalise; poor North Koreans, thanks to continuing communism, remain condemned; yet, in India, the killing fields of socialism are yet to be fully exorcised—socialism is still respectable in India, many advocating it are still considered intellectuals, while many socialists/communists continue to win elections. Nehruvian socialism has yet to be given a burial. *Unfortunately, several prominent members of even young political outfits like the Kejriwal's AAP mouth the same stale jargon that has taken India to dogs.*

But then, why does socialism-leftism continue to remain popular. It remains popular because it has very smartly been projected as pro-poor. Who popularise it to be so? Of course, the ones who have vested interest in it. The politicians and the babus have all the media and all the resources at their command.

What has been benefitting them, they publicise it as benefitting the masses. And they succeed!

Although liberalisation since 1993 has resulted in a sea change, it has not delivered enough, and the growth has not been inclusive enough. The reason is not liberalisation—it is very insufficient liberalisation. The necessary preventive, detective, regulatory and penal systems to control corruption have not kept pace with the massive economic changes post-1991, thanks to the rapacious politician-babu combine, who have retained the pre-1991 setup. The human cost of delayed economic reforms is tremendous—additional millions unemployed or under-employed, additional millions of infant deaths, additional millions in poverty and misery. But, all these, the Jholawallahs would not appreciate. They would stick to their self-serving poverty-for-ever agenda, lest they become irrelevant. People trapped in the mindset of Nehruvian socialism fail to appreciate that India's poorest would benefit substantially from economic reforms.

Communists, socialists, Nehruvians and leftists have been very inventive in labelling: "pro-poor" policies, "progressive" ideology, "inclusive" growth,.... What they say and propound is by definition "progressive", "pro-poor" and "inclusive". But, the question is why despite such policies for decades, there has been deficient progress, insufficient reduction in poverty and non-inclusive growth. Is it that the labels are actually the antonyms for what those socialist policies actually lead to?

Thomas Sowell, the American economist, philosopher and author, has rightly commented: "*Leftism or socialism in general has a record of failure so blatant that only an intellectual could ignore or evade it.*" Socialists strut around pretending they are pro-disadvantaged and pro-oppressed. Nobody can beat them in sheer hypocrisy. They are still engaged in their hopeless fight against progress, and are committed to make a West Bengal of India.

People need to be educated to realise that "Left=NOT Right" and that socialism means only this: Poverty, Millions in Hunger, Statism, No Progress, Pathetic Infrastructure, Actually-Anti-

Poor-Pretending-Otherwise, Hypocrisy, Rapacious Domineering State, Kafkaesque Bureaucratic Controls.

It is worth noting that it is the fast growth that saves lives and keeps people from hunger and misery—and socialism ensures what people mistakenly call the "Hindu" rate of growth.

### Misnomer: The 'Hindu' Rate of Growth

India's poverty is self-inflicted, thanks to the self-destructive policies followed, even though prescriptions for prosperity were available off-the-shelf for many years, and there were any number of real, practical examples to go by. Had Nehru's government focused on its primary responsibilities and desisted getting into business, had it allowed the freedom to public to do business, India would have shot into double-digit growth rate in the 1950s itself—such were its advantages over other countries—and would long since have been a part of the developed first world, rather than still being a poor, pathetic, third-rate third-world country.

While the developing countries of SE-Asia, which had been far behind India in 1947, raced ahead at over 9% growth and became highly prosperous, with infrastructure rivalling western countries, India plodded along at what was derisively referred to as the *Hindu rate of growth* of just 3%, and became a basket-case, begging aid and food from all.

However, the term "Hindu rate of growth" is highly inappropriate and unfair, besides being derogatory. Let us examine why?

*One, the "Nehruvian rate of growth"*. The low rate of growth was thanks to Nehru-Indira-Rajiv's policies. If rather than the "Hindu rate of growth" it was called the "Nehruvian rate of growth" or "Nehruvian socialistic rate of growth" or "NIDP [Nehru-Indira-Dynasty policies] rate of growth", one would have no quarrel.

*Two, the "Colonial rate of growth"*. The rate of growth during the pre-independence period, the colonial period, was even less! In fact, it had even turned negative during several long periods!! Why was the rate of growth then not called the

"Colonial rate of growth" or the "Christian rate of growth" in a pejorative sense?

As per an estimate by Angus Maddison, a Cambridge University historian, "India's share of the world income fell from 22.6% in 1700, comparable to Europe's share of 23.3%, to a low of 3.8% in 1952."

Hindu-India had been highly prosperous in the past, thanks to its *massive* "Hindu rate of growth", which is why first the countries to the northwest of India, and then the Western countries invaded it. Until the rise of the West, India was possibly the richest country in the world, which is why it presented an irresistible target for the ravaging Mongols and their descendants, and then the West. Why then was the term "Hindu rate of growth" not used in an adulatory sense?

*Three, how do you explain the recent growth rate of over 9%?* The same India, after only part junking of the Nehru-Indira-Rajiv socialistic policies, reached a growth rate of over 9%! Junk more of the Nehru-Indira socialistic policies, and the growth rate will rise to double-digits.

*Four, absurdity of religious-cultural connotation.* Many Islamic countries prior to the world demand and discovery of oil were very poor. Was their growth rate called the "Islamic rate of growth"? The growth rate during the dark ages of Europe was static or negative, when during the same period India was immensely rich and progressive. Was it ever called the "Christian rate of growth"? Sri Lanka and Myanmar have had long periods of no growth or measly growth. Were they castigated for being under the spell of the "Buddhist rate of growth"? China's growth rate after going communist and till the end of the Mao-period was pathetic. Was it termed the "Atheistic rate of growth"? Why associate "Hindu" with a rate of economic growth unless there is an ulterior motive of deliberately showing Hinduism in bad light? Of course, many use the term unfeelingly, without being conscious of its implications.

*Five, Nehru vs. Hinduism.* Nehru was an agnostic, and was more English than Indian, more western than eastern, more "something else" than a Hindu, and therefore it is grossly inappropriate to name a rate of growth, which was thanks to him and his dynasty, as "Hindu".

*Six, why not "Secular" rate of growth?* Nehru, Nehru-dynasty and company have raved ad nauseum on "secularism", without ensuring it in practice. Why not credit the growth rate thanks to them as the "'Secular' rate of growth"?

*Seven, Socialism vs. Hinduism.* Hindu-India has had long tradition of free international trade and commerce, and of liberal religious and world view. Such an ethos can never accept the Big Brother denouement or the run-up to it. There is an age old Indian proverb: *Raja Vyapari taya Praja Bhikhari.* That is, people become beggars when government enters into business. A belief in self-reliance and an overweening socialistic state on the part of Jawaharlal Nehru and Indira Gandhi actually did India in, rather than something that had anything to do with Hinduism.

*Eight, Socialism vs. Mahatma Gandhi and Others.* Mahatma Gandhi was no socialist. Nor were the other stalwarts like Sardar Patel, Rajaji and Rajendra Prasad. All the four—Mahatma Gandhi, Sardar Patel, Rajaji and Rajendra Prasad—quite unlike Nehru, could be considered as also representing the Hindu ethos, and perhaps precisely for that reason they were against socialistic claptrap of Nehru.

*Nine, a camouflage.* In any case, using "Hindu" as in "Hindu rate of growth" in a pejorative sense is not only insulting, it camouflages the real reasons—socialistic claptrap was never going to give you a respectable growth rate to enable you to ameliorate the lot of the poor.

But, the question arises as to why did the term "Hindu rate of growth" gain currency? Well, here are the reasons.

*One. Raj Krishna.* The term was reportedly coined by the economist Raj Krishna to draw attention to the embarrassing rate of growth during the Nehru-Indira period. India being predominantly populated by the Hindus, he called it the "Hindu rate of growth". But, of course, he didn't mean it to be insulting to Hinduism. He just used another term to represent India. It would have been more appropriate had he used the terms like

"Nehruvian socialistic rate of growth", which would have been really representative and meaningful.

However, what is interesting is the way it was lapped up, used, and made popular by the Nehruvians themselves, the socialists, and the leftist intellectuals; and also by the India-baiters and the colonialists.

*Two. Blame Hinduism rather than Socialism.* Indian politicians and bureaucrats never wanted to admit that the fault lay with the socialistic apparatus. Why blame self? Especially, why blame something on which you have fattened yourselves? The leftists, socialists and communists got prized slots in the government or government-aided organisations, societies and universities, and dominated the intellectual discourse in India: professors, historians, economists, journalists, and so on. Socialism and Marxism could not be wrong—what was required was more of it! The whole band, be it politicians or bureaucrats or intellectuals, didn't mind the blame shifting to the religious-cultural heritage. Someone coined the term, the next one picked it up, and it spread.

*Three. The Secularists.* For certain class of intellectuals the touchstone of secularism is whether you can be abusive to Hinduism. The term "Hindu" in "Hindu rate of growth" serves that purpose. It serves for them the double purpose: camouflage the ills resulting from socialism, and be also hailed "secular" the cheap way—by casting a slur on Hinduism.

*Four. The Colonialists and the India-baiters.* Other groups, which received the term with glee, lapped it up, and enthusiastically promoted it to disparage India, were the colonialists or those with the colonial mind-set or the brown sahibs, or the India-baiters. Give power to the Hindus, and what you will get is the "Hindu rate of growth"! Had the British Raj continued, things would have been better!!

## The Apologists

DEDs, the unabashed Defenders and apologists of the Establishment and the Dynasty (that has ruled India for most of the period after independence) highlight the changes since

1947 to tom-tom the achievements. Well, with passage of time, things would change. The right and the honest way to evaluate India's progress since independence is not to talk of changes in a general and absolute way, but in a relative way and compared to what it could have been.

We have to compare ourselves with nations who were about as good or as bad as us, or were worse off than us, around the time India got independence—like China, Japan, South Korea, Taiwan, Singapore (formed later), and so on—but are now far ahead of India. Compared to them, we cut a sorry figure, having been left far, far behind!

However, the DEDs are careful to compare India only with such nations as Pakistan, Bangladesh, Nepal, Afghanistan. Bangladesh and Nepal are better than India on a few indicators, and should they do better in future, these DEDs would have to give examples of African countries. However, they would need to be careful on that score too—on several indicators, certain African nations are ahead of India. If the ambition of these DEDs doesn't go beyond these countries, one can only pity their dreams and vision for India—unfortunately, these DEDs even include a famous lyricist who is professionally supposed to dream!

DEDs even come up with "it could have been worse" counterfactuals: India could have fallen apart, it could been a military dictatorship, it could have gone the way of Pakistan, and so on—and thanks to the Dynasty, it is not as bad. What if one advanced a counterfactual: India would have been a prosperous first-world country by 1980s had the Nehru-Indira-Dynasty not been in the saddle.

## Socialism and the AAP

The AAP has people with various strands of thoughts: stale-socialists, liberated-free-market-proponents, pragmatists, populists, opportunists. One only hopes that with the exit of Prashant-Yogendra duo stale-socialists are history in the AAP; and liberated-free-market-proponents and pragmatists would ultimately dominate for the sake of better India.

# 8

# SOCIALISM, BABUDOM AND CORRUPTION

**(Does the AAP understand the connection?)**

*S3: Save Society from Socialists.*
*SSCC: Save Society from Crony Capitalists.*
*SIFB: Save India from Babudom.*

—to paraphrase Raghuram Rajan's book title
*Saving Capitalism from the Capitalists*

*The government of my country snubs honest simplicity but fondles artistic villainy, and I think I might have developed into a very capable pickpocket if I had remained in the public service a year or two.*

—Mark Twain

It is unfair to only target the politicians. The greater culprit is the Babudom—the IAS-IPS-IFS-IRS combine, those from the criminal-justice system, and the bureaucracy lower down. Babudom is very intimately related to socialism, poor rate of growth, continued poverty, injustice and misery. The venal politicians, particularly the dynasts and the dynacracy, that is, the dynastic democracy; the poverty-perpetuating socialistic claptrap and populism and the crony capitalism that goes with it; and the callous, incompetent, ineffective, kleptocratic babudom are intimately inter-related. These three nodes are interdependent and feed one another.

Isn't it strange that while political parties excoriate one another, TV and print media pans the political class, and

NGOs and Civil Society groups fulminate against them, hardly anyone highlights the venality, lack of probity, incompetence and corruption of the babus, without whose complicity or negligence no scam is possible. Khemka, a capable and honest IAS officer who has been at the receiving end, had commented, "If bureaucrats did their duty, there would be no scams."

Indeed, Babudom is a strong pillar of the foundations of India's misery.

### Who is Responsible for the Misgovernance Mess?

When a private company fails or does badly you blame its top-executives, who are generally made to resign. The top executives of the government are IAS-IFS-IPS-IRS combine. You have to blame them for failure of India both at the Centre and in the states. Sadly, these non-performers continue irrespective of their performance.

They sit at the top of the dung-heap, and are in many ways more powerful than the politicians, who come and go every five years, while they continue, irrespective of their performance, on account of their constitutional sinecure. ICS prospered under the British, while the nationalists suffered jails. Post-independence, the top babus—not all, but an overwhelming majority—have been having a good time: making money, misusing power, contributing little, taking the country to dogs, and then blaming the politicians for all the ills, and how they are not allowed to function! The babus indeed have very low IQ—low *Integrity Quotient.*

### Why have Babus been Supporters of Socialism?

Most of the babus have been supporters of socialism or significant state controls and regulations, not because they think it would do any good to India, but because it results in enhancement of their powers and importance and opens avenues for making money.

### To Hell with Primary Responsibilities!

The primary duty of any government is to provide justice to all, ensure internal and external security, and build infrastructure and institutions of good governance. Nehru dynasty did the reverse. While it miserably failed to deliver on all the primary counts, it arrogantly went into business, which is none of government's business. It sought to be a trader and an industrialist—with no qualifications or expertise whatsoever. The generalist IAS babus salivated at the opportunities for power and pelf. Primary responsibilities went for a toss.

## Babus and the Failure of the Criminal-justice System

Justice to all? The powerful and the rich and the well-connected can get away with murder and huge scams and corruption; while the poor—and not just the poor, anyone bereft of power and right connections—can go to dogs: the state of the police and the judicial system being what it is.

The kind of criminal-justice system the governments, predominantly run by the Nehru-Gandhi dynasty since independence, have managed to build is exemplified by this story that was reported in newspapers in May, 2013. A poor lady, Vijai Kumari, living in a village in Aligarh district was arrested and imprisoned, and later granted bail by Allahabad High Court in 1994. However, she could not fulfil the bail conditions of a personal bond and two sureties. Nobody came to her help, and she had to stay behind bars. She was pregnant when arrested. She gave birth to a son in the jail. Her son, whom she named Kanhaiya, grew up in jail and then in Children's home. Upon turning 18, he was sent to a rehabilitation centre. He had received training in garment manufacturing. With his earning he arranged for a lawyer and bail amount and finally got his mother released after 19 years! Can a state and criminal-justice system be more callous?

## Babus and the Colonial Culture

Nehru and subsequent governments have done nothing to change the babudom and make it people-oriented, service-oriented and development-oriented—they continue with their feudal class consciousness and arrogant ways, ill-suited to public service. The pre-Independence babu culture of living like a rajah, misusing power, exploiting people, becoming rich at their cost, and aping the British ways to look cultured, continues.

## How the Babus Lord it Out

As per 15 October 2013 *Times of India, Mumbai news-item '2,600 cops serve in homes of IPS officers in state'* by Prafulla Marpakwar: "*...The question now is whether [the government] will withdraw the 2,600-odd police personnel deployed at the residences of 280 IPS officers across the state [of Maharashtra].... At least seven to 10 constables are deployed at the residence of an Indian Police Service officer, a senior IPS officer said. If this number is reduced, the state will get enough policemen to fill up at least 10 to 15 police stations.... [A conscientious] IPS officer said, 'I am shocked that so many constables are deployed. Occasionally I feel we are still in the British Raj....'*" The report states that 5 to 9 constables, 3 orderlies, 1 cook, 2-3 telephone runners and 2 drivers are deployed at the residences of SPs/Commissioners; while 2 to 5 constables, 2-3 orderlies, 2 telephone runners and 2 drivers are deployed at the residences of other IPS officials. The report continues: "*'Many officers have even more staffers, depending on their influence. In Pune, a high-ranking officer in the prisons department had 15-20 constables at his official residence,' said a senior IPS officer.... What was more shocking, the officer said, was that the staff remained the same even if the officer were to be shifted to another city, and even after an officer retired, the police personnel continued to serve him for a period ranging from three months to a year.*"

So, while the citizens may remain insecure and crimes against women may be a growing menace, the IPS babus, like their IAS counterparts, must lord it out. Which other democratic country in the world would allow such shamelessness, brazenness, colonial luxuries, feudal lordliness, priority of services to self over services to people, and utter contempt for the general public! And, can an abysmally poor country like India where millions go hungry afford this? Only a feudal, dynastic democracy like India, where those at the help similarly lord it out in utter contempt and disregard of the people, can permit such gross insult and indifference to the public!!

## Babus Care too Hoots About their Subordinates

The way the IPS babus allow their subordinates to be treated is astounding. There are many shocking examples. Here is a sample, a report in *The Indian Express* of 11 March 2014 titled '*No beds or bathrooms at SRPF's training base in Mumbai*': "*There are no beds or bathrooms, and the toilet facilities are almost unusable. About 700 personnel of the State Reserve Police Force are living in such conditions in the SRPF training base in Mumbai's Aarey Milk Colony. They sleep on dirt floors in the barracks....*" Why can't IPS babus or their associations take up the cause of their subordinates? Or, are they concerned only with their own luxuries?

## Why "Service" Attached to their Names?

What has the Babudom done—especially the IAS at the top, who ought to be accountable for it—to transform the state from a callous exploiter to one that serves citizens. One wonders why that "*S for Service*" is attached at the end of IAS, IPS, IFS and IRS, unless it signifies only self-service or service to their masters. Do they serve the public? Or, do they get served? Has the Babudom cared to evolve a system that provides incentives and rewards for desirable behaviour for their fraternity; and penalties for undesirable behaviour? They can't just put the blame on the political class. If they can't do all this as individuals, they can surely attempt it as a group—they have their own powerful associations. What do they do?

In the mid-1930s Nehru denounced the ICS—Indian Civil Service—as "*neither Indian nor civil nor a service*". He further said it was "*essential that the ICS and similar services disappear completely*". Unfortunately, after independence, with himself in power, such pledges, like other promises, faded away. The term 'Indian Administrative Service' is a misnomer considering the criminal absence both of "administration" and of "service" to public.

## Attributes of Indian Babudom

The Indian babudom is authoritarian, arrogant, callous, unfair, heartless, insensitive, ill-mannered, indifferent, incompetent, inefficient, ineffective, uninnovative, nepotistic, rude, sloppy, sluggish, self-seeking and shamelessly corrupt. Bureaucracy is now Kleptocracy. The only thing that partially saves us from the bureaucracy is its inefficiency. Even if politicians are willing, the babus are incompetent in executing anything positive or constructive, or delivering reforms on the ground—how can they, when they are unable to reform themselves?

Wrote Kuldip Nayar in 'Beyond the Lines' about the Emergency: "*Only a handful of civil servants stood their ground, others were too scared to lose their jobs. Some found in it an opportunity to occupy high positions on the understanding that they would carry out illegal orders. Sanjay Gandhi converted the civil servants into a servile breed; the willing tools of tyranny. They have not to this day recovered from the loss of esteem in the eyes of the public if not their own. They wield authority, not respect. Their political masters know that bureaucrats are beholden to them because they are partners in the loot in which both of them indulge without a twinge of conscience.*"

## Are all Babus Corrupt and Incompetent?

*Of course, not all babus are bad. It is only 99 per cent of babus, as someone said, who give the rest a bad name*! There are a few like Kiran Bedi who are fighting for better systems. Also, persons like T.S.R. Subramaniam, the ex-Cabinet Secretary, who has written the book, *Journeys through Babudom and Netaland*. It is worth reading.

## Babudom and the Metamorphosis of Franz Kafka

Babudom reminds one of Franz Kafka's *Metamorphosis*. What if Kafka was born in India and was witness to post-independence India; and what if he wrote *Metamorphosis* in the current Indian context? Would it still have the undertone of absurdity and alienation, and of a random and chaotic universe with no governing system of order and justice? Would it still have Gregor, a travelling salesman, metamorphose into a gigantic insect? Or, would it rather have the undertone of a crass, callous, corrupt, rusted, unjust system—all man-made; with Gregor, a babu rather than a travelling salesman, metamorphose into a gigantic cockroach?

## Indian Babudom Independently Evaluated

PERC (Political and Economic Risk Consultancy: www.asiarisk.com) rates Indian bureaucracy as one of the worst bureaucracies in Asia responsible for, as an article in *The Indian Express*, Mumbai of 16 October 2013 states, "*bottlenecking key policies, widespread red tapism in everyday affairs, massive corruption, being uninnovative and insensitive, and harbouring generalist officers who lack expertise.*" A report "*Corruption's Impact on the Business Environment*" for 2013 for Asia-Pacific was published by PERC. It grades countries on a scale of 10, 0 being the best and 10 being the worst—most corrupt. Singapore came at the top with a score of 0.74, Japan and Australia tied at number 2 with a score of 2.35, and India came at the bottom with a score of 8.95!

## What should be Done About the Babudom?

The India bureaucratic system is beyond reform. The only remedy is to dismantle it completely and put up a new system in its place. It is badly in need of creative destruction.

## Should Babus be Employed Post-retirement?

No. Because, the carrot of post-retirement assignment makes them compromise on their pre-retirement responsibilities. Besides, why let retirees block available positions. Give those in service a chance. Make way for the young. In case the retirees are keen to serve the country, let them come on as honorary advisors, without payment or perks.

## For Nation's Doom: Indians Always in Service (IAS)!

As if their normal service-period is not sufficient to ruin the country, a large number of retired babus manage a government position in some establishment or the other, and never really retire. No wonder Indian Express [IE] in its series of articles in July, 2012 expanded IAS as "*Indians Always in Service*". The probability of procuring a "*confirmed gravy train ticket*", as

IE called it, is predominantly influenced by the extent of one's servility to the powers that be.

Although politicians are largely blamed for India's misery, the babudom is as much or perhaps more responsible. In fact, political class and babudom, mainly IAS, have co-opted each other. Politicians can't amass wealth, handout favours and perpetuate their rule and that of their dynasty without the cooperation of the top babus; and the top babus, in turn, can't keep getting plump postings, a cut in the moolah and gain indemnity for their misdeeds without the kind intervention of the politicians. Being a mutually beneficial combination, the top babus seek and the politicians facilitate their continuation even after retirement. In expectation of life-long employment and/or opportunities of making of money, most of the babus have practically sold their souls to the politicians and are free from all scruples. They serve not the nation, but the politicians, and in the process, actually serve themselves.

## Why Generalist where Experts Required?

Indian Babudom predominantly harbours generalist with expertise in nothing except in bottlenecking key policies, holding or pushing files, red-tapism and corruption. However, thanks to the prevailing system of political patronage, powerful, pliant, generalist babus have long since expanded their tentacles to capture not only governorships, but also most of the critical positions requiring specialist expertise, such as position of RBI governor, CAG, head of TRAI, CCI, NDMA, CERC, and so on. It is worth noting that almost all top positions require high-level expertise, and the generalist IAS (even if they have done some course or taken some training or gained some little experience just to corner those posts) are gross misfits, because top-level expertise demands years of focused work in a particular field, which the IAS can never gain. IAS therefore has nothing worthwhile to contribute in those areas, and become mere file-pushers passing their time. Why shouldn't the head of TRAI be a telecom expert rather than an IAS babu? Why should the CAG be from IAS rather than from the Indian Audit and Accounts Service? Why shouldn't the RBI governor be an accomplished, experienced economist (like the current one)—why should he be an IAS babu? How come the USA manages to have high-level experts from the concerned fields to head the relevant positions; while in sharp contrast, we put in the IAS babus as square pegs in round holes in all top positions.

Why is it so? Actually, politicians require compliant people who would do their bidding; and IAS babus more than meet that requirement. Why take academic, judicial, social, financial, revenue, security, disaster management, law-enforcing, business, trade, management, information technology, telecom or other technical experts from outside to head those positions and run the unnecessary risk of having honest, conscientious and forthright persons? IAS babus are safe bets, more so the retired ones begging for assignments.

With the economic liberalisation post-1991 it was expected that the bureaucratic stranglehold would loosen. But, sensing the vastly enhanced scope of making the moolah with the unprecedented expansion of the economy, the politician-bureaucratic combine ensured that the plethora of new bodies, especially the regulatory ones that came into being, were hijacked by the babus. With a nod from the politicians, serving and retired babus have captured practically all important decision-making bodies. With IAS babus as heads of regulatory bodies, autonomous, independent, honest, competent and sane regulation is a chimera. Babudom, as it has existed, is incapable of delivering, as the experience of over six decades after independence bears out. There have been some babus who have tried to do good, but that's a miniscule percentage and an exception, and even they could not go very far, as they stood check-mated by the establishment, including their own colleagues.

An article, '*Revenge of the Babus*' in India Today of 27 September 2013 states: "Of the 12 economic regulators created since liberalisation, nine are headed by retired bureaucrats. Appointments to constitutional bodies like CAG, Central Vigilance Commission or RBI inevitably come from their ranks. In 20 states, the chief information commissioner is the state's former chief secretary. They head human rights commissions, SC and ST commissions and finance commissions, and are even part of bodies like the National Disaster Management Authority (NDMA).... Two decades after liberalisation, Babu Raj is back as India's only permanent establishment... [For the] Competition Commission of India (CCI), a new regulatory body...instituted in 2003...a technocrat was apparently considered for the job but retired commerce secretary...was picked instead. The appointment was challenged in a PIL.... Then chief justice V.N. Khare was quoted as saying, 'At this rate, a day would come, maybe after 20 years, when the 26 judges of the apex court would be replaced by bureaucrats' [that's what the corrupt politicians and babus would love!].... At the central level, there has been a near-complete dominance of IAS appointees to head regulatory bodies, a 'regulatory capture'.... In the same month that Khullar [former commerce secretary] was appointed chairman of TRAI, the Federal Communications Commission in the US appointed two young commissioners, Ajit Pai and Jessica Rosenworcel. Both had extensive experience in communications law. So why aren't young domain specialists heading regulatory bodies in India?... According to S.L. Rao, a senior economist who was appointed chairman of the first CERC in 1998, the top post was kept vacant for 10 months after his term ended in 2001 so that the incumbent power secretary, Ashok Basu, could take over the job after his retirement.... S.L. Rao explains that part of the reason that electricity regulation hasn't taken off in the states is that bureaucrats heading the regulators refuse to take tough decisions on pricing...."

IAS and the like should be banned from all top-level appointments requiring special expertise; and there are many such areas: Defence, Education, Electricity, Energy, Environment, Finance, Information Technology, Mining, Nuclear Energy, Regulatory, RBI, SEBI, Telecom, and so on. In fact, practically all departments at the top-level (not just the top-most level), except perhaps a few, require high degree of expertise which can be earned only by almost life-long work in the chosen field.

## Should Outsiders/Experts be Inducted?

Yes. Top-level assignments in all categories discussed above must be of specialists taken from outside. They can be given say a one-month course to familiarise themselves with the Babugiri, that is, the government working. IAS-officers may be appointed as their PAs to take care of the nitty-gritty of administration and file-movement.

## Bureaucracy Needs to be Competent Like the Chinese

Most of China's bureaucrats are engineers, scientists, professionals, and experts in various fields, who have risen up the hard way—by merit and performance. Compare that with file-pushing expert-in-nothing babus in India rising up the ranks on the basis of seniority and chamchagiri. This has to change. India can't afford to carry on with its existing Babudom. It has to drastically change itself and transform into an accountable, innovative, efficient, meritocratic machine. It has to learn from the Chinese.

To take care of SARS-infected patients in 2003, China built a 1000-bed hospital in Beijing in just 7 days—excluding, of course, the time for planning, design, blue-prints and approvals. Using 500 construction machines, over 4000 construction labourers worked non-stop during April 24–30 to build the giant hospital. It was made operational within days, with 1200 medical staff procured nationwide from military hospitals. Such is the competence of Chinese managers.

At its fastest growth-period, the US was doubling its living standards every 30 years; something which China has been doing every 10 years for the last 30 years! Consequent to a mega annual meeting of Chinese leaders in Beijing on March 5, Prime Minister Li Keqiang declared the country's war on pollution, and the anti-pollution campaign commenced. Do we see such huge political-neutral initiatives in India.

What takes decades in other countries, China does in mere years. In the recent past, it extended pension coverage to an extra 240 million (!!) in the rural area in just two years. Public-pension system in the US, that took decades, covers lesser numbers!

## Socialism + Babudom = Corruption

*Among a people generally corrupt, liberty cannot long exist.*

—Edmund Burke

Insufficient, halting and reluctant liberalisation thanks to continued socialistic way of thinking, coupled with lack of transparency and institutions of good regulation and governance, thanks to crony capitalism benefiting the political and the bureaucratic class, has pushed India into an abyss of corruption.

To minimise crony capitalism and the opportunities for gain from bribe-driven decisions, non-discretionary rules and strong open competitive market structures are required, coupled with transparency of rules and processes. That requires doing away with socialist mindset and socialistic-bureaucratic machinery.

# 9

# POVERTY AND PROSPERITY

**(What AAP and its supporters ought to know.)**

*Poor countries are poor because those who have power make choices that create poverty.*

—Daron Acemoglu and James A. Robinson

## Do Climate, Geography, Race, ... Matter?

*Are one or more of these factors that make a country poor or prosperous: climate, geography, location, abundance of natural resources, race, history, "type of people", "character of people"?*

No. None of these.

Daron Acemoglu and James Robinson in their book ***Why Nations Fail**: The Origins of Power, Prosperity and Poverty* demonstrate, inter alia, that climate, geography, location, history, race, "type" of people are NOT the reasons a country is rich or poor.

They take examples of neighbouring countries with identical climate, geography, location, history, race and "type" of people, where one-side is poor and the other prosperous: Mexico and the states of the US bordering it like Texas; North Korea and South Korea; Haiti and the Dominican Republic in the Caribbean region. One can add to these comparisons the Mainland China till the early eighties versus Taiwan; and Malaysia versus Singapore.

The determining factor, the authors say, are the institutions: human-made systems, rules and regulations, and how they are implemented on the ground. '*Extractive* Institutions' cause poverty and misery, while '*Inclusive* Institutions' lead to prosperity and freedom.

What are *extractive* institutions? Characteristics of *extractive economic* institutions are: lack of law and order, insecure property rights, entry barriers and regulations preventing functioning of markets and creating a non-level-playing field. Characteristics of *extractive political* institutions are: concentrating of power in the hands of a few without constraints, checks and balances or rule of law. *Extractive* institutions exist because there are powerful vested interests who stand to lose if the institutions were to become *inclusive*. *Extractive* institutions are normally the feature of monarchy, feudal system, political or military dictatorships, fascism, socialism and communism. Capitalist societies that are not fairly capitalist, or where crony capitalism prevails, may also lead to *extractive* institutions.

*Inclusive* institutions are the opposite of the above. Their characteristics include: encouragement of investments; harnessing the power of markets by better allocation of resources; allowing entry of more efficient firms; ease of starting businesses and provision of finance for them; and generating broader participation in the economy through education and ease of entry for new entrants. Growth under inclusive institutions involves both creative destruction (replacement of the old methods, technology, industries by new) and investment in technology.

*Inclusive* institutions are not compatible with socialism, communism and feudal societies, or with dictatorships and monarchies. Only a society with *competitive capitalism* is capable of having *inclusive* institutions.

## India a First-World Country by 1980?

Yes, certainly. Extrapolating the time it took Singapore, South Korea and Taiwan to become first-world countries by adopting competitive capitalism, and the time it took West Germany and Japan to rise from the ashes of the Second World War by adopting capitalist economy, it seems reasonable that India would have been a prosperous, first-rate, first-world country by 1980 had it too adopted competitive capitalism and befriended the West.

Unfortunately for the crores of starving Indians and millions of others who had great hopes for themselves, their families and the nation after independence, Nehru guided India into a poverty-and-misery-perpetuating socialistic-bureaucratic black-hole. His descendants, Indira and Rajiv Gandhi, by doing much more of the same, made the situation worse. UPA-I and II, by part reverting to the Nehru-Indira disastrous ways, have reversed the Narsimha Rao—Vajpayee upward trend.

### "Unless People Change... Can't Progress!" Argument

"People are like that... Unless people change... Unless the society improves,... Unless the society takes active interest... nothing would change.... Politics is but a reflection of the society..." goes another argument.

However, there is little evidence to show that the prosperous countries have become prosperous thanks not to the competence of its leaders, but to its amorphous public and civil society which suddenly decided to improve itself and take active interest in the well-being of the nation. There is no evidence to show that it was not Lee Kuan Yew and his band of competent leaders, but the suddenly awakened common Singaporeans, who, by themselves, took Singapore to such heights. Yes, good leaders choose competent teams, inspire people, motivate them and take the nation ahead with their cooperation; but it is rare that general public by itself, without a competent leadership, transforms a nation. India's tragedy has been a lack of genuinely competent leadership. Our so-called great leaders were really Lilliputs.

Common man is busy earning his or her livelihood. They are working on their chosen vocations and thus contributing to the society. They have outsourced supply of water, electricity and other utilities to companies at an agreed payment. Similarly, they have outsourced development of the nation and maintenance of towns, villages, cities, provision of security, and so on to elected politicians and appointed bureaucrats and technocrats. Each of them, whether a politician or a bureaucrat or a technocrat, is getting paid by the public (indirectly through taxes) to perform its allocated work. Just as each member of the public is doing its job (as a banker or an IT professional or a factory worker, and so on), so also each of its (indirectly) appointed persons (a politician or a bureaucrat or a technocrat) ought to do his or her work. It is because these appointed or elected politicians and babus, whose cost is borne by the public, are failing to perform their tasks that the nation is going to dogs. Hence, it is illogical to blame the society or public. Of course, having elected or appointed these politicians and babus, it is the duty of the electing/appointing authority—the general public—to take them to task for non-performance and ensure they serve them and do their allocated task.

## Spurious Reasons for India's Failure

Why has India failed? There are any number of spurious reasons: problem of national character; people not being hard-working; lack of discipline; corruption; colonial baggage; democracy, which is "soft"—what is needed is dictatorship, preferably military dictatorship. Those who advance such pleas should be asked: "Why was the economy doing relatively much better after 1993? Had the lazy of the old days suddenly became very hard-working? Had the national character changed for the better? Were people suddenly more disciplined? Why the Indian software professionals proved themselves to be highly competent and hard-working?" The real reason for the woes had nothing to do with those spurious factors. It was a plain, bad, borrowed Nehruvian economic model of socialism that did us in. There was a brisk progress even with marginal liberalisation.

## Unless "People with Character", Can't Take off!

So goes the plea of many. Including that of the organisation devoted to "character building", and which claims monopoly on patriotism, on "what is good for India", and on prescriptions for setting the country right.

These advocates of "character building" need to be asked: "Has the Indian character changed for the good or for the worse during the last 66 years after independence? Their answer would mostly be: it has changed for the worse. If so, where is the guarantee it would improve in the future. And, what if the character continues to remain the same for the next 1000 years? Is India then doomed for another millennium?"

Among the best cities in the world are several from Australia, which is now a first-rate, first-world country. It has no great civilisational heritage. Nor can it boast of "character" that has propelled it to where it is now. Their "character" heritage comprises murderers, rapists, dacoits, thieves, debtors, fraudsters, and the like, who were herded in ships in Britain and brought to Australia to undergo their jail terms. January 26 is celebrated as Australia Day, because in January 1788, eleven ships packed with convicts from Britain landed at Botany Bay in Sydney leading to the formation of the colony of New South Wales in Australia.

Priests, reformers and character-builders did not land in Australia to uplift the characters of the settler-convicts who made Australia their home. However, Australia dramatically progressed despite the "bad" characters and despite the absence of "character-builders". Why? How? That's what one must try to understand, and apply the lessons learnt to India, where applicable, rather than advancing silly pet theories like "requirements of character". Competitive capitalism lies at the root of their prosperity. They never touched socialism even with a long pole.

Lee Kuan Yew and his band of competent leaders of Singapore were not "Character-Builders". They didn't have that luxury of time, nor did they believe in those crazy notions. They knew what mattered was forward-looking economic policies and good governance. They therefore focused on implementing solid competitive capitalism, coupled with developing well-paid, merit-driven and competent bureaucracy.

In the process of building and enhancing competitive capitalism, and with increasing prosperity and peace both in Singapore and Australia, the "character" automatically "improved"! It is well to remember that character is also shaped by economic condition. You can't have millions in hunger and poverty and in wretched condition and with little to look forward to, and expect people to develop "good character"!

### What is Required is "The Spirit of Sacrifice"

No true.

It would suffice to quote Ayn Rand: "*America's abundance was created not by public sacrifices to 'the common good,' but by the productive genius of free men who pursued their own personal interests and the making of their own private fortunes. They did not starve the people to pay for America's industrialization. They gave the people better jobs, higher wages and cheaper goods with every new machine they invented, with every scientific discovery or technological advance—and thus the whole country was moving forward and profiting, not suffering, every step of the way.*"

Said Adam Smith in *The Wealth of Nations*: "*It is not from the benevolence of the butcher, the brewer, or the baker, that we expect our dinner, but from their regard to their own interest.*"

### "Scientific" Socialism a Contradiction in Terms!

We have already covered socialism-marxism in an earlier chapter, and have seen how Nehru-Indira-Rajiv poverty-perpetuating and misery-multiplying socialism took India to dogs. In fact, globally, no country has prospered under socialism-marxism-communism-maoism. Dismal fate of all nations that went socialist proves the point. This we have discussed for various socialist-communist countries.

### Why Things not Worked out Before Independence?

One finds it immensely distressing that while we succeeded in doing all the wrong or mostly wrong things after independence be it the socialistic economic policy or the external security matters or internal security; we failed to carry through any of the needed reforms or rectifications or restructuring be it babudom or police or criminal-justice system or our outdated laws or our past or contemporary history or our slavish colonial culture. What is amazing is that Nehru, and after him, his dynasty, had a field day doing as he (or they) pleased unconstrained by any policy constraints. Hence, the baffling question. Why had the freedom-fighting greats and the Congress not studied each important segment in sufficient detail and why were they not ready with a blueprint well before the actual independence.

They could have formed separate study/expert groups on policies on economy, finance, transport infrastructure like railways, airways, waterways and roads, power and energy sector, mining, environment, heavy industries, small and medium industries, village industries and handicrafts, trade and commerce, agriculture, allied-agricultural activities, literacy, education at various levels, specialisation in arts, medicine, engineering, science and other fields, research, historical research and recording of correct past and contemporary history, industrial and agricultural training and research, India's borders with neighbours and their status and steps to be taken after independence to firm up borders and ensure peace, foreign relations, defence and external security, internal security and firmer integration of all states, language policy, popularisation of Sanskrit, compulsory English for all, massive mass-campaigns across India on sanitation, hygiene, garbage-disposal, keeping environment clean, healthy and garbage-free, and mass-campaigns to root out casteism and communalism, and so on.

The study/expert groups should have visited other countries, particularly the prosperous ones like the US (unlike the conducted tours of the USSR designed to impress Nehru, and bias him into copycat Indian disaster), and studied what could be applied in the Indian context. They should have started building foreign relations with various countries, particularly the US, as part of the independence movement. It would have helped the freedom movement itself. The exercise would have thrown up many experts in diverse fields who could have steered India right after independence. It would have greatly helped mitigate the risk of letting only one person like Nehru have his way.

The list given above is long, and the scope vast. But, the freedom-fighters and the Congress had all the time in the world for it. Their major agitations were only once-in-a-decade affairs:

early 1920s, early 1930s and early 1940s. There were long gaps between the major agitations to do the suggested studies and to discuss and thrash out the details. Even in jails during the agitations, they had plenty of time. Some did spend time reading and writing. Some experimented with home remedies and food and fasting. The remaining passed the time in various other ways. However, no set of individuals or groups engaged themselves on any of the vital matters enumerated above. You have volumes full of Gandhi's writings, Nehru-Gandhi correspondence, and voluminous writings by others. But, hardly anything worthwhile on what really mattered for the independent India! So irresponsible, and so surprising! What was the result? Post-independence, whatever Nehru fancied, he did, and we know the result!

## Socialism Benefits only the Vested Interests

Socialism and leftism is something which benefits large sections of vested interests, but not the intended beneficiaries. Why do poor, who can ill-afford, prefer private schools to government schools, private hospitals to government hospitals? They know that this socialist claptrap is for the babus and politicians to make money, not to help them. Communism and socialism assume the State as a kind, empathetic *mai-baap*, meant to do good for the people; when the experience and the practical reality is that very often it is the State—through its agency of politicians, babus and police—that is the biggest *exploiter* and *mafia* around.

## Why Socialism Remains Popular?

It remains popular because it has very smartly been projected as pro-poor. Who popularise it to be so? Of course, the ones who have vested interest in it—the politicians, the babus and the leftist intellectuals, who have spawned the academe, the establishment, the NGOs and the media. What has been benefiting them, they publicise it as benefiting the masses. And they succeed!

## Predominance of Leftist Claptrap

It is India's tragedy that rational, bold, no-nonsense, rightist leadership and influential intellectual class that unapologetically supports competitive capitalism is absent. It is a crucial handicap in tackling poverty and in India's rise to a prosperous first-world nation.

It is high time the general voting public was educated to realise that leftism, socialism and sops would take them nowhere and would condemn them further to a life of want and misery; and that the jholawallahs, like the religious and communal fundamentalists and the casteists, belong to the past, and have no relevance for modern India.

Sadly the leftist "intellectual" brand and the leftist politics predominate in India. It's a vicious cycle. Leftist/socialist vote-catching-sops create poverty and misery. In turn, poverty and misery fuel further socialism and sops. The worse you get, the more leftist and socialist you become!

Practically all regional parties (SP, RJD, JDU, Trinamool Congress,...) profess to be socialists. The Congress is anyway an opportunist socialist and "electoral secular" party. Even the BJP had once professed to be a Gandhian socialist party. AAP, a young party, with many young professional faces, was expected to be different. But, they plan to be more socialist that all the other parties put together!

Is it that Indian intellectuals and politicians—both young and old—lack courage, and want only to play the safe, populist way, and socialism comes in handy.

That's why when people say why does one have to hark back to Nehru-Indira, who are long dead, one has to assert that their malinfluence still prevails, and afflicts intellectuals too.

## Democracy Compatible with Socialism?

Many say they don't like capitalism, but they want democracy. Many talk of democratic socialism. But what is the historical origin of "democracy"? Did socialism give rise to democracy? Did communism give rise to democracy? No. Historically, all socialist and communist societies have curbed freedom, democracy being a far cry. Did a feudal system or a monarchical system or a dictatorship give rise to democracy? No.

It was the mercantile-industrial capitalism that led to democracy. Democracy and capitalism go together. Competitive capitalism needs democracy to thrive. Vice versa, Democracy can thrive where competitive capitalism exists. Of course, vitiated forms of capitalism, like crony capitalism, can go along with dictatorships and oligarchies.

However, socialism and communism, where the state dominates and predominantly controls the means of production, can't have real democracy, because true democracy is unsuited to those systems. That's why when India went more socialist under Indira resulting in difficult economic conditions, she had to wind up democracy and declare Emergency.

## What to Follow? Socialism, Capitalism, Gandhiism...

Most Indian political parties profess to be socialists, and presumably want some kind of socialism. Maoists in the red-districts of India and their "intellectual" supporters want Maoism/communism. Gandhiites would like Gandhian Gram Swaraj. Some say, "neither Marx not Market", but some form of "Ram Rajya". Ultra-nationalists want something uniquely Indian. Some ignoramuses would even like to go back to the pre-independence days of the British! Then, there are the capitalists.

As many groups, as many systems. If this does not work, try that. Funnily, no group poses questions relevant to arriving at a satisfactory solution. For example, which system has triumphed in the world? Let's not be frogs-in-the-well, let's look around in the world, let's look at other countries. Let's check which countries are prosperous and rich and why? How they achieved that? Which of them also have freedom and democracy, and which don't, and why? Which countries are struggling like India and why? Which countries are poor and why are they so?

If one examines the above, one finds that socialist or communist countries are invariably poor or struggling or not so well off. China progressed very fast after it junked Maoism/

communism and adopted competitive capitalist practices. Certain countries are rich on account of mineral wealth (like the Arabs) but their people have no freedom, and are ruled by kings, monarchs, dictators or oligarchies. The rich countries, whether of the West or Asia or elsewhere, like the US, the UK, France, Germany, Canada, Singapore, Taiwan, Japan, South Korea, Australia, New Zealand, have invariably both competitive capitalism and democracy. This being the case, does it not make sense for India to also adopt competitive capitalism. In fact, India has no alternative if wants to rise from its grinding poverty, become prosperous and join the first-world.

As for people advocating Gandhiism or some form of "Indianism" or some other prescription, it would be good to ponder over these questions: To purchase a car, does one go for a tested model of a reputed brand of car, or does one choose a car merely by its listed features, ignoring the fact of its not having been well tested on the road? Does one take that risk? However, you don't mind crores being guinea pigs in your experiments with Gandhiism or some form of "Indianism" or some other prescription! Even if it has to be given a chance, try Gandhiism in a district, and monitor the results. It is another matter that if any reasonable person were to read Gandhi's economic prescriptions that he wrote in "Hind Swaraj" in 1909 and later, he would get a shock.

## Capitalism Evolved Organically. Others: Artificial Constructs

It's not as if there is a menu of systems, and one can choose which to adopt. Constructivism does not work in the field of economics. A set of complex economic, mercantile, industrial, societal, survival, cultural, psychological and organisational factors have led to the evolution of free enterprise and capitalism. Free enterprise and capitalism were not something that were first theorised, then planned, and then implemented or rammed down. They evolved as a sequence of civilisational growth, were taken cognizance of, and then theorised after the fact. Facts and practice led to the theory, and then the theory enhanced the practice. Thereafter, it was a beneficial evolving cycle, each helping enhance the other. Democracy, in turn, evolved out of free enterprise and capitalism; and again there was a cyclical effect between the two, each helping enhance the other.

In comparison, there is nothing natural, organic or evolutionary about Socialism, Communism or Gandhiism. They are all artificial constructs. You first theorise. Then you plan how the theory could be implemented in practice. And, when you implement you find there are just too many variables, too many unknowns, and too many practical difficulties and unforeseen human factors and frailties to contend with. Russians tried it for over 70 years, failed, reverted, and have since been struggling to implement capitalism. Same with the East European countries that went communist thanks to Russia. China wisely junked its Maoism before it was too late, and steered itself capably into a version of capitalism.

Gandhiism! Nehru, Gandhi's chosen disciple, shuddered even to try it, despite Gandhi's persuasion. It is another matter that Nehru tried another bad artificial prescription—imitating the Soviets. In fact, Gandhi could not implement his own prescriptions satisfactorily even in the restricted environment of his own ashrams.

# 10

# AGENDA FOR CHANGE: A PARTIAL LIST

**(Would AAP take note?)**

*Cowardice asks the question: Is it safe?*
*Vanity asks the question: Is it popular?*
*Expediency asks the question: Is it political?*
*But conscience asks the question: Is it right?*
*There comes a time when one must take a position that is neither safe, popular, or political; but because it is right.*

—Dr Martin Luther King, Jr.

Here are a few among the many things that need to be done or undone by the political parties, going forward.

### Junk Poverty-Perpetuating Socialism

As has been established earlier in this book, socialism guarantees permanence of poverty. High time the vote-catching gimmicks of socialism were exposed and the pro-poor competitive capitalism was given respectability and adopted.

Mercilessly demolish all socialistic claptrap.

### Introduce Systems to Root-out Crony Capitalism

Eliminate or reform or redesign all those Sarkari processes and systems that give rise to crony capitalism.

### Eliminate/Minimise Corruption

Introduce effective preventive, detective and punitive systems to eliminate or minimise corruption.

Prevention is better than cure; and hence preventive systems are more important than the punitive systems. Preventive systems include elimination of possible avenues of corruption. That requires a number of steps. Electoral reforms. Government has no business to be in business—disinvest and sell off public sector units. Shrink the government. Formulate transparent rules. Put them up on the web. Eliminate discretion and discretionary quota. Reform and restructure the Babudom and the Criminal-Justice System.

Detective and punitive systems include an independent Lokpal and an independent investigative agency.

## Electoral Reforms

There has to be complete transparency about the funding of the political parties. All sources of funds, irrespective of amounts, must be declared and also audited by an independent auditor.

While most of the other areas should be denationalised or privatised, election funding and political activity could be one area that could be nationalised by creating a Common Central Election Fund (CCEF). Corporate funding could be to CCEF, rather than to individual parties. A criteria could be devised to apportion funds to parties. Provide TV and radio time, and publicity in the print media from the national fund for the purpose. Allocate public grounds and construct platforms for election rallies. Provide funds for political activity. Create a level-playing field for the parties. There should be stricter norms for candidates, so that proper candidates come in the fray.

## Judicial Reforms

Even though the Law Commission had recommended there be at least 50 judges per million population, we hardly have between six to fifteen—the correct figures are not available—which is less than even Bangladesh! Augmentation of numbers, so necessary for expeditious delivery of justice, would require massive intake of judges, and ramping up of infrastructure.

Creation of an independent *National Judicial Commission* has been gathering dust.

## Governance Reforms

We are plagued by woeful, substandard governance. Selection and promotional system in the civil and other services has to be drastically overhauled. You can't have promotions predominantly on seniority. Competence and performance have to be given greater weightage.

All post-retirement assignments for IAS-IFS-IPS should be banned. It would help curb continuance of pliable officers after retirement.

IAS and the like should be banned from all top-level appointments requiring special expertise; and there are many such areas: Defence, Education, Electricity, Energy, Environment, Finance, Information Technology, Mining, Nuclear Energy, RBI, SEBI, Telecom, and so on.

## Police Reforms

Police reforms have been pending for decades. They need to be expedited. The living and working conditions of the constabulary have to be drastically improved.

## Open, Competitive Market Structures

To minimise crony capitalism and the opportunities for gain from bribe-driven decisions, non-discretionary rules and strong open competitive market structures are required, coupled with transparency of rules and processes.

## Transparency

There has to be transparency in all processes of the government. All rules and regulations should be made simple, clear, open and accessible on the web. High time the colonial legacy of keeping things under the wraps is abolished. RTI should be made stronger. Discretionary powers have to be done away with.

## No Retrospective Changes in Law

India touts its democracy and 'rule of law' as its edge over China, but when it comes to crux, its debilitating socialistic-leftist-bureaucratic mindset, the incapacitating legacy of the Nehru-Indira raj, doesn't hesitate going back retrospectively 25 years to change the law and tax a global company, Vodafone, that is one of its biggest investors. Retrospective changes in rules and laws should be banned.

## Shun the Dole-out Economy

The Congress and other parties, including AAP, have been indulging in hand-outs, not out of any compassion for the poor, but to garner votes. Dynasties only think survival and are driven by the short-term vision of winning elections. Part indulgence in such short-cuts can be understood as a political compulsion, but to elevate it to the level of economic policy and to completely ignore the far more important task of reforming the system can only be understood if one makes due allowance for the incompetence of, and the irresponsible nature of the Dynasties.

Both the rural employment scheme and the food security bill demonstrate a paternalistic, feudal, *mai-baap sarkar* approach. After six decades of independence all that India can promise its poorest are wages for 100 days of employment in a year—less the leakages. It does not even plan to provide 365 days of gainful employment to as many as possible. That requires too much of planning and efforts and management that dynasty-led governments are incapable off. Find an easy way out.

In MGNREGA, the create-useless-work-scheme for the poor, Sonia-NAC had already frittered away over ₹ 1,70,000 crores, of which only a fifth (₹ 34,000 crores) went as wages, while four-fifth (₹ 1,36,000 crores) went to well-off as overheads and swindle. What kind of Sonionomics was that where nation builds no productive assets, poor get meagre wages and a major amount is siphoned off.

Wrote Minhaz Merchant in his article 'Rich MPs, Poor Voters' in *The Economic Times*, Mumbai of 9 June 2012: "A study by Shikha Jha of the Asian Development Bank and Bharat Ramaswami of the Indian Statistical Institute has shown that only 10% of the benefits of the public distribution system (PDS) reach the 'deserving poor'. Around 43% is siphoned off illegally,

28% goes towards administrative costs of the Food Corporation of India (FCI) and the balance 20% is misappropriated by other vested interests. Pouring more money into this leaky system without first fixing it—as the NAC, to its credit, has suggested in its detailed submission on the proposed food security Bill—will lead to the worst possible outcome: the poor remain poor even as politicians become richer."

Subsidies and give-aways that UPA and many state governments practiced does not lead to inclusive growth, it results in making beggars of all, and ultimately national bankruptcy.

*The Economic Times*, Mumbai of 27 February 2014 reports under the heading '*Food Delivery Spend Thrice the Cost: Independent Evaluator*': "The government spends ₹ 3.65 to deliver ₹ 1 worth of food, the Independent Evaluation Office (IEO) under the Planning Commission has pointed out. The IEO, which was formally launched on Wednesday, says despite this high cost incurred on distribution, less than 50% of the subsidised grains reach the intended beneficiaries. Over a third of the food-grain is pilfered from the supply chain...."

Economists like Amartya Sen who have generally been supportive of the Congress and the Left, including the CPM, had been pushing for the UPA-II's Food Security Bill (FSB). It allows them and the political parties to project themselves visibly as pro-poor, and as doing something concrete to fight poverty. Strangely, these "pro-poor" political parties and leftist intellectuals and economists have rarely fought against the disastrous economic policies since independence that have condemned millions into poverty in the first place; nor have they campaigned for pro-growth economic policies that are the real panacea out of poverty. Anti-reform NAC-driven dole-out Sonianomics had ensured millions remained submerged in poverty, rather than emerge from it, with productive jobs that genuinely boost the country's wealth and allow them a dignified existence, rather than remaining beggars at the receiving-end of the crumbs thrown at them. Faster growth is much more effective in curbing hunger and poverty than the Food Security

Bill. However, for politicians, FSB is much more visible a tool for garnering votes than the invisible growth-rate.

## FDI, FII

Why the senseless socialistic-bureaucratic restrictions like 16% or 24% or 49% or 51% FDI? Why not 100% for all sectors deemed worth inviting investments for.

If foreigners want to invest in your country, which would thereby boost your economy and infrastructure and would provide jobs, should you welcome them with open arms and make it easy, smooth and red-tape-free for them to invest, or should you shun them and put up hurdles. All right-thinking countries of the world openly welcome and encourage foreign investment, including China, but here we are, the inheritors of the irrational self-damaging inward-looking socialistic legacy of Nehru-Indira, suspicious of all things that might benefit us.

Nehru, Indira and descendants see the ghost of the East India Co in every foreign investor. As if foreign investors are free to tag along an army, like the East India Co, nurture and expand it, which in turn would help them expand their business empire, and who knows, political empire too! Are we simpletons?

Besides, many Indian capitalists have been increasingly investing abroad, finding the Indian investment climate discouraging, and corruption and red-tape a huge burden. Their investments abroad are FDI from India. Are we then saying that FDI abroad by India is fine, but FDI by foreigners in India is not so?

## Discourage Industrialisation of Food

Unhealthy packaged food and industrialisation of food, like in the West, is something to be discouraged and shunned on health, taste and medical grounds, and also on account of the possible long-term damages to the land by inadvisable farming practices, and the cruelty to animals for "efficient" production of non-vegetarian food. FDI for such purposes should be banned.

We should NOT go the ways of the West in the area of food, whether through FDI or otherwise. Even unhealthy packaged food like potato chips and Kurkure, and soft drinks like Coke and Pepsi should be heavily taxed so as to discourage their consumption. Their advertising should be banned like for cigarettes.

However, we must build infrastructure of warehouses, cold storages, transport and supply-chain for food-items, excluding that for unhealthy packaged food.

### Govt. has no Business to be in Business. Privatise PSUs

Air-India and PSUs are kept under the government only so that they could be bled to make money for the politicians and the babus. Government has no business to be in business. It is incapable of managing them. It must disinvest and get out. PSUs are no family-silver or crown-jewels as the leftists-socialists like to term them, they are actually bleeding ulcers, as Arun Shourie called them.

### Industry-Friendly, NOT Industry-Hostile

The Nehru-Indira-leftist tradition that still prevails considers it legitimate, and even 'intellectual' and empathetically pro-poor, to be abusive to capitalists and industrialists. That gives them cheap cheers from the public—like AAP is getting lately. It has not dawned upon them that it is thanks to capitalists and industrialists that jobs get created and poverty can be fought. Of course, no one is thereby defending the cosy-crony-capitalism practised between the socialist politicos and babus and the business-persons. But, it is the nation's patriotic duty to encourage healthy, competitive capitalism to get us out of poverty and make India a prosperous nation. It also requires showering appreciation and according dignity and respect to entrepreneurs, capitalists and industrialists, so that more and more young professionals are motivated to become entrepreneurs rather than employees or babus.

Here is a telling example from an article '*The Regulation Raj*' by Jaithirth Rao in *The Indian Express* of 5 May 2012: *"The irony is that in 1947 we had a decent share of the world market for textiles and the Chinese had zero market share. The rhetoric of the times cast mill owners as evil, blood-sucking capitalists (remember the Bollywood movies of that time? [Currently, at the drop of a hat, both Rahul Gandhi and Arvind Kejriwal & Co yell against Ambani and Adani—just to get cheap popularity!]). The very first economic legislation of free India's government was the Textile Industries (Development and Regulation) Act. We created a czar known as the textile commissioner who told mills how much inventory they could hold, what their product mix should be, how many spindles and looms they could have and so on. We taxed the industry mercilessly. We wilfully destroyed a glorious industry. Today the Chinese textile industry is several orders of magnitude ahead of us. In 1947, we had a dominant share in the world tea market. Tea-planting in Kenya grew fast after India imposed export duties (believe it or not we had duties on exports!) on Indian tea."*

Deny land, deny mining, deny electricity, deny motorable roads, deny flexible labour laws, do little for skill-development and for making skilled-labour abundantly available, put back-breaking road-blocks by stipulating plethora of permissions to be obtained and then delay or deny those permissions, unleash inspectors of all kinds looking for their pound of flesh, invent new ways of harassment, change laws adversely and retrospectively, and be as insulting, as defamatory and as abusive as you like, and yet expect Indian manufacturing to take off and compete with China!

## Implement Land Acquisition Bill (LAB) and GST

Implement both the Land Acquisition Bill (LAB) and the Goods & Services Tax (GST) asap. (LAB is covered separately in this book.) BJP has introduced the bill in the Lok Sabha. All parties must support it.

However, as expected the Congress is coming in the way. It appears that the Dynasty and their slave Congress has decided NOT to let anything good happen for the country. Why? If the country progresses fast, Prime Minister Narendra Modi and the BJP would get the credit, and would hence become more popular and stronger, while the Congress and the Dynasty, which in their 10-year misrule had brought the country to its knees, would look even worse. What is the priority? Dynasty or the nation? Obviously, the Dynasty! Hence, oppose all good steps.

At least the AAP should see through the game of the Congress and the Dynasty, if indeed they (AAP) have good of the nation at their heart.

## Encourage Entrepreneurship

As per a World Bank report on ease of doing business, India ranks 166 among 189 countries. Plethora of permissions are required, besides greasing of palms. And, it takes too long to get all permissions. The whole process must be made simpler and must be put online so that it is transparent, fair, fast, and free of corruption.

## Bring Back Black Money Stashed Abroad

Billions of dollars of Indian money is stashed abroad. Many countries, including the US, have aggressively gone against their country's money illegally kept abroad, have arm-twisted the Swiss and other banks, and have recovered billions.

Why not India?

Congress never tried. UPA was brazen enough not to even set up an SIT for Black Money despite the Supreme Court instructions!

The BJP was quick off the block in setting up the SIT on the very first day of its taking charge! Arun Jaitley, the Finance Minister, has been promising results for close to a year. No results yet, though.

## Mining

Politicians and babus indulge in massive corruption, and when there are unsavoury disclosures, the nation simply shuts down the mining sector. That's no way to manage economy. Leftists and NGOs target principally the supply-side of the corruption—the mining barons and capitalists. They do not as much focus on the demand-side, the recipients—the politicians, the babus and the faulty laws and the discretionary powers that make corruption possible. It's not a pleasure for the industrialists to give rent. It's the corrupt system that forces them into it.

Mining is a very vital segment of the economy that can't be stopped or discouraged. Yes, environment has to be protected and the affected population has to be taken care of. But, it is not as if it is a choice between the two. If sensibly managed, environment can be protected even as mining is expanded, and the consequent development can be a boon for the affected population, enhancing their income and prosperity. Also, mining is a huge employment generator.

India has the world's fourth-largest deposits of coal, yet we are importing coal! Why? Because, we are unable to mine sufficient quantity to fuel our power and steel plants and other infrastructure requirements. Why? Because only Coal India Limited (CIL), a state-owned company, was allowed to mine coal. The companies related to coal-scam were to mine coal for captive purpose only. And, CIL is unable to mine enough. Thankfully, Modi government has taken welcome steps in the matter.

India imports nearly 1000 tonnes of gold. Needful has to be done on the gold-mining front. Setting right the mining sector would give a major boost to the economy and employment.

The iron-ore deposits of Australia and Brazil are almost the same as India's, yet their iron-ore mining output is respectively six times and four times as much as India's 100 MT, when India needs increasingly more iron and steel for its infrastructural and industrial growth. In 2012, against China's steel output of 717 MT, India's was mere 77 MT—about 10th!

SAIL has said investments of $200 billion would be required to achieve the steel production target of 300 million tonnes by 2025.

But, can the above be done without tackling issues related to raw-materials, mining, power, land acquisition and environment. UPA had been engaged in making all these issues tougher to resolve. Modi government is now actively engaged is resolving these issues. It has successfully done coal blocks auction. The Land Acquisition Bill (LAB) is another positive step in that direction. But, what are the Congress, the other opposition parties and the AAP doing: opposing a sane move!

### Energy Crisis

India has a severe power shortage, yet it allows coal-fuelled power plants to remain starved of coal, despite having fourth-largest deposits of coal in the world. Stark mismanagement! Thousands of crores of power projects worth thousands of MW of power are remaining stuck for lack of environment clearance. Why should setting up of a power plant require plethora of permissions that take 5 to 7 years when the need of power is so urgent. Shows that netas and babus see no urgency in the urgent requirements of the nation.

In the last decade, the cumulative debt of Indian power utilities, rather than decreasing, has risen from $4 billion to $45 billion, thanks to free power to agriculture and mismanagement. Gujarat had been facing problems similar to all other states, but it has managed to tackle them. It has segregated its feeders and now provides 24 × 7 three-phase power supply to all its 18000 villages! Why can't other states imitate the Gujarat model?

### Grains Storage

It's shocking callousness that huge quantities of grains are allowed to rot even as millions go hungry. It's shameful that the government has failed to construct sufficient number of modern warehouses to properly store grains, nor does it have schemes in place to distribute to the needy the grain it is, meanwhile, unable to store properly.

As per an Assocham study, up to 30% of food-grain harvest is wasted on account of inadequate storage capacity, unprofessional storage and deficient logistics.

### Link Rivers

Linking of rivers had been proposed long back. It has tremendous positive potential for drinking water and irrigation. Also for water-transport and related businesses. Besides, it would help tackle both the problem of flooding and of drought. The proposal needs to be revived. It would be very positive for the economy and growth, and for employment generation and poverty elimination.

## Indian Railways

Look at any government-run or government-controlled organisation. Its condition would always be pathetic. Take *Indian Railways* [IR], the major undertaking, which is India's lifeline and transports millions daily. How ill-kept and dingy are majority of the railway stations and trains. While most of the countries, except countries not worth comparing with, boast of fast, smooth, comfortable trains and bullet trains, we force our millions to take risks with slow, ill-maintained, accident-prone, bone-rattling, rickety tracks and trains.

IR is in dire need of massive investment and competent, enlightened management, free from political interference. Apart from tracks that need replacement, 25% of railway bridges are over 100 years old, requiring urgent repairs/replacements. IR's *Vision 2020* document estimated the required investment at 14 lakh-crores. IR modernisation requires 5.6 lakh-crores over the next 5 years as per the Sam Pitroda committee report. IR's urgent safety requirements alone require one lakh-crore, as per the Kakodkar-Sreedharan committee.

China's railway network length (27,000 km) was about half that of India (53,000 km) in 1947. We have since added just 12,000 km, an increase of 22% in 65 long years since independence amounting to an average of just 185 km per year! Meanwhile, China's network length has touched a whopping 1,00,000 km.

China's indigenously built high-speed trains run at speeds up to 350 kmph, while India's fastest train runs at 150 kmph. Railway stations in China and other countries are spic-and-span like airports, while ours are mostly decrepit and dirty.

IR had been a neglected sector under the UPA. Now, with Suresh Prabhu at the helm as the Railway Minister things are likely to look up.

## Garbage-free, Clean India

In March, 2014 there was an excellent episode of *Satyamev Jayate* on Garbage management. All-out efforts ought be made all over India for "Clean India, Garbage-Free India!" It should be taken up as a mass campaign, and all the states should be involved. Targets should be set for each district.

Lots of buzz has been generated around *Swachh Bharat Abhiyan*, and that's a good thing, but there is as yet little concrete plan or systems in place or laws and penalties to ensure cleanliness. Talks and publicity have to give way to definite targets and action.

## Open Up the Education Sector

Education sector deserved to be delivered from the clutches of the government and the babus and from the business-politicians running their educational establishments for making money.

We are in dire need of quality colleges, universities and research establishments, yet the government, rather than encouraging the private sector, remains a major road-block. Quality of graduates from engineering and management colleges is so poor many remain unemployable. Not a single Indian university or institute of higher learning, including the premier IITs, figure in the top 200 universities of the world, listed by the QS World Rankings 2012! The only ones close to the best are IIT-Delhi at 212, IIT-Mumbai at 227 and IIT-Kanpur at 278. India remains the only BRICS nation without a university in the top 200.

We need gear up our literacy campaign, and have to drastically overhaul our primary and secondary education. In literacy, India is 183 among 214 countries—below many African countries. Reports *The Economic Times* of 18 January 2013: "The Annual Status of Education Report (ASER 2012) by NGO Pratham shows that the number of Class V students who could not read a Class II level text or solve a simple arithmetic problem has increased. In 2010, 46.3% of kids in this category failed to make the cut and this shot up to 51.8% in 2011 and

53.2% in 2012.... In 2010, 29.1% children in Class V could not solve a two-digit subtraction problem without seeking help. This proportion increased to 39% in 2011 and 46.5% in 2012."

Singapore and Finland recruit teachers in schools from among the brightest 10% of graduates and offer them salaries on par with engineers. And, in India?

India needs to drastically increase its budget on education and to have a really competent person as its HRD minister—someone like Suresh Prabhu for the Railways. Why Modi has not thought it fit to offer this important portfolio to a genuinely competent person like Arun Shourie is a mystery.

## Writing Contemporary History

Our contemporary history since independence has many gaps and the little that has been written is highly flawed. This is because the government has refused to make available relevant documents. Academics, researchers, historians, journalists, army-men, bureaucrats and others who may be interested are thus handicapped. How do you record authentic history, how do you discover and analyse your good deeds and misdeeds, and how do you ensure you rectify your shortcomings and don't make the same mistakes again, unless you have access to the original material.

All democratic countries declassify their documents after a set period as per their law, but not India. Even where the provision exists, politicians and babus find some excuse not to declassify on the pretext of "national interest". They want the official version and the wall around the lies to remain intact. The colonial Official Secrets Act of 1923 still rules. The RTI Act notwithstanding, there are many departments and organisations that are specifically exempted from disclosures. Besides, documents that could "prejudicially affect the sovereignty and integrity of India, the security, strategic, scientific or economic interests of the State, relation with foreign State or lead to incitement of an offence" are also exempted. Thousands of documents including the Henderson-Brooks-Bhagat Report on the India-China War 1962, Netaji Subhas papers, Shimla

Agreement with Pakistan have therefore been kept "top secret". Nothing has been done regarding the Mitrokhin Archives.

By ensuring secrecy, the vested interests—politicians (especially, the Dynasts) and babudom—have managed to ensure they are not exposed. This must change. A healthy democracy can't permit secrecy calculated to shield the vested interests in the name of protecting the national interests.

# 11

# LAND BILL, RAHUL'S RANTS AND AAP'S TAMASHA

*What is right is not always popular and what is popular is not always right.*

—Albert Einstein

## Land Bill: Brief History

Land Bill is a short term used here for the law relating to land acquisition by the government for economic development and infrastructure.

Land acquisition in India was governed till 2013 by the British era ***Land Acquisition Act of 1894.***

The revised land act, *The Right to Fair Compensation and Transparency in Land Acquisition, Rehabilitation and Resettlement Act, 2013* (RFCT-LARR Act, 2013), in short, the ***2013 Land Act***, framed by the UPA government came into effect from 1 January 2014.

The Modi government sought to amend the 2013 bill. They got *The Right to Fair Compensation and Transparency in Land Acquisition, Rehabilitation and Resettlement (Amendment) Bill, 2015*, in short, the ***2015 Land Bill***, passed in the Lok Sabha on 10 March 2015, following an ordinance on it on 31 December 2014. The bill is being opposed by the Congress, the AAP, and the socialist and communist parties of various shades, and is yet to be passed by the Rajya Sabha.

## Problems with Earlier Land Bills

Land acquisition in India since independence was governed by the British era Land Acquisition Act of 1894. It is shocking that India carried on with that unjust British era act right till 2013. During that long period of 66 years since independence ruled mostly by the Congress there had been a large number of cases of land acquisition for dams, irrigation, industries and other economic activities where the compensation paid for the land was meagre and little or no rehabilitation of the displaced was done.

The revised 2013 Land Act sought to correct the injustice. However, the social activists, assorted NGOs and the NAC, who too were involved in its framing, went overboard in correcting the historical wrong, and settled for the other extreme. They incorporated such onerous conditions in the act and made the approval process so laborious, involved, complex, taxing and time-consuming, and the cost of the process itself so high (leave apart the cost of land itself) that land acquisition became almost impossible, and many projects, including the critical defence and road and infrastructure projects, came to a halt. If there was one single UPA minister who caused maximum setback to India's economic growth it was Jairam Ramesh who as Rural Development Minister piloted this 2013 Land Act, and who as the Environment Minister halted critical projects. He was, of course, backed by Sonia-Rahul who hoped those actions would project them as pro-poor, pro-farmer and pro-tribal, and would help them garner votes to help continue their damaging Dynasty rule.

Profusion of onerous clauses in the UPA's 2013 Land Act not only adversely affected the industrial, infrastructural and mining projects, it severely affected projects for rural prosperity: irrigation, village roads, rural-infrastructure and rural housing projects. Economic growth crashed. Supposedly pro-farmer measure boomeranged—it turned out to be effectively anti-rural-prosperity, anti-farmer, anti-infrastructure and anti-industrial.

In view of the above, the Modi government had no alternative but to amend the Act if they had to fulfil their election promise of faster economic growth, massive job creation and rural prosperity.

## Proposed Amendments and their Rationale

Let us look at the main amendments to the *UPA's 2013 Land Act* in the *NDA's 2015 Land Bill*, and also the critical provisions on fair compensation and rehabilitation that remain unchanged.

***Does the 2015 Land Bill make drastic changed to the 2013 Land Act?***

No. It retains almost all the provisions. It amends only some provisions.

***What are the specific amendments brought-in by the 2015 Land Bill, and what are their rationale.***

Here are the amendments along with their reasons:

### (1) *Five Special Categories*

It creates five special categories of land use: Defence, Rural Infrastructure, Affordable Housing, Industrial Corridors, and Infrastructure Projects including Public Private Partnership (PPP) Projects, where the central government would own the land.

*Clarification on Industrial Corridors*: By industrial corridors is meant industrial corridors set up by the government and government undertakings. Further, land can be acquired up to one kilometre on both sides of the designated railway line or road of the industrial corridor.

*Rationale:*

All the above five categories are for pressing public good, and for defence and security, and NOT for enriching the corporates at the expense of the farmers, as Rahul Gandhi falsely alleges. These categories indeed deserve special treatment. They need to be freed from the onerous, time-consuming, cost-adding, cost-escalating and project-delaying clauses of the 2013 act if we desire faster project implementation for our defence preparedness and security, proper infrastructure for economic development and affordable housing for the poor.

### (2) *Exemption from Consent for Special Categories*

It exempts the above five special categories from the requirement of consent of the land owners whose land is to be acquired. (That requirement as per the 2013 Land Act is 70% of the land owners whose land is to be acquired for PPP and 80% for others.)

*Rationale:*

Special category projects, which are critical, can't be held up just because 20% of the land-owners choose not to give their consent. Take for example a highway project connecting the two ends that are 500 kilometres apart. For an aggregate of 400 kilometres you obtain land-owners permission through whose land the highway would run. But, for the remaining aggregate of 100 kilometres you fail to obtain permission. Should you then abandon that vital road link?

### (3) *Exemption from SIA for Special Categories*

It also exempts the above five categories from the requirement of *Social Impact Assessment* (SIA).

*Rationale:*

SIA under the 2013 act is so broad and complex that the process may go on for years delaying the projects and massively shooting up the costs. Can the critical special category projects of defence, etc. afford such delays and enhanced costs?

Need one do SIA for a rural housing project or a rural electrification project or a rural road project or a defence road highway?

However, for a project such as a cement factory or a car factory or a fertilizer plant, SIA would continue to apply.

### (4) *Exemption for Irrigated Land for Special Categories*

There was a limit to the acquisition of irrigated multi-cropped land and other agricultural land under the 2013 act. That restriction stands removed for the five special categories above.

*Rationale:*

The government has assured that it would resort to such acquisition only as a last resort, when there is no alternative. Critical requirement of land for Defence and other special categories may make it incumbent upon the government to acquire such land, in the absence of less fertile land.

### (5) *Term "Private Enterprise" Replaces "Private Companies"*

It substitutes "private enterprise" for the term "private companies" in the 2013 act. A private enterprise is an entity other than a government entity, and could include a proprietorship, partnership, company, corporation, non-profit organisation, or other entity under any other law.

*Rationale:*

This is to make it more encompassing, and not restrict it to only one type of legal entity.

### (6) *Bringing Other Acts on Par*

There are 13 other acts that deal with land acquisition having their own separate provisions, that were excluded from the UPA's 2013 Land Act. The 2015 Land Bill brings all of them on par with itself in respect of provisions for compensation, rehabilitation and resettlement, making them as generous.

The 13 Acts are as under:

The Land Acquisition (Mines) Act 1885, Indian Tramways Act 1886, Resettlement of Displaced Persons (Land Acquisition) Act 1948, Damodar Valley Corporation Act 1948, Requisitioning and Acquisition of Immovable Property Act 1952, National Highways Act 1956, Coal Bearing Areas Acquisition and Development Act 1957, Ancient Monuments and Archaeological Sites and Remains Act 1958, Petroleum and Minerals Pipelines (Acquisition of Right of User in Land) Act 1962, Atomic Energy Act 1962, Metro Railways (Construction of Works) Act 1978, Railways Act 1989, Electricity Act 2003.

*Rationale:*

This brings in uniformity and massively benefits farmers and land-owners, who would get much higher rates of compensation for land acquired for metros, railways, roads and highways, coal and mining projects, nuclear projects, and so on, compared to what they would have got under the acts they are governed by.

### (7) *Return of Unutilised Land*

The acquired land needs to be returned to the owners if it remains unutilised for five years, as per the 2013 act. As per the 2015 amendment, it can be five years or any period specified at the time of setting up the project, whichever is later.

*Rationale:*

Some big projects take longer to complete, hence the necessary amendment.

### (8) *Land for Private Hospitals and Educational Institutions*

The 2013 Land Act excluded the acquisition of land for private hospitals and private educational institutions from its purview. The 2015 amendment bill drops this restriction.

*Rationale:*

Hospitals and educational institutions serve a critical public purpose, hence the amendment.

### *Are the Amendments Meant to Favour the Corporates, as Rahul Gandhi-Congress-AAP Allege?*

No, certainly not. From the very nature of the five special categories it is clear that they are not meant for private profiteering. They are all for public good and would be those where government would be the land-owner or would take the initiative.

Creation of a spectre of corporate-favours or sarkari largesse for the corporates is therefore totally misplaced.

### *Are the Amendments Anti-farmer, as Rahul Gandhi-Congress-AAP Allege?*

Even in the worst case scenario, the 2015 Land Bill may end up affecting 2% to 3% of land-owners. But, it would benefit the rest, as all land acquisitions result in enhancing the value of the neighbouring land. And, even those 2% to 3% of land-owners would be getting two to four times the market price of their land plus other benefits, including guaranteed job for one member of the family.

The numbers who would benefit from land acquisition would far outstrip those who might lose (if at all).

### *Any Extra Benefit to Farmers/Land-owners on Account of the Amendments?*

Yes. Please see amendment (6) above.

### *Do the Amendments Lessen the Compensation Paid to Farmers, Land-owners, Affected Persons?*

No. Please see details below.

## Generous Compensation for Land Acquisition

The Land Act provides for generous compensation and rehabilitation.

As per the act, *compensation* for acquiring an *urban* land would be *twice its market value*, while that for *rural* land would be *four times its market value*!

The above compensation is more than adequate considering the following:

Land prices in India have almost quintupled in the last decade making them the highest in the world. Farmland prices currently vary from rupees 5 lakh an acre to as high as 1 crore an acre in regions around big cities and in prosperous rural regions. In contrast, the average farmland price in the US is only around rupees 2 lakhs an acre, even though those farms are far more productive. The price of farmland in India is a huge 2 to

50 times more compared to the West than can be justified by its productivity!

In addition to the monetary compensation, the act provides for *employment for at least one member of the affected family*, and for appropriate resettlement.

### Would Rural Population be Adversely Affected?

No.

Overwhelming majority of rural population would stand to gain. Even the minority whose land would be acquired would gain on account of the generous compensation and rehabilitation package that we have discussed above.

Creation of rural infrastructure with the land acquired would benefit all. It would spur economic activity in the rural areas, spawn small businesses and would create jobs sorely needed. As it is, agriculture is not a remunerative occupation for a majority of farmers, and most people in the rural areas would be happy to have an alternate occupation.

As per National Sample Survey Organisation (NSSO), major income of 56% of small farmers (having land less than 100 square metres) came from wages from an external job rather than from agriculture. While 82% of the landowners do not earn much from the land anyway, 75% are marginal croppers with an average holding of 0.6 hectare. As per a survey, only 10% of rural population felt farming meant a good life; 62% said they would give up farming given an alternative; and 76% of the children of farmers did not wish to continue as farmers. Another survey reported that 65% of farmers having sub-hectare holding were not able to break-even. It is worth noting that Indian agricultural productivity is very low, contributing only 18% to the GDP; even though 50% of the population is engaged in agriculture.

### Boon for Dalits and Landless

Dalits who have migrated to cities know that their freedom, emancipation, progress and prosperity lies in moving out of the shackles of their debilitating rural misery into an urban setting.

The 2015 Land Bill, which would help development and urbanisation, would be a step in that direction.

It is queer that most opposition parties and leaders—be they Congress or AAP or socialists or communists or Bahujan Samaj Party or Rahul/Sonia Gandhi or Arvind Kejriwal or Mayawati—are outdoing one other in blindly opposing the 2015 Land Bill hoping to win over the rural population by appearing to be their saviours, protectors and well-wishers riding on the intensely and widely propagated mischievous misinformation that all of them would be adversely affected by the legislation.

The question is how many among the rural people own land that may be acquired? And, how many are landless? The fact is that a majority are poor and landless, and a large number among them are dalits. They don't stand affected. They may be indirectly affected by agriculture-based job loss (income from which is meagre, seasonal and uncertain), but they too have not only the assurance of adequate compensation, but hope of a more remunerative job on account of the economic opportunities that would be opened up. Those dalit families that are land-holders have actually very small land-holdings barely enough for them to eke out their living. They stand to get generous compensation, and an assured job.

The NSS survey reveals that 52% of the scheduled caste households are engaged in casual labour in rural areas, while 33% are self-employed in agriculture.

Dalits must know that Dr B.R. Ambedkar would have been indeed very happy with any step that would have helped pull Dalits out of the darkness of villages and into the freedom of urban setting. He was of the opinion that '*these village republics have been the ruination of India*'; and was '*surprised that those who condemn provincialism and communalism should come forward as the champions of the village. What is the village but a sink of localism, a den of ignorance, narrow-mindedness and communalism?*' Ambedkar never believed dalit-upliftment could come about in a rural setting.

Dalit writer, journalist, political commentator and an advisor to the *Dalit Indian Chamber of Commerce and Industry*

Chandra Bhan Prasad has repeatedly stressed that urbanisation is the real road to salvation for Dalits. Opportunities coupled with the anonymity in urban centres enable Dalits to chalk out a career for themselves free from the debilitating oppressiveness of the village life. Chandra Bhan and the Dalit industrialist Milind Kamble are the moving force behind the *Dalit Capitalism Movement* whose central thesis is that free markets and entrepreneurship are the route for salvation for Dalits.

One tends to agree with what Chandra Bhan Prasad and Milind Kamble state in their article "*Manifesto to End Caste*" that appeared in the *Times of India*, Mumbai of 23 January 2013. As per the article, the obliteration of caste in a major way would be when caste, that evolved from a feudal, rural setting, transforms into class through capitalism, industrialisation, professionalization, modernisation and mechanisation of agriculture, and urbanisation. Class is not hereditary, there is no stigma attached to it, and one can move up or down. They say, "*Capital is the surest means to fight caste. In dalit's hands, capital becomes an anti-caste weapon.... The manifesto demands that India embraces capitalism publicly as its official ideology....*"

The truth and effectiveness of the above proposition is the proof contained in the book *Defying the Odds: The Rise of Dalit Entrepreneurs* by Kapur, Shyam and Prasad that profiles the phenomenal rise of twenty Dalit entrepreneurs from poverty to prosperity.

Rather than parroting one tutored jibe after another on land acquisition and farmers, Rahul Gandhi would do well to read Ambedkar: the salvation for Indian rural, including its Dalits, lies outside its rural setting.

But, what about the farmer suicides? Let's look at the issue.

### Are Farmer-suicides Abnormally High?

As per the National Crime Records Bureau (NCRB) data, farmer-suicides are 8.7% of the total, considerably less compared to their share in the total population. It is also not as if the rate for farmer-suicides has been increasing; actually it has been coming down.

The number of farmer-suicides were 1109 in 2014, 11,772 in 2013 and 13,754 in 2012. They didn't increase during the Modi-period in 2014, they drastically came down. Figures of 2015 have yet to come out, but, based on newspaper reports, they do not appear to be large.

Incidentally, the overall suicide rate (farmers + non-farmers) of India is about 11 per lakh, that is, 0.011%. Compared globally, it is not high, despite India's poverty—if poverty, penury and want are considered as the likely main reason for suicides. In fact, it is rather low. Countries such as Belgium, China, France, Germany, South Korea, UK have higher suicide rates compared to India. China's suicide rate is almost double that of India.

Further, out of this suicide rate of 11 per lakh for India, the proportion for farmers is less than that of non-farmers. The main cause for suicides is depression and not poverty and want. Depression is caused by various factors, only one of the many factors being poverty.

Why then the alarmist ear-splitting hullabaloo in India on farmer suicides. Enlightens S.A. Aiyar in his *Swaminomics* in *The Times of India* of 3 May 2015: "*Because presenting farm suicides as a single mass tragedy can win awards for journalists, TRPs for TV anchors, donations for NGOs opposing commercial crops and globalization, slogans for leftists attributing everything to class war, and* ***votes for opposition parties....***" No wonder Rahul Gandhi, the Congress, the AAP and others have jumped into the fray.

## No Link Between Land Bill and Farmers' Suicides

There is absolutely no link between the Land Bill and the farmers' suicides. Farmers' suicides have been on account of the crop failures for various reasons like unseasonal rains this time. Relating the proposed land acquisition legislation to issues such as crop damage or farmer indebtedness or farmer-suicides defies logic, as these problems have plagued farmers for decades. What is relevant is to tackle the related policy failures.

In fact, the said bill (2015 Land Act) is not even in force, so how could it be the cause. The bill in force is the 2013 UPA Land Bill. Is that the cause of suicides?

Purely for misleading the public and getting political mileage, Rahul Gandhi, Arvind Kejriwal, the Congress, the AAP and the opposition are trying to establish a spurious link between the amended 2015 Land Bill and the sorry position of farmers in distress and farmer-suicides. Politics over farmer-distress is not new, but this time it is being used to stall a bill that would augment the efforts to reduce that distress itself in the times to come.

## Agriculture and National Economy

The global trend in agriculture is this. By and large, rate of growth of agriculture is always much less than that in other sectors like manufacturing and services. In developing economies, while rate of industrial growth of 7% to 9% is common, agricultural growth is generally between 1% to 5%. Over the years, the effect of this gap in the rate of growth of agriculture and industry is that the share of agriculture in the total GDP of a country gradually reduces. For example, in North America and Europe, agriculture accounts for less than 5 per cent of the nation's GDP. In China, the share of agriculture in the total GDP went down from 27% in 1990 to 11% in 2010. There has been similar reduction in other countries. In India, this share has gone down from 31% in 1990 to 14% in 2012.

The other global trend is increase in agricultural productivity over the years. With better seeds, irrigation, fertilizers, pesticides and mechanisation the agricultural productivity has been increasing and you are able to produce more in less land and with less labour. India is, however, a laggard on this front. We have among the least agricultural productivity on an average. As per an estimate, the US produces as much food with 8 million farmers as India does with 200 million! That's a ratio of 1:25!! That is on account of many factors. Much of our land is either unirrigated or insufficiently irrigated. Modern techniques are yet a far cry. There has been little investment in agriculture. On top of it, there is abnormally high wastage on account of lack of adequate storage.

Although we are producing enough, we still have hungry millions. That is not because of paucity of grains and other food items, but on account of insufficient purchasing power in the hands of many. What we need to do is to provide gainful employment to the hungry millions so that they have sufficient purchasing power to feed and house themselves. That employment cannot come from agriculture.

The solution is to increase agricultural productivity and produce more food with less land and labour; and utilise freed-up land for agricultural infrastructure—like dams, canals, irrigation works, roads, storages, etc.—to enhance agricultural productivity, and to set up industries and businesses.

Globally those farmers and farm-dependent people have progressed in life who managed to become non-farmers. Not all, but many, especially the landless and those with small land-holdings. Future of majority of farmers is not in farming. They need to learn new skills and move on into industries, services and other businesses.

It therefore does not make sense for the politicians to support steps that keep the farmers tethered to land. Why continue to trap them in barely remunerative occupation. Of course, the uninformed like Rahul Gandhi may continue to talk hoarse on the issue hoping to garner votes in future, but it would not work.

Like China, we need to establish a number of agro-based industries in rural areas to gainfully employ the underemployed and the unemployed.

Crop-insurance should gradually cover entire crops. The coverage is a pathetic 10% currently. It should grow to 100%. That can happen with economic development and better resources and revenues. Like China, the crop land should be linked to a bank account and insurance policy; and in case of crop loss, the compensation and/or insurance amount should get expeditiously credited to the accounts within days. It shouldn't take months to assess and pay.

## Why Amended Land Bill is Good and Necessary

The proposed amendments in the Land Bill would make it easier for the government to acquire land, whether agricultural or non-agricultural, for industrialisation, infrastructure projects, roads, defence and rural housing, without reducing the compensation to the landowners.

India cannot develop without massive infusion of capital. However, the competition for capital is fierce. In this era of globalisation, if India is unable to attract capital, it would go elsewhere to other nations. To get capital you have to have investible projects. Projects require land. And, if land cannot be made available or takes too long to get or is too cumbersome to acquire, projects would simply not come in.

Take the case within India itself: Singur in West Bengal, for example. Land issues came up. The project shifted to Sanand in Gujarat. Sanand has since developed into an automobile hub with many more industries having come up there. Who gained? Gujarat and the people of Gujarat: farmers got very good compensation, excellent economic development followed, thousands got jobs and Gujarat gained in revenues from taxes. Who lost? West Bengal and the people of West Bengal. Similar scenario obtains among countries. If India fails to provide the necessary infrastructure the industries and businesses that could come to India would go to an alternate country.

It is estimated that about $300 billion worth of projects have been stalled owing to problems in land acquisition.

Nearly 12 million young people are joining the workforce each year. Agriculture cannot absorb them. Only manufacturing and services can employ them. That requires land for setting up of industries, offices and service centres. You need accommodation to house them. For that, you need to create new towns and cities and urban centres and inter-connecting infrastructure. There is a plan for 100 smart cities and Delhi Mumbai Industrial Corridor

(DMIC). How would all that be possible without acquiring of land?

There is actually no alternative but to ensure faster and smoother land acquisition, without of course short-changing the landowners.

The only alternative is to continue in the Nehru-Indira-Dynasty-bequeathed poverty and misery, and make it worse.

### *BJP/Modi Has-to-Do Responsibility*

BJP cannot again come to power in 2019 and Modi can't get a second term unless there is rapid economic growth and massive job creation. And, that can't happen given UPA's 2013 Land Act.

BJP should not wilt under the opposition onslaught and misinformation campaign. It should bear in mind that slow growth and slow job creation would hurt it much more by way of both urban and rural votes than what it might lose thanks to the opposition's name-callings and possible resentment, if any, in a small section of society owing to land acquisition.

Looking to the opposition of the leftist, communist, Congress, AAP and reforged Janata Parivar, a section of the BJP and allies might want to backtrack weighing the possible political costs, but that would be cowardly and against the interest of the nation. They need to be brave and must demonstrate their guts. If they carry the act through and ensure development and jobs; rather than the imagined political costs, the act would result in bumper political benefits.

If the BJP wilts, people will lose faith in Modi and in what they expected him to accomplish. As it is, one is not too happy with average to below average performance of some critical ministries like Finance—this would add to the grouse.

### Why Opposition to the Bill is Effectively Anti-farmer?

As detailed above, the amended bill would help acquire land with lesser hassles (while providing generous compensation and rehabilitation) for the five critical sectors, that include enriching rural facilities. It would help accelerate economic growth and generate jobs both in the urban and the rural areas. Rather than adversely affecting them, it would greatly help rural folk. There would be no losers. It would be a win-win situation for all.

Opposition to it is either driven by ignorance or by vested interests who wish to exploit it for spreading misinformation to gain vote banks at the expense of the nation.

Opposition to it is therefore effectively anti-poor, anti-farmer, anti-development, anti-prosperity, and pro-vote-bank-politics, and hence mischievous and ill-intended: it amounts to working against national interests.

### *Reaction to Amendments: A Sample*

Welcoming the changes made to the land acquisition act, former NAC member NC Saxena had himself commented that the 2013 UPA Land Bill moved by the then Minister of Rural Development Jairam Ramesh was effectively both anti-industry and anti-farmer.

## Congress/Sonia-Rahul's Irrelevant Rants

No party can beat the Congress in sheer hypocrisy. If there is one party which has gained massively through crony capitalism and corporate-favouritism it is none other than the Congress. The "*suit-boot ki sarkar*" accusation of Rahul Gandhi is therefore totally unfounded, mischievous and irresponsible, and is a case of "*Ulta chor kotwal ko dante*", because it is the Modi-sarkar which by putting-in sensible systems in place like 2G and coal auction is minimising the scope of crony capitalism and corporate-favouritism—the channels that many allege resulted in truck-loads of grease money for the Congress and its allies.

After having deprived the national exchequer of mountains of money through a series of scams, which effectively amounted to depriving the millions of poor of the benefits of that money, the Congress, in the most hypocritical way, went about further massively impoverishing the national exchequer by way of MGNREGA, FSA and farm loan waivers (where major amounts were defalcated) mainly to get votes and to continue in their misrule and corruption.

Like the term "*suit-boot ki sarkar*", the term "*anti-farmer*" used by Rahul for the Modi government actually fit the Congress like a glove. Why are the farmers in distress? Why are they committing suicides? Why just one failed crop destroys many rural families? Why is a small farmer worse off than a city beggar? Why is there endemic poverty in rural areas? Why the rural infrastructure is so pathetic? It didn't become so in the last one year of the Modi rule. It is thanks to the criminal misgovernance, neglect and faulty agricultural policies of the Congress since independence, and their poverty-perpetuating and misery-multiplying socialism.

Congress-Sonia-Rahul realise that Modi's amended 2015 Land Act has the potential to accelerate the economic growth, create jobs, give a fillip to rural infrastructure and growth, and ultimately add to the broadening support base for the BJP and Modi—all of which would mean further marginalisation of the Congress. Hence, oppose the bill. What is good for the nation is not important. What is important is the survival of the Dynasty. Priority is for the Dynasty and the party, in that order, and not for the nation.

Congress-Sonia-Rahul are hoping that by their vigorous misinformation campaign on the bill they would be able to get back their rural votes. It exposes their bankruptcy of ideas. Apparently, the Dynasty is unable to think of anything positive to prevent or delay their becoming history.

Rahul is too self-centred to realise the damage he is doing to business sentiment by railing against corporates. Is it not irresponsible on his part to tar corporates and businesses in general just to score political points and retrieve his own pathetic position. Corporates work hard, provide jobs to millions, and bring prosperity to the people and the nation. What does Rahul do? Frequently fly off for holiday jaunts, spend tons of money on himself, and in the intervals between his jaunts, empathise with poor farmers, and curse and defame all those who had been working hard while he was having fun.

Rahul has lately been touring the countryside lamenting the condition the farmers are in and blaming the ruling party for their misery. Does he think people at large are fools that they would believe him. Don't they know the current rulers are less than a year in the saddle. That the previous decade was the decade of the Congress and the UPA. And, that for most of the years since independence it has been the Congress and his Dynasty that has ruled, or rather misruled, India.

*Hence, the public knows that their miserable, pathetic condition is thanks to the Congress and the Dynasty. If Rahul and the Congress-persons feel distressed and angry at the condition of the farmers they must slap themselves real, real hard; and must box and kick themselves each time a farmer commits suicide.*

Rahul's constituency Amethi has lost about 80% wheat crops due to unseasonal rains and hailstorms, and has also reported a number of suicides. But, Rahul is careful not to go for a padyatra there. He is answerable there. He would go only to the opposition-rules states of Punjab and Maharashtra where he can create a tamasha.

As per *The Times of India*, *Mumbai* report of 2 May 2015, pomegranate farmers of Karnataka are so desperate that they have written to the governor of Karnataka, "*No yield, no money to repay the loans. The only option before us is to die.*" Has Rahul Gandhi cared to go there? No. Because, Karnataka is ruled by the Congress, and Rahul does not wish to go to any place where he may be answerable. The hypocrisy of the Congress and the Dynasty knows no limits.

The fact is the Congress has never ever given a damn about farmers—since the Nehruvian times. The Congress and the NCP have reportedly been the biggest looters of farmers and farmlands. The CAG had found a huge scam even in their the loan-waiver of over rupees 50,000 crores in 2008, which helped them win votes and power. The mind-blowing irrigation scams under the Congress-NCP government in Maharashtra are well-known, so also land-grabs by their partymen. Land-scams in Haryana and Rajasthan under the Congress government are public knowledge. What have Sonia-Rahul done about them? Nothing. What is more, there are serious allegations regarding improper land-dealings against Sonia's son-in-law and Rahul's brother-in-law Robert Vadra. That being the background, with what face Rahul projects himself as a saviour of the farmers? And, why doesn't the media question such claims?

### *Congress-ruled States can Modify Central Act*

Land acquisition is done by the states. If Congress-Sonia-Rahul do not like the amended 2015 Land Act, the Congress-ruled states can modify the act and stipulate their own conditions, or let the terms of the Congress/UPA 2013 Land Act govern land acquisition. They have that freedom. Why crib then. Why deprive non-Congress ruled states of the benefits of the new act?

The fact is the Congress state governments themselves had problem with the 2013 Land Act of the Centre. They realised it would make land acquisition almost impossible and would halt all development in their state.

Let the Congress state governments not implement the new 2015 Land Act. BJP and Modi would love it: they have nothing to fear, and much to gain. Let the Congress-rub states' development suffer. Let the people throw the Congress out in the next election for lack of progress.

## BJP Losing the Perception Battle

For a PM contestant and a party which so successfully managed the 2014 Lok Sabha election campaign and for a PM candidate who was able to create magically positive perceptions about what he and his government would do if elected, it is surprising that post-elections while they have not been able to adequately leverage their good performance and policies to project an impressive image, they have been getting enough flak for all the wrong reasons and even on fictitious or made-up grounds. And, yet, they have failed to fight back.

Why is a section of the main stream media (MSM) so hostile to them? Why do they give such bloated publicity to the inanities or plain nonsense of people like Rahul Gandhi or Digvijay Singh? Why the white lies or illogical or wild statements of Rahul Gandhi and the Congress not properly questioned or exposed by the media? Why the BJP is unable to effectively put its points across?

If the Congress and the AAP, if Rahul and Arvind can effectively use rallies, media and other platforms to spread misinformation and falsehoods on the amended 2015 Land Bill and its linkage to the farmer distress and suicides to the extent that it is snowballing into massive political cost; how is it that the BJP and its leaders have been watching it helplessly allowing goals after goals to be scored.

Why can't the BJP take up the cudgels and expose the falsehood and the dirty political game of the opposition? It's not difficult. They have the truth and the logic on their side. What the bill seeks to do would be good for the farmers and the nation. Why are they unable to put it across to the public? Why this gross failure? What is the I&B Minister, Arun Jaitley, doing? It's not enough to answer questions logically in an interview on an English channel. The public at large must be explained the true picture. The benefits and the truth must be publicised at twice the intensity of the falsehood.

What took the cake were the white lies and allegations of Rahul Gandhi in the parliament that strangely went unresponded or inadequately responded by the treasury. And, surprisingly his uncalled for jibes like "*suit-boot ki sarkar*" (which is actually a self-description of UPA) that were lapped up by the media went unreplied or tamely replied. The belated counters to the Congress were "*suit*case sarkar", "un*suit*ed sarkar *boot*ed out", and so on. But, they were not enough. Given their 10-year long misdeeds, there is enough that can be coined on the UPA, the Congress and on Sonia-Rahul.

High time the Central Government and the BJP realised they are losing the perception battle, and did something about it.

### *Mysterious Ways of the MSM*

Granted, of course, that not much sense can be expected from a section of the MSM, who have been lapping up the nonsense spouted by Rahul, and have even been conducting debates on them during the prime time on TV channels, without having the spine to cross-question him on his lies, or educating the public on the same. Further, how can you give a wide berth to a fellow just for some sound bites when he has nothing to show for his actual work on the ground. How can you contrast a mere blabber who has never taken any responsibility as a minister or otherwise with a person like Modi who has handled a state as a chief minister for over a decade and made it a foremost state or who has been capably handling his job as a prime minister. But, strange are the ways of a section of the MSM!

## AAP's Pointless Tamasha

In view of what is stated above, one would not expect any right thinking party or person to oppose the 2015 Land Bill. If they have the good of the country and farmers in their heart they would support the bill.

If Arvind Kejriwal, the AAP, Rahul Gandhi, the Congress and others were genuinely concerned about the plight of the farmers in distress, they would focus on the policy and implementation failures in the agricultural sector since independence, rather than continuing to shackle desperate farmers to land by grandstanding against the 2015 Land Bill through mega rallies and yatras.

The AAP was supposed to be a different type of political party. Unlike the usual run-of-the-mill parties comprising hard-boiled political oldies, the AAP's backbone was a large band of young educated professionals committed to change India for the better. The AAP was not formed to pursue vote-bank politics like the others; and to oppose or support for the sake of opposing or supporting. It was expected to think through and evaluate each issue, and then take a principled stand.

Why then did the AAP choose to line up alongside the other opposition parties? Why did it try to link farmer-suicides with the Land Act? Why it chose to oppose in the hope of getting farmers in its favour? Why did it play the same game as the other opposition parties? What then is the difference between it and the others? It is a case of disappointing similarity.

However, to make a show of being different they tried to impress upon the public that while they were sincere and honest in their sympathy for the farmers, such was not the case with the Congress and the others who were opposing the act. To buttress this claim of theirs they went about exposing the misdeeds of the Congress when in power and their anti-farmer policies, and made a lot of sound and dance about the few farmers (Metro Delhi does not have many) they were compensating for the crop loss on better terms.

One view on the AAP's rally was that it was a way for them to divert attention away from their internal strife, and washing of dirty linen in public by the their two warring groups.

In any case, insincerity has a way of exposing itself, and it did expose itself in this particular case—unfortunately.

## Gajendra's Unfortunate Death

In the AAP's rally against the 2015 Land Bill at Jantar Mantar in New Delhi on 22 April 2015, a person named Gajendra Singh from a village in Rajasthan climbed up a tree a stone's throw away for the stage from which the spirited pro-farmer speeches were being made. He had the AAP's election symbol "broom" in his hand. His ostensible intention was to attract attention, get captured on the TV cameras that were in profusion near the stage, be seen on TV screens all over India, create some drama, and given a chance, perhaps make a short speech either from the tree top or after descending down to the stage nearby.

His climb and antics were a long drawn out affair, and not something sudden. There was all the time in the world to persuade him to climb down. But, apparently, there was more interest in his drama and remaining hung up than in his coming down. As per the subsequent police report, people around had even egged him on.

Rather than firmly ensuring he climbed down for safety, rally and the speeches continued; and hung up, he remained a curiosity, with a few half-hearted calls for him to get down.

Later, in the process of staging a drama of a fake suicide by hanging, he put a *gamchha* around his neck and tied ends to a branch of the tree. In the process of enacting this drama he accidentally slipped, and the fake suicide act became real!

He was brought down from the tree, and taken to a hospital.

What was bizarre was that the unfortunate event that took place just a little distance away from the stage where all the top leaders of the AAP, including Delhi's CM and Dy CM, were sitting, was not allowed to mar or interrupt the rally or the speeches. Not only that, the leaders, assuming the poor person had died and that he had actually committed suicide on account of crop failure and farm distress, promptly began exploiting his death to blame the police (Delhi police being under the Central government) for dereliction of duty and the ruling party at the Centre for their anti-farmer Land Bill that was making the farmers like Gajendra Singh commit suicide!

It occurred to none of the top AAP leaders sitting on the stage so near to the scene or their members attending the rally or those of them witnessing the antics of Gajendra Singh on the tree that if they had taken just a little initiative they could have easily prevented the unfortunate incident. Were those AAP-persons, claiming to represent aam aadmi (common man), especially the distressed and the deprived, conveying that even if a horrid thing were happening right before their eyes, they would only expect the police to do the needful, and that they shoulder no responsibility or accountability? What kind of empathy was that?

Does politics make people so heartless? Even AAPians. It was a shocking public display of irresponsibility, insensitivity and political immorality.

Events surrounding Gajendra Singh's unfortunate death have raised suspicions and a number of questions. For example: How did AAP get Gajendra's "suicide note"? How come Kumar Vishwas "read" out from the alleged "suicide note" matter that didn't exist in it? What of the claim of Gajendra's sister that the handwriting on the so-called "suicide note" was not his? What of the wordings of the so-called "suicide note" that nowhere mention suicide or the intention to die? Why no clarification from the AAP on Gajendra Singh's alleged meeting with Manish Sisodia that day morning, before the rally? Why the AAP took a U-Turn on its allegation on conduct of Delhi Police? On what evidence did leaders of the AAP claim there was a conspiracy behind Gajendra's death? What made a leader of the AAP tweet Gajendra's death before medical confirmation from the hospital? Why the tweet sought to exploit the death politically? Besides, what kind of persons choose to promptly tweet such things than to rush and try to save the poor person or take him to hospital or worry about his well-being? Inappropriate gestures of Kumar Vishwas and Manish Sisodia on Gajendra's death? Usage of the term "Latak Gaya?!" by Kumar Vishwas. What made several top AAP leaders make political speeches exploiting the assumed suicide? Why was Gajendra projected as a farmer in distress when (although from rural background and having agricultural land) he was more of a businessman and an aspiring politician, and had no crop-failure related distress? Why assume suicide for a person who, as it turns out, had absolutely no intention of killing himself?

Desperate to extricate themselves from the embarrassment and the consequences of Gajendra's death under suspicious circumstances, the AAP despatched post-haste its leader Sanjay Singh to the Gajendra's village in Dausa, Rajasthan on an SOS mission to handover a cheque of rupees ten lakhs to Gajendra's family. The Delhi government under the AAP has since named the farmer compensation scheme as '*Gajendra Singh Kisan Sahayta Yojana*', and compensation cheques were distributed to the affected farmers from Bawana in Delhi in the presence of Arvind Kejriwal and the family members of late Gajendra Singh.

The Delhi government has also decided to build a memorial of Gajendra Singh; and the cabinet has reportedly declared him a martyr! One could understand such crazy steps by Mayawati of BSP or SP or such parties, and be dismissive about them—resigned to the notion that those parties were beyond rectification. But, for the AAP to indulge is such tactics—plain crazy! Or, do they carry so much genuine guilt? The Delhi High Court on 6 May 2015 sought the Delhi government's response on a PIL challenging its decision to declare late Gajendra Singh as "martyr".

## Would AAP Learn and Change?

Would the AAP learn from at least this tragic incident? Would they understand that politics is not a series of tamashas or allegations or name-callings? Would they stop their dramas? Would they get back to their original roots of principled and responsible politics? Would they realise that people are not fooled by unfounded allegations or false propaganda or illogical, unprincipled positions. That grandstanding like that of Rahul Gandhi does not help. It makes you look non-serious and ridiculous. Populist positions may temporarily help garner votes, but they harm the nation, for whose good the AAP was claimed to have been formed in the first place.

# 12

# DISSIDENCE IN AAP AND EXIT OF LEADERS

*We learn from history that we do not learn from history.*

—Georg Wilhelm Friedrich Hegel

*May we never confuse honest dissent with disloyal subversion.*

—Dwight D. Eisenhower

*Managing dissent is about recognizing the value of disagreement, discord and difference.*

—Noreena Hertz

*We may be so eager to protect the right to dissent that we lose sight of the difference between dissent and subversion.*

—Richard Perle

## Initial Exit

It was sad to see a party that had claimed to be unlike others, and had won the 2013 assembly elections on its planks of principles, probity and propriety to be so soon embroiled in ego clashes, betrayals, back-stabbings and ugly manoeuvrings.

Among the first AAP member, who was also an MLA, to rebel was Vinod Kumar Binny. He was later expelled from the party. Binny was not a novice; he had twice won the elections in Delhi as an independent before joining the AAP. He became a third-time MLA in 2013 defeating Ashok Kumar Walia of the Congress from the Laxmi Nagar constituency in Delhi. What was the apple of discord? Considering that he was the senior most among the MLAs (having won a third time) he should have found a place in the cabinet. But, Kejriwal had not obliged. Why? It was perplexing the AAP let go of a popular person and an experienced and capable hand who would have been an asset in the cabinet—all other MLAs being mostly novices. Ego clash? Is Kejriwal an egoist? Is Kejriwal uncomfortable with those with an independent base? Does he shun those who are more experienced and capable? Or, does he lack the skill to take others along? Binny finally joined the BJP in 2015. The AAP's inability to keep an asset like Binny with them showed their political inaptitude.

Resignation of their founder-member, prominent leader and TV face Shazia Ilmi reflected further on the political immaturity of the AAP, and the weaknesses in the essential attributes of political leadership in the top echelons of the AAP. It also exposed the lack of internal democracy in the AAP, their tom-toming of "swaraj" notwithstanding, and all that Kejriwal had himself written in his book by that name. Shazia had solid grounds to be unhappy with the party leadership, yet the party did little to assuage her hurt. The fault did not lie with her; the fault lay with the way the party leadership treated her. Shazia Ilmi was an indisputable asset for the AAP, and losing her again exposed AAP's inability to self-correct its weaknesses. Much later, Shazia Ilmi too joined the AAP rival—the BJP.

Many well-meaning and competent professionals like Captain Gopinath and others had joined the AAP. However, an ambitious coterie within the AAP that included people like Yogendra Yadav refused to give any quarters to them or use their talent. They allowed the talent to fade away from the AAP. Were they afraid they would get marginalised if people with proven credentials and much more capable than them got on to important positions? Ideological considerations might have also played a part. People with stale and failed socialist ideology were preferred by people like Yogendra Yadav and Prashant Bhushan. And, enlightened talent from outside could have never subscribed to an ideology that was a proven failure and a prescription for continued poverty.

After the unprecedented electoral victory and formation of the government in early 2015, rather than staying newsworthy in a positive way, the AAP began dominating prime time news for all the wrong reasons, as its internal dissentions came to the fore and it began to implode, climaxed by the expulsion of two of its most prominent members, Prashant Bhushan and Yogendra Yadav.

### Bhushan-Yogendra Exit: A Case of Good-riddance?

As per one scenario, Prashant Bhushan (**PB**) plus Yogendra Yadav (**YY**) vs. Arvind Kejriwal (**AK**) & Co (PB+YY vs. AK&Co) feud was made out to seem principled, while as per another it was purely farcical and a struggle for power. So, let's examine.

*Did PB-YY match the TAA-AAP spirit?*

While the Team Anna Agitation (TAA) and its offshoot, AAP, had universal support, the engine that fired them comprised the young, enthusiastic, tech-savvy middle class—employed in the information technology industry, finance, management, marketing and so on, they were the products of capitalism. They were never against free enterprise and liberalisation, only they hated crony capitalism, corruption and the likes of Kalmadi and Raja. They certainly did not look forward to the public sector at the commanding heights or a control-freak state of a socialist's dreams. PB-YY were actually a paradox in that setting. Both are wedded to the stale Marxist-socialist thought.

Also, the TAA-AAP engine was fiercely nationalistic, like Anna Hazare. They didn't have stomach for the wild ideas of plebiscite-in-Kashmir of PB, or for his Maoist-defence.

The only matching ground was anti-corruption.

*Were PB-YY elected?*

They were not elected. They were handpicked by the *National Convener* Arvind Kejriwal (AK) and inducted at his instance by the *National Council* into the *National Executive*. They were basically the beneficiaries of the largesse of AK.

Was PB-YY revolt a noble struggle for inner-party democracy and "swaraj"?

PB-YY never really bothered about inner-party democracy when others were eased out before them, rather they actively collaborated and even took initiatives to throw out several, freely subverting internal democracy. They began crying out when the tables turned against them!

As per reports, PB-YY have had a record of manipulating to prevail over others, circumventing democratic norms. Their lamentation lately over lack of democracy in the party is therefore baloney.

Even otherwise, communists-socialists-marxists-maoists are not known for their love for external or internal democracy. They all think they alone are right, and prefer dictatorial and violent methods to have their way.

*Weren't PB-YY the victims deserving sympathy?*

The media and well-meaning individuals, in their natural tendency to support what seemed to be the underdogs, sympathised with PB-YY; ignoring that appearances may often be deceptive: that the persons who appeared to be sinning (AK & Co) may actually be those heavily sinned against! They lost sight of the fact that PB-YY & Co engaged in unpardonable anti-party activities, even as they tried to hijack the AAP ideologically.

*Were PB-YY removed undemocratically?*

They were removed by a majority vote. So, how was that undemocratic? Even if the complaint is that the AK-faction managed the numbers, it has to be admitted that, in case of a showdown, the democracy is indeed about managing the numbers!

*Were PB-YY removed because their views differed?*

Not really. What their views have been were rather well-known. If those were the reasons they should have been removed long back. The AAP as a whole is more on the pragmatic and the populist side, and on what works, be it leftist or rightist or otherwise, rather than being strictly ideological. They went along with PB-YY even though all their views were not aligned.

*What then was PB-YY revolt really about?*

It was to encash their contribution, rise up the hierarchy, leverage the AAP brand, extend their influence and power, and steer the party in the direction of their stale leftist-socialist-good-for-nothing ideology.

*What were PB-YY really up to?*

PB-YY had brought in many socialists-marxists-communists-maoists-JNU-types or their sympathisers in the AAP. Some examples: Prof. Anand Kumar, Kamal Mitra Chenoy, Medha Patkar.

BB-YY & Co, that included the JNU-bred leftist elites, planned to steer the AAP in their own ideological way—far removed from the philosophy of those who had led the Jan Lokpal movement and founded the AAP.

They had been endeavouring to colour AAP red or pink. It effectively amounted to hijacking a movement of young, energetic, idealistic committed patriots ready for sacrifice for their country wanting a prosperous, clean and corruption-free India. To hijack that spirit and try to steer it back into the bad old miserable Nehruvian-Indira-Rajiv socialistic 50s, 60s, 70s and 80s was not just devious, improper and unethical, it was criminal, for it amounted to playing with the future of India and pushing it back into the gray to dark ages of 50s to 80s.

*Was PB-YY exit good riddance?*

Surely yes. It also meant thankful exit of other socialists-marxists-communists-maoists-JNU-types like Prof. Anand Kumar and Medha Patkar. One platform—and an important, effective platform like the AAP—less for this coterie whose overall approach to the national issues is harmful and dangerous.

Of course, this is not to paint all their work and actions with one brush. Most PIL (not all) work of PB is commendable.

Many of these marxists-socialists-leftists may be well-intentioned. However, what matters is the thinking, policy, ideology and approach; and it is well to remember that *road to hell is often paved with good intentions*.

Stalin and Mao can't be faulted for bad-intentions, but what was the net result of their ideology and actions? Socialists-communists Che Guevara and Fidel Castro may be held as heroes, but what is the fate of Cuba and its citizens: as per a recent survey about half the population of Cuba wants out of the country if they can manage it! Loud-mouth Hugo Chavez was another socialist messiah, but what has been the unfortunate fate of his country, Venezuela, and its citizens! Widespread misery and poverty and millions in hunger was the net result of Nehru's 17-year long tryst with socialism. His daughter Indira indulged in more of the same socialism and took the country further into the dark ages. One can't fault Nehru or Indira on bad-intentions. They were well-intentioned. But, what was the result of their faulty policies? And, how do intentions—which are internal to the person, and may not be correctly gauged by the outsiders—really matter. What matters are the results. We would not mind even bad intentions if the results are good!

# 13

# AAP: IRRATIONAL EXPECTATIONS

*There is always a right and a wrong way, and the wrong way always seems the more reasonable (for getting votes).*

### Parallel with V.P. Singh?

Looked from one angle, the machinations of AK & Co appear to be not too different from the farce of V.P. Singh in the late 1980s.

Just as a series of mega scams led to Team Anna agitation, which then morphed into the AAP, so also V.P. Singh came in the limelight on the back of the then mega corruption scandal of Bofors. Just as the AAP tom-toms its high moral standards, honesty and uprightness, and has raised the banner against corruption, so also had V.P. Singh projected himself as an honest, holier-than-thou politician out to uproot corruption from public life. Just as the AAP railed against the Dynasty, so had V.P. Singh railed against them. Just as the AAP flaunts its aam aadmi credentials, so also had V.P. Singh popularised a catchy slogan to project himself as pro-poor: *Raja (V.P. Singh) Nahin Fakir Hai, Desh ki Taqdeer Hai.*

After the people of the country sold on his publicity brought him to power and looked forward to the promised rosy results, the bickering for power within the V.P. Singh camp began and soon developed into an ugly war. The masks of honesty, probity and public-service began to crumble, and before long they all were exposed as power-hungry frauds masquerading as pro-poor messiah.

The internal dissentions within the AAP camp therefore worry you. Would a promising outfit like the AAP go the V.P. Singh's way? Most probably not. V.P. Singh was an ex-Congressman who had spent long years in the Congress. Arvind Kejriwal and group come from non-political, devoted social-activist background.

### AAP = "Corruption-free" Congress?

On many issues you find the AAP to be chillingly like the Congress, only they claim to be honest and corruption-free.

The Dynasty-Congress—which has promoted the Dynasty at the expense of the nation and at the expense of the much more capable leaders of the party, and thanks to whom India is one large gigantic stretch of garbage dump with run-down infrastructure, and because of whose policies the vast majority of India is still pathetically poor and wretchedly miserable, even as the Dynasty lives it out in the Lutyen's luxury and the Dynasty and the Congress party-persons have cornered riches, benefits and privileges—used to shamelessly publicise itself as an aam-aadmi (common man) party, and had therefore even protested the "aam aadmi" name they claimed the *Aam Aadmi Party* had usurped. But, it now appears the AAP has "usurped" far more from the Congress.

Be it pro-poor affirmations, be it pro-common-man claims, be it pro-farmer rants, be it anti-corporate harangues, be it secular credentials, be it minority-appeasement, be it socialistic nonsense, you find it difficult to distinguish if you are hearing the scamsters of the Congress or the voices of the AAP.

It is true that the AAP has come to power in Delhi by displacing the Congress: while the vote-share of the BJP remained almost the same as in 2013 assembly elections, that of the Congress shifted en bloc to the AAP. But, having usurped the Congress vote-bank, should the AAP usurp its policies too: something that has taken the nation to dogs?

People are certainly not looking forward to an equation:

AAP = Congress – Corruption. Because, corruption is a function of time. The AAP is new to power. But, as the AAP spends more and more time in power; like the Congress, it too would pick-up corrupt-practices on the way; and the equation would revert to AAP = Congress – ~~Corruption~~.

Another area where the AAP is going the Congress-leftist-socialist-communist-party's wayward way is with regard to the foreign policy. The AAP demanded that both Houses of Parliament should immediately pass unanimous resolutions condemning Israeli attacks on Gaza and should not allow the Modi government to reverse the decades-old policy on Israel. The AAP also wanted the Indian government to stop purchasing arms from Israel. It would take too many pages to go into the details and expose the erroneous stand of the AAP, the Congress and the Indian communists, socialists and leftists. If interested, the reader is requested to read the blog-series *"Israel & the Jews"*, *Part-I to IV* available at http://rajnikantp.blogspot.in.

## Raising Relevant Questions

*What is it about the AAP that gives hopes?*

The AAP still comprises honest, dedicated, committed and well-meaning persons. The party is still corruption-free. Despite exit of many good persons, there are still many competent persons in the party. So far, the party is performing well in Delhi. All kind of negatives keep floating in the media, but what really matters is this: Is the AAP focused on doing good for the people of Delhi? The answer is a resounding "Yes!".

*What is it about the AAP that concerns you or disappoints you?*

Many among the AAP leaders come from an assortment of left, far left, socialist, radical socialist, communist, Marxist, Maoist or Maoist sympathiser or similar background. It's a mystery why despite the global experience and proof that no socialist or communist nation has ever prospered, and that socialism, communism, Marxism and Maoism as political thoughts are totally irrelevant and defunct, even a new party like the AAP have people who profess such stale, poverty-perpetuating ideas.

Back in 2009, Arvind Kejriwal, then a social activist, had signed a letter (whose main author was Suzzana Arundhati Roy, notorious, among other things, for her support to Kashmiri separatism, for her support to the terrorists of *2001 Indian Parliament Attack*, and for her activism to derail the *Sardar Sarovar Project*, which has been a boon to the people of Gujarat and MP) by Sanhati, a leftist organisation, condemning the proposed *Operation Green Hunt*, a military offensive against the Maoist (their so-called fight against exploitation is all a smoke-screen—they just want to capture state power and take India to dogs like Mao had done for China) insurgents. The other signatories of the letter included the leftist Noam Chomsky and Prashant Bhushan. No wonder Prashant Bhushan reportedly wanted to bring-in Maoists within the fold of the AAP. Thank God he is no more in the AAP! Another prominent socialist was Yogendra Yadav, who too, thankfully, is out of the AAP. But, there are still many of the same or similar ilk.

The AAP has tried to be one up on the populist giveaways to gain vote-banks cheaply on which the Congress and the leftist parties had the monopoly. They have offered giveaways not just to the poor but also to the middle-class.

*Given the above, is it irrational to expect that the AAP could be a panacea for India's problems?*

Yes.

However, it is hoped that good sense would prevail upon the AAP. There is enough fresh and rational blood in the AAP to do course correction.

Talking about honesty and corruption; mouthing slogans on poverty and economy similar to the Congress, communists and socialists, and distributing freebies like them; and remaining populist can only make them a xerox copy of the Congress, communists and socialists, no more!

They must also realise that their irrational and opportunistic u-turns do not enhance their image. Some examples are given below.

## AK and AAP's Disconcerting and Opportunistic U-turns

*Many of us believe that wrongs aren't wrong if it's done by nice people like ourselves.*

—Anonymous

### *Democracy*

The AAP prided itself in being democratic both externally and internally. However, the way it got rid of many of its prominent members without due internal discussions has been shocking. Shazia Ilmi had regretted lack of inner party democracy, that had made her leave the party. If you don't allow internal discussions and debate, free voicing of different opinions within the party forums, and treat criticisms as expressions of disloyalty to the party then where is the question of inner-party democracy?

### *Swaraj*

The concept of "swaraj" was integral to the AAP. Among other things, "Swaraj" envisages genuine democracy where the power of governance and rights of democracy will be in the hands of common people of India. Kejriwal had penned a book titled "*Swaraj*". However, in practice, it is already a dead concept within the AAP itself.

Wrote Prashant Bhushan in his letter to the AAP in April 2015: "You accuse us of having conducted a 'Swaraj Samvad' and you label that as an anti party activity. As you know and as I have written in the open letters to the Volunteers and Arvind, and also in the letter given to the members of the National Executive on 26 February, there has been a very serious drift in the party away from its founding principles of Transparency, Accountability, democracy, clean politics and Swaraj, during the last year. We have not only refused to bring the party under RTI contrary to the law declared by the CIC, and contrary to our boast; we have not been transparent on our expenditure, our members, our office bearers, the decisions of our party, what to say of minutes of meetings. None of these are there on our party website. Far from being transparent, we seem to have developed a fear of transparency."

The "*Swaraj Samvad*" movement launched by the expelled ex-AAP stalwarts, Yogendra Yadav and Prashant Bhushan, has since made the AAP so allergic to the word "Swaraj" that it has gone to the ridiculous extent of deleting the entire para that contained that word from its webpage that enrols members and volunteers for AAP: "...Democracy is popular self rule, but the current practice of democracy negates this ideal and reduces the citizens to mere subjects.... Aam Aadmi Party (AAP) aims to restore power to the people, so as to realise the promise of *Swaraj* enshrined in our Constitution." (Although, the word "Swaraj" remains in its constitution.)

### *Law on Defamation*

Many defamation cases had been slapped on Kejriwal for making wild, unsubstantiated allegations against others, the prominent ones being those against Nitin Gadkari of the BJP and Kapil Sibal of the Congress. Pushed into a corner, Kejriwal had petitioned the Supreme Court to decriminalise the sections (499, 500 under IPC) in the law relating to defamation.

Lately, stung by the media raking up issues that are giving the AAP a bad name, Kejriwal has got a circular issued to the Delhi's government departments that media reports be scrutinized, and where deemed appropriate defamation suits be filed against the media under the very same sections (499, 500 under IPC) of the law Kejriwal had earlier wanted decriminalised!

### *Lokpal*

Kejriwal and the AAP had vociferously campaigned for Lokpal, and had panned all those who had not supported them. However, they chose not to refer certain relevant cases to their own internal Lokpal, Admiral Ramdas, that they had themselves appointed. Sensing he might not give judgement on the lines they desired, they not only refused to refer certain cases to him, but had him replaced by their own chosen coterie.

As Prashant Bhushan alleged in his letter to the AAP of April 2015: "But instead of referring those serious allegations against you to the Lokpal as required by the Party Constitution, you have now removed Admiral Ramdas!... You say that I have defamed the party by comparing the purge of NE members and others including the Lokpal to a 'Stalinist Purge'. What else would you call the action to suspend/remove virtually anyone prominent who was objecting to the manner of our removal from the NE. When you remove NE members and even a Lokpal for merely questioning the illegal and unjustifiable actions of the Convenor or those who are in control of the party, when you label every dissenter as a traitor and charge him with anti party activities, when you try to instill fear among members of the party for merely questioning the drift of the party away from its founding principles, it does remind one of a Stalinist purge where similar things were done."

### *Hypocrisy*

If you support something as principled when it suits you, you can't go against the same thing when it does not suit you. Else, you are a hypocrite.

True, politicians tend to be hypocrites, like Zulfikar Ali Bhutto of Pakistan had remarked in an interview to the Italian journalist Oriana Fallaci: "...*The only thing I accept from the philosopher John Locke is this statement: 'Consistency is a virtue of small minds.'*..."

Or, like Khushwant Singh had written about Krishna Menon in his autobiography '*Truth, Love and a Little Malice*': "*He was also a congenital liar and regarded truth as good enough for the simple-minded and lying as the best exercise for the mind.*"

However, we know the fate of both Bhutto and Menon.

It doesn't pay to be a hypocrite.

# 14

# AAP: HOPES AND EXPECTATIONS

*We are confronted by insurmountable opportunities.*

Having given them an overwhelming unprecedented majority of 67 seats out of 70, the people of Delhi have high expectations from the AAP. With no excuse of insufficient numbers in the legislature to fulfil its promises, it is up to the AAP to deliver, come good on its manifesto, and distinguish itself as indeed a party with a difference.

Proving what you have projected yourselves to be to win votes and fulfilment of election pledges and promises to people requires honesty, sincerity, competence at good governance, and, of course, resources. It is one thing to lure voters with freebies, but quite another to find the money to afford it. The former is easy, the latter the real test of one's ability. It is easy to spend money, but difficult to earn it. You have to find new sources of revenue, you have to collect the revenues more efficiently so as to reduce the cost of collection and plug leakages. It is this area of revenue augmentation that demands innovative, out-of-the-box thinking. The AAP has so far mostly focused on the innovative ways to spend. It has now to focus on the revenue side.

Unless the AAP wishes to be bracketed within the unenviable club of other 'socialist' (socialist is actually an obnoxious, unprincipled, self-seeking, corrupt, cunning bully leveraging poor to get rich and powerful) parties, it can't just go on a spending spree of freebies to show it has fulfilled its election promises, and then demand grants from the Centre, and shift the blame to the Centre if it fails to extract money from them. Financial plan of bleeding the national exchequer dry is no plan. Even if the national exchequer shows indulgence, it would necessarily be at the cost of other states, whose allocations it would have to cut, and who may be much poorer states. That would be transferring resources from the poorer to relatively less poor or rich. Even though those poor would belong to a state other than Delhi, they are after all Indians. So, your so-called kind act of helping your poor would be at the cost of making other poor poorer!

We all know that a responsible individual earns, and then saves, invests and spends. What would you say of a person who spends beyond his means on himself and on his spouse and children, and then expects his father to make good the deficit? Even if his father is generous enough to help him once, is the habit sustainable?

Like a responsible individual, a government also has to wisely budget its revenues and expenditures.

The Delhi government would have to ensure self-sufficiency of finances. Voted-in on "Transparency" as one of its planks, the AAP government must share its plans with the people on how it intends to bridge its revenue deficit, both in the short-term and in the long-term, accounting for the current and proposed subsidies, and proposed social, educational and developmental plans.

Genius, hard work and competence lies in garnering revenues, not in spending them. Because, augmenting revenues to enable you to better the lot of the people brings to fore your economic philosophy and framework, your grasp and understanding of "*what really makes a nation and people prosperous*" based on the knowledge derived from "*why some nations and states have succeeded and why others have failed*", and your financial strategy.

It would test whether you are a moribund, stale socialist like Yogendra Yadav you have thrown out, or a pro-poor ranter interested only in self and the Dynasty like Rahul Gandhi, or like the host of leftists, socialists and communists whose only achievement has been to collectively keep India's poor in permanent poverty even as they have cornered perks and privileges for themselves. The AAP must measure up to the freshness of its youth and have fresh, free-market ideas to propel the poor to prosperity.

~ ~ ~

Tired of the corrupt Congress misrule, and the inept, rent-seeking Municipal Corporation of Delhi (MCD) under the BJP, voters in Delhi whole-heartedly welcomed the AAP. So far, the AAP has NOT been a disappointment. It is hoped the AAP would do well, and would not allow the corrupt Congress to claw back, and would displace the BJP from the MCD if the BJP continues with its unreformed ways.

Well-meaning and patriotic people all over India look forward to the success of the AAP in Delhi. That would give them a hope and an option that if the BJP fails to perform and deliver they have another party to look forward to, rather than to revert to the incorrigibly incompetent and corrupt Congress.

The next state that people would look forward to for the AAP to be in power would be Punjab, where the next assembly elections are scheduled for 2017. People of Punjab have had a very bad experience of the misrule of the Congress, whom they booted out. Little did they realise that the parties they were replacing the gone-case Congress with, would turn out to be no better. The people of Punjab are now the unfortunate victims of the misrule of the Akali-BJP (SAD-BJP) combine.

Punjab is down with drugs. The heart-rending Moga bus case of 29 April 2015, in which a Dalit woman and her teenage daughter were molested and thrown out of a running bus, leaving the girl dead and mother seriously wounded, was not an isolated incident. It was a pointer to a deep-rooted malaise. There have been many other incidents, including the shocking one at Jalandhar where a cop was thrashed on 3 May 2015 by a group of youths in broad day-light for confronting daughter's stalkers! A news report "*Getting to a village in Moga: The bus stops here*" in *The Indian Express*, Mumbai of 10 May 2015 (may please check on the web) is an eye opener. What a shocking state of affairs? What kind of shameful culture has taken roots? Girl students and women passengers suffering indignities every single day! The politicians, equally of the Akali Dal, the BJP and the Congress, and the Police of the state must hang their heads in shame. There are many unbelievably alarming incidents given in the report. To give just one example: A girl details the daily harassment she faces, the indignity that is heaped upon her, and the risk she takes in commuting for her coaching for IELTS (International English Language Testing System), but is bravely tolerating it all in the hope of clearing the examination that would allow her to move out from India to a "country safer for women"! Don't the people responsible for the safely of people—the concerned ministers, politicians, IAS officers, IPS officers and police-persons—deserve to be sacked?

When one comes to know of such a sad and shocking state of affairs, and knows that both the national parties, the Congress and the BJP, and the joint ruling regional party, the Shiromani Akali Dal (SAD) are guilty of misrule and have utterly failed to provide even safety to its citizens, one has no alternative but to hope the AAP metes out a crushing defeat on all these parties in the 2017 assembly elections, à la Delhi, and provides succour to the people of Punjab.

If the AAP prevents further internal dissensions, continues to remain clean and corruption-free, shuns populism and socialistic nonsense, goes beyond freebies, charts a sane free-market developmental agenda, delivers in Delhi, demonstrates ability at good governance; its political future is secure; it won't have to do much to get votes, the aam aadmi of Punjab would itself come forward and welcome it into power with resounding majority like in Delhi, and thereafter it can spread country-wide.

Rather than having a dynastic party like the Congress as a national alternative to the BJP, one would hope it is the AAP, but without the socialistic economic policies of the Congress that have kept India wretchedly poor.

People have lots of hopes and expectations from the AAP, and the AAP has a great responsibility to come up to those expectations. They must guard against the temptation to descend to populism-socialism-leftism for the sake of votes and thereby become indistinguishable from the Congress, the CPI, the CPM, the SP, the RJD and the JDU.

One hopes that the young blood in the AAP, and the professionals who form its part, would keep the AAP on the right economic track—that being the most critical part, looked at from the angle of India's poor. Not that there are also young people, including several in the AAP, who harbour the good-for-nothing marxist-socialist-communist political philosophy. They should be questioned: "Has any nation or society anywhere in the world prospered on socialism or communism?" The AAP would need to internally resolve such issues.

If the AAP combines its rare quality of honesty and probity in public life, selfless service, and commitment and dedication for the people, with a sane economic policy that would see India prosper, *then sky is the limit for the AAP*. Of course, that is subject to the AAP shunning unnecessary controversies, giving up its *tamasha* politics, and remaining in the news for wrong reasons: people are not impressed by them, they are put off. The AAP must stick to its principles and support what is right and good for the nation, rather than being populist.

# 15

# AAP'S POLITICAL INNOVATIONS

*To lead the people, walk behind them.*

—Lao Tzu

The AAP has been highly innovative in many respects. Behind those innovations is the young blood in it—a dedicated group of professionals for whom AAP is their first brush with politics; and who joined the AAP not because they wanted to be in politics, but because they desired to change India. The traditional parties like the Congress and the BJP have much to learn from the AAP. What to speak of the young blood and innovative ideas, the Congress is not able to even wrench itself out of the clutches of its debilitating Dynasty. The BJP has thankfully jettisoned the old-guard, but it has a lot of ground to cover to induct young, innovative professionals, who may also help it displace its conservative cabal.

Here are some examples of the AAP's political innovations.

## Agenda with Wide, Universal Appeal

The AAP has not been just another run-of-the-mill political outfit, playing on caste, class, community, region, religion, rich-poor, urban-rural, language, east-west, north-south, this-that-ism to carve out its vote-bank. It has been innovative in choosing non-sectarian, non-divisive agenda with universal appeal. And, that are among the major reasons it has been so successful in so short a time. Corruption and bad governance affects all, so make them the main planks. Parties forget about the people after the elections, so highlight AAP's distinguishing feature of participative democracy and "swaraj".

## "Non-Political" Members with Fresh Faces

The AAP was not formed by defectors from some established political parties, or by some disgruntled politicos denied share of power, or by coming together of some disparate political groups. It was not old wine in a new bottle. Or, a cocktail of several with a new brand name. The AAP was formed by people who had been "non-political", but who had a proven track-record of doing good, selfless work for the society through NGOs or otherwise. That is, they had a reputation as good, well-meaning, dedicated people. Many young professionals from Information Technology and other domains also became members and volunteers for the AAP purely out of their inner call of doing good for the nation, and not for any political ambitions or power or for making money.

The political character of the AAP was therefore different and unique among all political formations since independence. Composition-wise, in terms of the nature of people who formed the initial AAP, it was a grand organisational innovation.

## Innovative Name

The choice of name of the party that itself conveys who the party stands for was a master stroke. Co-founder of the Aam Aadmi Party (AAP), Manish Sisodia, said they zeroed-in on the name because the AAP is a party "of the people, by the people and for the people of India". Not only is the name *Aam Aadmi Party* self-explanatory; its acronym AAP is a synonym for the pronoun "you", used when you address someone with respect in Hindi. The name thus allows room for beautiful word plays.

Parties like the Congress who have been fooling the common man (*aam aadmi*) that they stand for them were obviously rattled, and raised objections to the name. "The *aam aadmi* is synonymous with the Congress since 1885 when the party came into existence. Nobody can hijack, skyjack or bicycle-jack the intrinsic relationship between the Congress and the people of this country", commented the verbose Congressman Manish Tewari used to laboriously deploying "big" words inappropriately and engaging in jarring word-play wearing a smug smile and harbouring a self-deluding impression of being grand in oratory, repartee and caustic comments. In response to the Congress claim of "copyrights" on *aam aadmi*, Kejriwal had tweeted: "*Congress ka haath kabhi bhi aam aadmi ke saath nahin tha. Lekin ab Congress ye jhooth kehna bhi band kar degi.*"

No one gave any weightage to the cribbing of the hypocritical Congress, and the *aam aadmi* lapped up a party after its name. The transformation from *Team Anna* to *Team Kejriwal* to the *Aam Aadmi Party* was both smooth and dramatic.

## Innovative Symbol

The AAP scored yet another hit, after its hugely popular name *Aam Aadmi Party*, with its election symbol.

Declared AAP's web site: "Aam Aadmi Party is happy to announce that the Election Commission has allotted the party a reserved symbol of '***Broom***'.... With this the party has crossed the second milestone (after party's registration) *on its way to cleaning up the polity of the country. With the Broom which symbolizes dignity of labour, the party hopes to clean the filth which has permeated our government and our legislature. The country needs a clean sweep of its corrupted main stream political parties.*"

Deceptively humble "broom" actually aggressively and derisively casts the opposition as so much political dirt meant to be swept away by "you" that is "AAP" that is public that is voters! Could there have been a more meaningful and evocative symbol, that was also very easy to remember and recall by the general public, including illiterates?

"*Every Indian household cleans their house in the morning*", said AAP's Manish Sisodia. "*This Parliament and these assembly houses are also your houses. Select the broom to clean the houses.... This was the ultimate symbol.... Politics of the day has become too dirty in India. There is so much dirt. You talk about crime, you talk about corruption. Rapists, murderers are there in politics.*"

The symbol "broom" also helps identify the AAP with the poor humble section of the Indian society engaged in cleaning and sweeping, and through them, with all the poor and deprived.

Unlike the symbols of the other parties, holding this symbol of broom in hand is easy, demonstrative and useful, and lends itself to very effective publicity and marketing. Sweep of an area by brooms by a set of volunteers of the AAP during election campaigns serves double purpose: clean-up of the area and publicity for the AAP.

## Innovative Use of Technology

In its first election campaign in 2013, despite paucity of resources, the AAP pole-vaulted from nowhere to a leading contestant in the Delhi thanks to its several critical innovative strategies, one of which was intelligent and pervasive usage of technology.

For example, a cloud telephony start-up *Voice Tree* designed a convenient cloud-based telephony solution for the AAP that enabled a large team of AAP volunteers (that included students and housewives) connect with Delhi citizens through a toll-free number to persuade and convince them to vote for the AAP, while taking care that the calls were not duplicated. The calls went up to as many as 60,000 a day.

## Innovative Membership Drive

In January 2014, the AAP launched an open-for-all, free '*Main Bhi Aam Aadmi*' membership drive. Those interested to become members could just SMS their name, STD code and the name of their Vidhan Sabha to designated numbers, following which a response SMS was sent with the AAP membership number. Alternately, one could fill-in a simple online form at www.aamaadmiparty.org. Those unsure of how to go about becoming a member could give a missed call to a designated number, upon which they were sent an SMS guiding them on the process. Additionally, the membership form could be downloaded from the party's website, printed, made copies of, and distributed among those interested. Those without mobile could use voter ID to become members.

Within just four days of the launch of the drive, nearly ten lakh people had enrolled themselves as members; and soon thereafter the membership rose to fifty lakhs!

## Innovative Cap

White Gandhi caps with "*I am Aam Aadmi*" or its translation in Hindi or another regional language written on it, along with the symbol of broom, became popular and ubiquitous in no time. They were available in stores and online. There is also a video on the YouTube that illustrates how to make an aam aadmi cap.

It was a very thoughtful publicity innovation. The proof of its grand success were the plethora of imitators: the copycat job by the other political parties of using similar caps with a different colour and wordings.

## Innovative Publicity

The AAP's home-grown publicity innovations and marketing methods that fetched them huge dividends would not only give marketing gurus and top marketing companies charging multi-million fee a run for their money, but also effect in them a deep inferiority complex.

AAP's publicity blitzkrieg was multi-dimensional, and each dimension had plethora of innovative techniques. Usage of tailored cloud-based telephony application. Rich web portal. Intensive usage of facebook and twitter. Wide variety of attractive AAP merchandise available at stores and also online: AAP caps of various shapes and colours, AAP mugs, AAP T-shirts, AAP key-rings, AAP pen-drives, and so on.

## Innovative Funding

On 26 November 2012, the formal launch day of the AAP, the former law minister, Shanti Bhushan, donated rupees one crore. Since then, the party has used many innovative methods to raise funds. It has also been very transparent about them. Details of all funds received by the party are put up on its website for anyone to check. In that sense, the AAP is head and shoulders above all traditional parties in honesty and transparency. Through this, it has also shown the way forward for all political parties: clean, transparent funding for clean, honest politics!

The party does not have mega donors. It has to depend upon relatively small contributions from numerous well-wishers.

It had used an effective campaign "*I Fund Honest Party*" to collect funds. Pankaj Gupta, the national secretary of the AAP and the brain behind both its technology initiatives and innovative funding had remarked: "The *#IFundHonestParty* Challenge has ignited the imagination of our volunteers from across the world. Nearly every day we get a request to approve a new, innovative fund-raising initiative."

The party undertook various fund-raising programmes by its units in India and abroad, including the "*SelfieWithMufflerMan*" (that is, with Arvind Kejriwal) in Bengaluru; the *#FlameOfHope* in UK; and many lunch-dinner events at various locations.

The AAP also came up with a mobile application "*Aap ka daan*" for donations.

The AAP team has to be commended for being able to stand on its own through honest, transparent funding against well-funded propaganda of the Congress and the BJP through TV, print media and hoardings managed by professional marketing agencies charging astronomical fee.

A bad name was sought to be given to the AAP on certain irregular funding allegations. The media also raked it up. Opposition parties like the Congress and the BJP went full throttle against the AAP on it. What was the issue? Cheque of some 50 lakhs from an alleged bogus company. The information about the said contribution was put up by the AAP itself on its website. The receipt was by a cheque. It was unbelievable hypocrisy on the part of the Congress and the BJP who receive hundreds of crores of contribution, the details of which they never put up on their websites transparently as the AAP does, to cry hoarse on the issue.

The Congress and the AAP must rather publicly commend the AAP for their transparency on funding and must try to follow in their footsteps.

# 16

# AAP'S ACHIEVEMENTS

## Promises Kept

At the end of one month in office, the AAP claimed as its achievements the slashing power tariff by 50 per cent and free water up to 20 litres per month at an annual cost (subsidy) of about 1670 crore rupees to the exchequer, simplification of VAT payment, providing of licenses to 20,800 e-rickshaws, start of the process of installing of CCTVs in all its 1000 schools, exploration of the scope of utilising information technology to the maximum in various functions of the government, studying areas of reforms, among others. It promised to revamp its anti-corruption helpline that was launched during its earlier 49-day stint. It had already issued show cause notices to 200 private schools for charging exorbitant fees. Rent for anganwadi premises had been substantially raised: from 750 rupees per month to 4000-5000 rupees per month.

## Partial List of AAP's Innovative Achievements

### *Health Care*

The Delhi Government is planning to open 1000 new clinics in public-private-partnership (PPP). To better utilise existing infrastructure, it is considering evening shift in Government dispensaries; and allowing private medical practitioners to run their clinics in Government-run dispensaries.

### *E-Ration Card Service*

Delhi became the first state in the country to launch an e-ration card service. The scheme would link ration and

Aadhaar cards. Rather than making rounds of the government department and paying bribes, the eligible persons can apply online for the card at the government portal nfs.delhi.gov.in. The sub-title of the website reads: "*An e-Governance initiative to ensure Food Security to every eligible household in Delhi.*" It is worth looking at the website to appreciate the transparency in sharing information with the public and the nature of online facilities available.

### *Anti Corruption Helpline 1031*

The service can be used to lodge complaints of harassment for bribes. Trained persons run the 24/7 helpline and attend the calls in English and Hindi.

### *Participative Budget (PB) Making*

In *Participatory Budgeting* (PB), common people of an area discuss the budget allocations prepared with the help of experts, and decide (vote on) the priorities.

This type of experiment started with Porto Alegre in Brazil in 1989. Its success has since made it popular in hundreds of cities across Latin America, Europe, and North America. In India, this experiment was first tried, with great success, at Hiware Bazar, a village in Ahmednagar district of Maharashtra, by one Popatrao Baguji Pawar in 1990, who took inspiration from Anna Hazare who had turned around his village Ralegan Siddhi, which was just 35 kilometres away from Hiware Bazar.

The AAP kick-started this experiment, calling it "*People's Budget (Janata ka Budget)*" initiative, on 19 April 2015 from Delhi Deputy Chief Minister Manish Sisodia's Patparganj constituency. The AAP plans to gradually expand the exercise to the whole of Delhi.

### *Revamping School Education*

The AAP has taken up the revamp of school education system on a priority basis stressing both on the infrastructure and the quality of education.

It plans forming its own education board on the lines of Central Board of Secondary Education (CBSE) and National Council of Educational Research and Training (NCERT), but more modern and effective. The AAP is also working on dramatically upgrading the government-run schools and turn them into model schools that would be better than the private schools over the next five years. They are planning better training for the principals and teachers of government schools and are working on an incentive system for them.

### *Chalta-firta (Mobile) Office*

Introduction of mobile office on van to facilitate registration of aadhar card and voter ids is a public-friendly step appreciated by people. A day before visiting an area, announcements are made that a mobile office would be in the ward as per schedule, and that the interested residents may keep their documents ready. The mobile office is also used to register complaints of the residents.

# 17

# MEDIA AND THE AAP

*The COUNTRY is controlled by LAWS,*
*LAWS are controlled by POLITICIANS,*
*POLITICIANS are controlled by VOTERS,*
*VOTERS are controlled by PUBLIC OPINION,*
*PUBLIC OPINION is controlled by the MEDIA and EDUCATION, SLS*
*So, whoever controls MEDIA & EDUCATION, controls the COUNTRY.*

—William J. Federer

*There are people so addicted to exaggeration that they can't tell the truth without lying.*

—Josh Billings

Media ought to disseminate news and information from as wide an area and in as unbiased and objective a manner as possible. Media should not be deliberately selective in what it informs and what it hides; what it over-publicises and what it sweeps under the carpet. Overly negative orientation should be guarded against, just as tendency to cover up negatives of some is immoral. News, information and facts should be checked and cross-checked before circulated them. Giving out one part of the facts while suppressing the other part is not ethical. Giving spin to the news and headlines is mischievous. How you select news from a vast pool is also important. You can't focus on the inanities, ignoring the vital. You can't keep picking up the negative, ignoring the positives. National news can't be news just of Delhi and Mumbai. Biases should not be projected as honest opinions. Personal agendas and prejudices should not drive debates.... It's a long list.

Sadly, a majority of the Indian Main Stream Media (MSM) recklessly violates the "don'ts", while contemptuously ignoring the "dos".

One can say that if the politicians are not what they should be, or the bureaucracy is not what it ought to be, or the criminal-justice system is not what it is expected to be, or the medical profession does not measure up to the ethical standards of the Hippocratic Oath, or the teachers don't teach or teach well, and so on, then why expect media to be above board?

True. But, unfortunately, thanks to the pervasive TV, media is now the most intrusive element in a citizen's life—even an illiterate is not left untouched by it. That being the case, it is a very powerful medium of information, misinformation and disinformation. It can spread both truth and lies at an alarming speed. Hence, its responsibilities and its ethical standards ought to be higher.

But, is that the case? No.

Fortunately, the social media is a good counter to the MSM. But, then the social media is restricted to the literate, who are also technologically or gadget literate. Besides, the social media, being free for all, manufactures and spreads its own information, misinformation and disinformation.

For better news, information and opinion dissemination, there is no alternative but to have an effective news-regulator or news self-regulator. Those enlightened systems have to be in place. Till then, the public at large remain a helpless victim of the MSM.

Let's take the AAP itself as an example, before we move on to other examples.

## Media's Love-Hate for AK and the AAP

Lately, to the AAP's allegation of *supari-journalism* against it, the MSM was up in arms remonstrating the AAP's ingratitude to the media-boost for the AAP, and the invaluable role that the media claimed it had played in bringing the AAP to power.

Nothing can beat the arrogance and the smugness of the MSM, and the megalomania of its supposed strength in making or marring political career.

If they gave undue exposure to the AAP at a given time, it was because it helped them enhance their TRP. In a way, it was the AAP doing them a favour by helping them enhance their TRP, rather than the other way round. Sure, in the process the AAP too gained. But, that was not because the MSM was large-hearted in promoting them, or was doing them a favour.

Further, even if it is accepted for the argument's sake that the MSM indeed helped the AAP in a large-hearted manner, that supposition actually exposes the MSM for playing favourites and not being even-handed. What the MSM claimed was therefore self-incriminating.

On 3 May 2015, responding to an audience suggestion of putting media on trial at the launch of a news website Janata Ka Reporter, Kejriwal turned to the CEO of the portal and commented: "*This is a good suggestion. If you see a channel showing something factually incorrect, you must name the channel and raise the issue.*"

He said, among other things: "TV channels did not spare anything to ruin AAP before the election and even now they're trying to discredit us in all possible ways. However, people are very smart. The more the media shows us in a negative light, the more support we get. This time we won 67 seats and next time we may end up with 70 seats."

He further told the audience: "*Just as AAP had exposed politicians, we will expose the media. We won't tolerate blackmailing.... You can have a public trial as well. Fix 8-10 points and collect people there and say that a particular channel showed something wrong. Name the media.*"

These remarks were enough for all the TV channels to go ballistic on Arvind Kejriwal and the AAP during the prime time, launching an all-out attack on Kejriwal for daring to suggest scrutiny of the news-media. A neutral observer wondered at the empty fulminations. What was so holy about the news-media? Why it could not be questioned? If media had an agenda and gave out false or manufactured news, why shouldn't it be exposed? If there was no proper regulatory mechanism, and if the news-media self-regulation was ineffective, where was the alternative except exposing them publicly? Kejriwal had only talked against false news. If one could go against dishonest politicians, why not against dishonest and unethical news-media?

The media tried to project that Kejriwal had committed some kind of sacrilege by alleging that 'a large section of the media wanted to finish off the AAP', and by suggesting 'people trials' for those in the media indulging in agenda-driven, motivated journalism. The TV channels took it upon themselves to show Kejriwal his place. How could they, the holy cows, be questioned?

They forgot that the term "MediaWhores" was not uncommon in the West. So also the term "presstitutes" used in the West and deployed by Gen V.K. Singh to express his anguish. Narendra Modi has used the term "News Traders" for a section of the news-media indulging in unethical journalism.

The media may rage over Kejriwal's suggestion of people's trial being preposterous, but what redress does a common man, or even an uncommon man like Kejriwal, have against the false onslaught of a news-media with an ulterior agenda. As mentioned above, there is no effective regulatory or self-regulatory body for the news-media.

There had been unnecessary over-much publicity on Bhushan-Yadav rift, with the media projecting Bhushan-Yadav as the victims and Kejriwal-AAP as the perpetrators of the wrong done to them, without sufficiently highlighting the negative role played by the Bhushan-Yadav duo. The BJP and the Congress had a gala time taking potshots at the AAP along with the media buffoons, without appreciating it was an internal matter of the AAP, and that what was questionable was not why they were removed, but why they were tolerated for so long and why they were not ejected much earlier. You can't blatantly work against a party and yet expect to remain in its top positions or as its members.

The recent Kumar Vishwas affair is another example of a section of media crossing all limits of fair play, and rest of the media joining in for 24 × 7 time-pass. It was bizarre a lady demanding "*Kumar Vishwas declare he had no illicit affair with her*", and the media going full-throttle on it! Imagine the unenviable position of Kumar Vishwas in this. What remedy a person in his place have against such blatant media mischief?

The media has to introspect and self-correct; or an external body or a self-regulating body must take the responsibility to effectively control it and listen to grievances of complainants.

One queer thing is that when one political party or political person is wrongly targeted by a section of the media, the other political parties and their spokespersons, rather than going by the facts of the case, start blindly slamming the concerned falsely targeted person or party. If something wrong is done against Kejriwal or the AAP by a section of the media, the spokespersons of parties like the BJP and the Congress would promptly jump into the fray with the media and start slamming the target. If a section of the media wrongly targets Modi or the BJP, the AAP and the Congress would promptly contribute sound bites against Modi or the BJP. Why can't political parties criticise on merits. They don't mind being used by the media to target others.

## Media's Hate-Hate for Modi and the BJP

For reasons that are hard to fathom, the MSM has a chip on its shoulders against the BJP.

Wrote William Shakespeare: "*The evil that men do lives after them; the good is oft interred with their bones.*" Paraphrased for Modi and the BJP versus the news-media, it could read like this: "*The good that the Modi government does is either met with silence, or is given a spin so as to look otherwise; while its slips or deficiencies are magnified to form the headlines*!"

Despite his performance as the best chief minister ever of any state since independence, the media chose to only highlight the negatives they could pick on Gujarat and on Modi for over a decade, ignoring the remarkable achievements, and ignoring the judicial decision in his favour. In the run-up to the 2014 Lok Sabha elections, so as to hurt Modi's and the BJP's chances, they began unfairly panning the "*Gujarat Model of Development*" without ever comparing it with the proven disastrous "*Nehru-Indira Dynasty Model of Development*".

The current tenure of Modi as the Prime Minister has been reasonably successful. During the last one year, the Modi-government has been singularly blemish-free: there have been no scams or scandals. Modi's foreign sojourns have been highly successful. Economy is not doing great, but is on the growth path. There have been a number of noteworthy achievements like the *Jan Dhan Yojana*. A large number of excellent initiatives have been taken, but that will take time to fructify. India's action in Yemen and Nepal have been exceptional—lauded globally. Yet, you find a large section of the *Main Stream Media (MSM)* being not only lukewarm to the government's good work—often being silent about them; but inventive in picking holes, acting like a drain inspector (as Mahatma Gandhi had remarked about Katherine Mayo for her book *Mother India*), and even manufacturing stories or giving spin to news items to somehow tar the government. Granted there was much more that the Modi-government could have done, but then you highlight the good that has been done, and then mention what more was expected. Further, also stress that notwithstanding the not-as-great-as-expected performance of the Modi-government, it has been far, far better than the good-for-nothing Congress-led UPA.

Modi and BJP should also internally debate why the media is so hostile to them. Media is an important segment, and they can't afford to ignore it.

## Media's Love-Love for the Dynasty-Congress

It has been a mystery why a large section of the *Main Stream Media (MSM)*, along with a majority of the so-called opinion makers (political commentators, academics, intellectuals, business-persons, and the like) have been pro-Dynasty and pro-Congress: ***the Dynasty-lackeys***. Is it because the natural tendency of the elites is to remain on the right side of the power that be? It pays to be so. Although the Congress and the Dynasty are no more in power at the Centre, they have been in power for decades. The habits formed during those decades die-hard. Many are beholden for the favours done in the past, and cannot now turn around. What if the Modi-government does not last? What if the Congress comes back? That could be another consideration. Wait and watch. Only after they reckon the Dynasty is perhaps gone for good would they give up their self-serving reverence. It is like the "good" old days of the Raj, and the way the elite-natives behaved then, sucking up to the Whites. Those elites, or rather their descendants, and their feudal elite-mindset continues. The Raj was replaced by the Congress, and the Raj-rulers were replaced by the Nehru-Indira Dynasty.

Democracy and democratic norms are there for this class (*the Dynasty-lackeys*) only for hyperventilation—they are comfortable with their self-serving quid-pro-quo of feudal subservience. The good things that Modi does are of no consequence, but the inanities that Rahul blurts out deserve to be appreciatively highlighted and even debated during the prime time!

One can only hope and say: *Arise, O Dynasty-lackeys; you have nothing to lose but the chains of your feudal and mental slavery! Taste the liberation, freedom and democracy! Jettison the Dynasty bonds*!

## Poor TV Coverage and Quality

Looking to the miserable state of India, one would have expected a powerful medium like television, with its vast reach, to highlight problems and issues. But, no. The Indian TV channels are happy broadcasting inanities.

News for Indian news channels is only some odd things happening at New Delhi or Mumbai. It is as if India of the other metros, over thousand cities and towns and over six hundred thousand villages does not exist. News is mostly what some political bloke said or what negative happened! And, what sort of discussions they have on the prime time? Gossips based on guesses. 9 p.m. news and discussions on most news channels seems like post-dinner prattle and time-pass.

The anchors on TV, even when they take up an issue, generate lots of heat, but no light. You schedule half-an-hour. Some eight minutes go in the ads. That leaves 22 minutes. Over one-third time is hogged by the moderator, who should actually take no more than ten per cent of the time. That leaves only 14 minutes for the actual debate participants. If there are four participants, that works out to just over three minutes per person. What kind of worthwhile debate is possible in that much time. But, the idea is not to throw light on anything. The whole drama is just to generate as much heat and acrimony as possible by engaging in unsubstantiated, controversial statements.

Those good at one-liners leave triumphant. Those who have something worthwhile to say find their time is over just when they are about to begin on a critical aspect. "We have completely run out of time," the moderator would shout, and then take another few minutes putting words in somebody's mouth or giving the matter a controversial spin. The moderator does not like to be a moderator. He or she is the wisest know-all around, hogging maximum time: wasting time on giving unnecessary background, interfering when others are talking, commenting after each has his or her say, and blabbering his/her own meagre knowledge.

Most TV debates are a waste of time. They are, in fact, as pointless and predictable as the Saas-Bahu serials, especially after the preponderance of lawyers as spokesmen from all parties. It is rare to watch a debate on TV on any Indian channel after listening to which one could say with satisfaction: it was worth it, it enlightened me.

Though, one does find several debates on BBC TV to be good. First, unlike the moderators on Indian channels, those moderators only moderate, taking as little time for themselves as possible, and giving maximum time to the participants and the audience. Second, the debate participants show respect to one another. They listen to others in silence allowing them to complete. They do not cross-talk. They do not try to hog the time for themselves, or accuse others.

Even Lok Sabha and Rajya Sabha TVs have a number of well-conducted debates. These Sarkari channels beat the commercial ones hands-down when it comes to quality of discussions. They also have a better variety of topics. Part of the reason is that for many of their discussions, Lok Sabha and Rajya Sabha TVs call experts in the field, who really enlighten you, and not politicians. Commercial channels deliberately call politicians from the opposition and the ruling groups so as to generate as much heat as possible—that being their only motive! That's why you see the pathetic spectacle of each participant trying to be one up, interrupting others, and saying his or her own thing, without listening to the others. And, the moderator, rather conducting the debate in a civilised manner, joins-in in the noise, contributing to the racket.

You even have people like that fellow who was given no quarters by the wise Narsimha Rao, but who has now warmed his way back through *chamchagiri*: writing appropriate book and articles and becoming self-appointed defender and propagator of the Nehru-Gandhis, and their defunct socialism and disastrous foreign policies. The obnoxious fellow considers himself very wise and knowledgeable and even witty—and says so himself, with no one willing to put in a good word for him. This babu turned politician is so crude and arrogant that he freely insults other participants on TV. One wonder why moderators do not shut him up or throw him out or ban him from appearance on TV. He even came on one BBC debate, and true to his crudeness told a participant, "you are completely wrong!" One can understand somebody saying, "I beg to differ." But to dismiss another guy like he did—it was shocking. And, it was not as if he himself had anything worthwhile to say. The creep flaunts his having been a babu! As if that is an achievement! It exposes the bankruptcy of that character. He is just a lapdog of the Dynasty. However, it is a revelation to find that dogs can be arrogant too!

You have one-hour debates on some Indian channels where you collect a crowd and then let a score or more say a few sentences, and before anybody is wiser, an hour is over, and the moderator declares: "We are completely out of time." The participants in the debate and the TV audience waste an hour, and the moderator ends it in a grand manner as if some complex issues have been resolved, or some new light has been thrown on the topic under wasteful discussion.

Then there are some TV personalities who intimidate the person they are interviewing, behave in an aggressive and grossly ill-mannered fashion, and think they are great TV journalists—a particularly irritating journo among this tribe puts on a scowl, grits his teeth and growls menacingly to intimidate his guests. As if by behaving police-like they would ferret out information from the interviewee that the interviewee would not reveal if the interview was conducted in a cultured manner. Further, they do this in a selective manner. If this tribe perceives that the interviewee has the power that could bring harm to him or her or to the channel, the interview method changes, and takes a very pleasing, cultured form. However, if this tribe perceives the interviewee to be otherwise, and judges that by embarrassing or insulting him those in power would feel happy, the tribe sticks to its crude techniques.

Here is an extract from a "gem" of an article—an old one, but illustrative of the class—from a senior journalist Karan Thapar in the *Hindustan Times* of 9 May 2009:

"...*Priyanka Gandhi will be Prime Minister of India one day.... My hunch is we are going to see a messy outcome of the present elections.... And the pain of endurance will determine the outcome of the next election. That could be as early as 2011...the process that brings Modi to power will fracture or shatter the NDA.... And I'd say his government will probably serve its full term.... So it's seven years down the road that Priyanka Gandhi will step on to the political stage. It will be the shock of the Modi victory...that will overcome both her philosophical distaste for politics as well as her emotional reluctance to replace her brother.... Convincing Priyanka won't be easy and it won't happen quickly. In fact, she'll have to convince herself...by accepting, but perhaps never admitting, that Rahul, the brother she adores, cannot restore the Congress fortunes or India's self-image and self-respect. She'll have to convince herself that her party and her country need her. And now, why do I believe if Priyanka steps into politics she could end up as PM? Because she has a magical spark that makes her compelling. It's a combination of charm, charisma, presence, appearance and intelligence. You see it on TV, you sense it in her interviews and, if my colleagues are correct, it captivates the audiences she speaks to. She has one further quality which is particularly rare. She understands herself and is comfortable with who she is. It's a sort of Buddhist self-awareness and it's reassuring to encounter. It makes you want to believe in her. Yet this is why she will struggle and agonise over becoming a politician but, when she does, this is also why she will rise to the top....*"

Do you notice what the senior journalist thought were her credentials to become PM: '*charm, charisma, presence, appearance, intelligence.... Buddhist self-awareness.*' *The first four* '*charm, charisma, presence, appearance*' are all related to looks; 'intelligence'...this he senses; and finally, having run out of any further attributes, you have the mystical '*Buddhist self-awareness*'. The critical and the most vital attributes for becoming a PM do not seem to figure for the senior, "incisive", "To The Point" journalist at all: experience, proven achievements, competence for the job, track record, thought process, views on matters of national importance, ability to deal with complexities,... Only trivialities matter! Such are TVs top analysts and opinion makers!!

## Paid News

Based on the report of the Press Council of India and other sources, it can be said that in recent years, corruption in the Indian media has gone way beyond the corruption of individual journalists and specific media organizations—from "planting" information and views in lieu of favours received in cash or kind, to more institutionalized and organized forms of corruption wherein newspapers and television channels receive funds for publishing or broadcasting information in favour of particular individuals, corporate entities, political parties and candidates contesting elections, that is sought to be disguised as "news".

Writes Kuldip Nayar in *Beyond The Lines*: "...*Corruption is not confined to politicians, public servants, or the corporate world. The media too has blackened its face. Not only have reporters or correspondents changed their copy or withheld information for a consideration, but they are also involved in scams, vis-a-vis the appellate income tax tribunal.... I do believe there should be greater transparency in relation to editors. My suggestion to the Editor's Guild of India was that editors should annually file with the Press Council of India a list of their assets and that of their spouse.... Like Caesar's wife, editors should not only be honest but seen to be so. My suggestion was not to the liking of many editors.... Whether journalists believe in anything at all is difficult to say but my general impression is they are primarily interested in themselves. They may speak about values, and they ceaselessly speak about principles but it is material rewards that they hanker after....*"

# 18

# KEJRIWAL, RAHUL AND MODI

*The difference between a politician and a statesman is that a politician thinks about the next election while the statesman think about the next generation.*

—James Freeman Clarke

*Nearly all men can stand adversity, but if you want to test a man's character, give him power.*

—Abraham Lincoln

## Questions of Comparison

Comparison among Arvind Kejriwal (**AK**), Narendra **Modi** and Rahul Gandhi (**RG**), however misplaced, is not uncommon, especially by the media, and more so by those sections of the MSM (Main Stream Media) who have an incurable bias, either on account of their personal predisposition or their vested interests.

Why not then try and respond to questions of comparison often raised, and also those which ought to be raised.

### *What is their academic background?*

**AK**: AK has an excellent academic background, being an engineer (B.Tech.) from IIT, Kharagpur.

*Modi*: On account of his economic circumstances, Modi did not have the luxury of regular, proper education. However, while working as a *sambhag pracharak* (regional organiser) for *Rashtriya Swayamsevak Sangh* (RSS), he studied through distance-education and completed his graduation in political science from the Delhi University. Later, he did a Master of Arts (M.A.) in political science from Gujarat University.

**RG:** His educational details are not available with due clarity, although he is reported to be a graduate.

### *Did economic circumstances have an adverse bearing on their education?*

**AK:** No. He belonged to a middle-class family.

**Modi:** Yes.

**RG:** No. He had all the money in the world to do and study what he wanted.

### *Despite being well-funded, why are RG's academics below average?*

Deficient education is a Dynasty attribute, despite all the money, and all the facilities at their disposal.

Nehru's academic achievements were rather modest. He was a graduate and had passed the bar exams. Writes M.J. Akbar in *Nehru: The Making of India*: "Eventually when he [Jawaharlal] passed in the second half of the second class, Motilal was relieved enough to celebrate lavishly.... Motilal was acutely terrified that his son might fail, so even such moderate results were cause for celebrations.... Motilal had set his heart on sending his son to the Indian Civil Service.... He called the ICS the 'greatest of services in the world'.... But the weak Second [class of Jawaharlal Nehru] at the end of Cambridge persuaded Motilal that his son was unlikely to get through the tough ICS examinations...."

Indira Gandhi failed to complete her graduation despite spending considerable time and money in prestigious institutions in India, Europe and Britain.

Sanjay Gandhi never attended college!

Rajiv Gandhi did not do his graduation despite all the expenses at London. He was at Cambridge till 1965, but left it without a degree, because he did not appear for the examinations. He joined Imperial College, London in 1966, but again left it after a year, without a degree.

Sonia Gandhi? A graduate? Not clear. Most probably not.

Rahul Gandhi. Like his father he had the habit of joining a college or a course, and leaving it mid-way, perhaps finding the load too much to tackle.

All the members of the Dynasty, despite all the money, support and facilities, have been gross under-achievers academically. Yet, they are qualified enough to rule India! And naming educational institutes after their name is justified!

Another queer thing about the Nehru-Gandhi Dynasty has been pursuing studies and courses abroad at considerable expense when those courses of similar or better standards were available in India. Indira tried to engage in elementary studies abroad, Rajiv tried to do engineering in London. Why? Didn't the family, which flaunted its patriotism, find good schools and colleges in India! One could understand if they were academically brilliant and went abroad to do some specialised courses not available in India, or went to prestigious colleges abroad for their better teaching. But, no. They went for ordinary courses; and mostly, they whiled away their time there, and precious foreign exchange.

### *Do academics matter?*

It can of course be argued that academics is not all. It is not necessary to be highly qualified to be a good leader. That's fine.

If a certain leader was unable to go in for higher studies on account of paucity of money, or because of some special circumstances, one can understand. But, when you do take admission in a college, and have all the monetary support, and all the facilities, and yet you either fail to finish your education or do poorly, it does reflect on you as a person. Perhaps, you have no self-discipline, or you lack commitment, or you possess no determination, or you are too casual and irresponsible and while away time, or you have low IQ. You need not be a topper, but blessed with all the facilities, you do need to do reasonably well.

### *Did they have to struggle to come up in life?*

**AK:** No. His father was well-employed, being an electrical engineering from the Birla Institute of Technology.

**Modi:** Yes. He is an OBC belonging to the Ghanchi (oil-presser) community. He had to work in his childhood and teens. He helped his father sell tea at the Vadnagar railway station, and later ran a tea stall with his brother near a bus terminus.

**RG:** No. Never.

### *What were they doing before coming up as social or political activist?*

**AK:** He was with Tata Steel, Jamshedpur; and then, after qualifying in the Civil Services Examination, he joined the Indian Revenue Services (IRS) as an Assistant Commissioner of Income Tax in 1995.

**Modi:** He was helping his father in his tea stall; and later became a *pracharak* in RSS.

**RG:** Nothing. Reportedly doing time-pass dabbling in some business, awaiting the Dynastic call of parachuting onto a top position in the party or government.

### *Were they socially or politically active before coming into the limelight?*

**AK:** Yes. He was a social activists involved with several NGOs. He was the leading figure in the Team Anna Movement against corruption and for the Jan Lokpal Bill. He received many top awards including the *Ramon Magsaysay Award for Emergent Leadership* in 2006. He spent 12 long intensive years in civil activism and social service before jumping into the political fray.

**Modi:** Yes. Starting as a *pracharak* in RSS in 1971, he devoted himself selflessly for the nation and excelled in various positions in the RSS; and then moved on into the BJP in a number of important organisational assignments. He was an active underground worker during the 1975-77 Emergency declared by Indira Gandhi. Working sincerely and tirelessly for three decades (1971-2001) in various organisational and leadership position in the RSS and then in the BJP, he rose up the hierarchy to take up his first governmental position as the Chief Minister of Gujarat in 2001.

**RG**: No. Even in politics, he didn't have to struggle to prove himself. Entering the politics in 2004 as an MP, he jumped the hierarchy of many senior people, who had given their life to the party, to become the Congress General Secretary in 2007; and in 2013, without any achievement to his credit since entering politics, he took up the second highest position in the Congress party as its Vice President!

### *Did they sacrifice anything in the process of being socially and politically active?*

**AK**: Yes. He had a well-paying job as an Assistant Commissioner of Income Tax, which he left. He survived on his wife's salary. Kejriwal, Sisodia and Abhinandan Sekhri established the *Public Cause Research Foundation* in December 2006 in which they also inducted Prashant Bhushan and Kiran Bedi as trustees. He donated his *Ramon Magsaysay Award* prize money to the *Public Cause Research Foundation*.

**Modi**: Yes. As a *pracharak* in RSS, and then as an organisation man in the BJP, it was a life of hard-work and sacrifice for Modi—all you got was survival money.

**RG**: No. Question of sacrifice never arose. The Dynasty does not sacrifice. Either they sacrifice the nation, or the nation sacrifices for them—particularly the later generation.

### *Did they take initiative in doing things socially or politically useful?*

**AK**: Yes. He took a number of positive initiatives through his NGOs; and he jointly lead the Team Anna anti-corruption and Jan Lokpal movement.

**Modi**: Yes. As a *pracharak* in RSS, his had been a life of service and sacrifice; and as an organisation person in the BJP, he initiated a number of positive measures.

**RG**: No. The Dynasty is too self-centred to serve or sacrifice. They mostly do things that helps them remain in power.

***Did they come up the hard way learning things along the way?***

**AK:** Yes. He faced many tough challenges.

**Modi:** Yes. He had to work hard and struggle his way up.

**RG:** No. He has got where he is now by way of feudal "dynastic rights"; and not on account of any merit or performance.

***What has been their contribution in building up their political party?***

**AK:** He built his political party from scratch, and brought it up to great heights within a short period of one year—a highly creditable job: an achievement almost unmatched in the Indian political history after independence.

**Modi:** His contribution to building up the BJP has been exemplary. His becoming the Chief Minister of Gujarat was thanks to his proven competence and hard work, and not on account of any political manipulation or favours or *quid pro quo*.

**RG:** Under him, the party has suffered and has become much weaker.

***Did they head a responsible position in the government before reaching their current position?***

**AK:** No. He straightaway became the Chief Minister, such was the dramatically magical performance of his political party under his leadership.

**Modi:** He excelled as Chief Minister of Gujarat for over a decade before taking up the challenge as Prime Minister.

**RG:** No gradualism for the Dynasty. They always parachute to top positions.

***How had been their performance in their previous government position?***

**AK:** He was the Chief Minister of Delhi for 49 days in his first term. During that short-term his performance was good in many respects. Although, on some accounts, there was severe to mild criticism.

**Modi:** His performance as the Chief Minister of Gujarat for over a decade was excellent. He was perhaps the best chief minister India has had for any state since independence.

**RG:** He never took up a government/ministerial position. Was he afraid he would be exposed?

### *How is their performance in the current position?*

**AK:** He is doing well as the Chief Minister of Delhi.

Strangely, the media keeps highlighting mostly the negatives like the rifts and dissensions within the party. However, what really matters is what AK is doing for the people of Delhi as the CM. The media doesn't bother to cover the good work happening on this front.

Overall, the Delhi government is performing well.

**Modi:** His performance as the Prime Minister of India has been good and encouraging. Of course, more could have been done, but compared to the previous UPA government, his performance is far, far better.

**RG:** As the VP of the party, his performance has been disastrous. The Congress has been reduced to an all-time low of just 44 seats in the last Lok Sabha elections, and has been losing in most state elections.

### *Have they been willing to shoulder higher responsibilities?*

**AK:** Yes, definitely.

**Modi:** Yes, definitely. That's why he became the PM.

**RG:** He has been running away from responsibilities. He could have become a minister in UPA-I or UPA-II, but he didn't. Perhaps he is diffident and realises his own deficiencies. He is reluctant to get exposed.

## Attributes, Competencies:

### *Young?*

**AK:** Yes.

**Modi:** Yes, by Indian political standards.

**RG:** Yes.

### *Physically fit?*

**AK:** Reasonably fit.

**Modi:** Yes. Perhaps fitter than the other two younger persons, as was proved during his US visit where he remained intensely busy, even as he fasted.

**RG:** Yes.

### *Capable of working long hours?*

**AK:** Yes.

**Modi:** Yes. Certainly. He has not taken a single day off since becoming the PM, even though he had been exerting himself to severe exhaustion for many months in the run-up to the Lok Sabha elections.

**RG:** Highly doubtful. Keeps disappearing on long foreign jaunts periodically.

### *Patient and persistent?*

**AK:** Persistent—yes. Patient—doubtful, if one considers the impatience of the AAP to spread nationally in the last Lok Sabha elections: but, that could have been in deference to the ambitions of Prashant Bhushan and Yogendra Yadav duo, who have since been thankfully ejected. Reportedly, patient now, and rightly and wisely focusing on Delhi to come good on their promises.

**Modi:** Yes. Certainly. He has amply demonstrated this by working diligently, patiently and silently, away from the limelight, for the RSS and the BJP for three decades before becoming the Chief Minister of Gujarat; by his conduct through his trying times as the Chief Minister of Gujarat for over a decade, that included the terrible 2001 Gujarat earthquake and the slow and systematic rebuilding of the lives of its people; and now as the PM, even as a section of the MSM and intelligentsia, and the opposition parties keep ranting against him.

**RG:** Patience? As a dynast, he wants to pole-vault into top positions without working up his way patiently and diligently and by practically proving himself.

### *Financially honest? Not corrupt?*

**AK:** Yes. Certainly. As an employee in the Income-Tax department, he actually fought corruption. He and his ministers in Delhi are an exemplary demonstration that governments at the level of politicians can be honest too!

**Modi:** Yes. Certainly. Nothing against him despite a long political career spanning over four decades. He has even been donating savings from his salary for charitable purposes. He has auctioned all gifts received by him as chief minister or prime minister and given the proceeds to charities. He has also been instrumental in curbing corruption. His over a decade long administration in Gujarat and a year-long administration at the Centre has been remarkably scam-free. He is not only personally honest, he has taken steps and brought in changes in policies to minimise corruption. His conduct has been exemplary. How one wishes all politicians become like him in this respect.

**RG:** During the decade-long rule of UPA-I and UPA-II between 2004 and 2014 there had been a large number of mini, medium and mega scams. Some mega scams established a record for the mind-boggling amount involved. All the scams and wrong-doings were caught not by the internal processes of the ministries, but by whistle-blowers, external people or CAG. Each time a scam was brought to light, the government, rather than pursuing it and bringing the culprits to book in view of the massive financial loss to the exchequer, tried to pooh-pooh it or suppress it or make light of it or dismiss it. They even tried to defame the messengers or attribute motives to them. In certain cases they got vindictive.

All through, Sonia-Rahul called the shots. What was their role? Why didn't they exert to ensure the culprits who caused such massive losses to the nation were severely punished and made examples of.

One does not know if Sonia-Rahul are personally honest or dishonest. But, this much is clear: they have little to show for their action against the dishonest or for curbing corruption.

### *Mentally sharp?*

AK: Yes.

Modi: Yes.

RG: His responses belie mental sharpness.

### *Ability to comprehend complex issues?*

AK: Perhaps, yes. Though not fully tested as yet.

Modi: Yes.

RG: No.

During the Mayawati period in UP, Rahul Gandhi said in a certain context: "I feel ashamed to call myself an Indian after seeing what has happened here in UP." Sure, there is much to feel ashamed about, not only in UP, but elsewhere too. Six PMs of India have been from UP—three from his own Dynasty. Congress ruled it since the pre-Independence period, after the elections in the thirties. Post-Independence, Congress ruled UP for the first 40 years, barring some periods in-between. All through, since the late 1930s, the Dynasty members have been getting elected from UP, without a break. It is because Rahul's dynasty did little for UP that the other parties displaced Congress. So, if Rahul feels ashamed, it is a genuine sentiment. He ought to feel ashamed of how his Dynasty has shamed all Indians—in UP and elsewhere in India! He, his Dynasty and the Congress have plenty of reasons to feel ashamed: India's pathetic poverty, crores in hunger, millions of children victim of malnutrition, widespread illiteracy, poor infrastructure, wretched living conditions, yet crores looted through mega-scams—CWG, 2G, Coalgate, ...it's a long list.

### *Decisive?*

AK: Yes.

Modi: Yes.

RG: Not tested. Doubtful.

***Basically committed to doing good for the nation?***

AK: Yes.

Modi: Yes.

RG: Committed more to Dynasty rule than rule for the good of the nation.

***Familiar with Indian culture and traditions? Good understanding of India?***

AK: Yes.

Modi: Yes.

RG: Doubtful.

Here are extracts from Rahul Gandhi's gibberish at CII on 4 April, 2014:

"There is a tendency to look at India as a country. In our everyday life we see India as a national structure. But if you go back slightly more than that, go back a hundred, two hundred years, you would find that India is energy, it is a force. If you go back a thousand years, two thousand years, you would find that force came from our rivers, Ganga, Yamuna, Saraswati. We worshiped these rivers and the reason we worshiped these rivers was because that is where our energy came from, and everything we had was built on these rivers. Now we have gone way beyond that. We have built structures that are allowing this energy to rise, to explode...."

"...Democracy and technology have triggered a non-reversible chain reaction in India. This reaction is unstoppable. Nobody can stop it. We have to channel this reaction. We need to nurture it. We need to make it harmonious. We need to make this happen smoothly. We need to use the energy generated by this movement of people and ideas, the force this movement is generating, and we need to use it to empower everybody. Not one person, not almost everybody, but everybody...."

Can anyone beat him in sheer nonsense!

### ***Reasonable grasp on agricultural and rural issues?***

**AK:** Not known. Occasion to properly test it has not arisen. Currently mouthing Congress/opposition rants on farmers for the sake of vote-bank politics.

**Modi:** Yes.

**RG:** No. If what he says is done, Indian rural poor would be as poor and pathetic (maybe, more) in the future as they have been in the past.

### ***Reasonable understanding of the issues of the poor and Dalits?***

**AK:** Yes.

**Modi:** Yes.

**RG:** No.

Here is a gem from Rahul Gandhi:

"Yahan Hindustan mein hamara jaat ka concept hai. Is mein bhi escape velocity hoti hai. Dalit community ko is dharti pe Jupiter ki escape velocity chahiye.... (In India we have caste. Dalits need ***Jupiter's escape velocity on Earth***.)

"Isiliye agar aap history ko dekhe, jo dalit log hai, hum sab hai, Ambedkarji ko bahut garv se dekhte hai. Wo pehle aadmi hain jo escape velocity kar ke US chale gaye.... (Ambedkar was the first to achieve *escape velocity* and go to the US.)

"Jo leadership hai wo Mayawati ji ne capture kar liya hai aur doosre logon ko ubharne nahin deti. (Mayawati has captured the leadership and she does not allow others to emerge.)"

What about Rahul and his Dynasty who never allow capable Congress leaders to emerge, lest they threaten their position! Rahul seems to be so dumb the irony of what he says doesn't hit him.

### ***Reasonable grasp on non-agricultural and urban issues?***

**AK:** Yes.

**Modi:** Yes.

**RG:** No.

### *Reasonable grasp on economy and economics?*

AK: Not known. Occasion to test it has not arisen. Not yet properly articulated by AK.

Modi: Yes.

RG: No.

### *Leftist? Rightist? Centrist?...*

AK: Leftist. Socialist? Pragmatist?

Modi: Rightist, leftist, centrist, depending upon issues.

RG: Leftist. Socialist. Populist. Whatever is the short-cut to votes.

*Note*: Socialists, communists, populists can never do anything worthwhile for India.

### *Reasonable grasp on human resources and educational issues?*

AK: Yes.

Modi: Yes.

RG: No. Far cry.

### *Reasonable grasp on defence and security issues?*

AK: Not known. Occasion to test it has not arisen.

Modi: Yes.

RG: No. Doubtful if he understands. Mostly, he misunderstands.

As per the WikiLeaks, Rahul had told the US Ambassador to India in all seriousness that the Hindu terror was a greater challenge than the Islamic terror! What does it tell about his understanding of this serious issue of terror?

### *Reasonable grasp on social issues?*

AK: Yes.

Modi: Yes.

RG: No. Appears foreign to many Indian issues.

### *Reasonable grasp on foreign policy?*

**AK:** Not known. Occasion to test it has not arisen.

**Modi:** Yes. Excellent.

**RG:** No. Appears to be foreign to foreign policy.

In Gujarat, much before the last state elections, hinting at Modi, he said something to the effect that evil man like Mao Zedong also did development. This remark educated us on several things about Rahul. *One*, he has no historical knowledge. Mao's period was an economic disaster for China, like Rahul's father's, his grandmother's and his great grandfather's was for India. *Two*, he has no idea about world leaders. Mao was certainly not an evil person. Yes, many of his ideas, which he genuinely believed in, thinking they would benefit China, proved disastrous. But then, many of the things Nehru and Indira Gandhi and Rajiv Gandhi did also proved disastrous. Were they evil? *Three*, the person having ambition to be the PM of India seems to have no idea on diplomacy, and how to refer to leaders of other countries. China still reveres Mao. *Four*, Rahul does not know how to articulate what he wants to say. *Five*, anything impromptu, and Rahul is likely to blunder.

### *Reasonable grasp on what all India needs to do going forward?*

**AK:** Not yet well articulated.

**Modi:** Yes.

**RG:** No. Many of the things he harps on can only take India to the bad old Nehru-Indira socialistic days.

### *Overall, knowledgeable and well-versed with problems and issues?*

**AK:** Yes.

**Modi:** Yes.

**RG:** No. Hasn't demonstrated yet.

Like his mother, Rahul Gandhi has never held forth on any topic of importance, nor has he participated in any TV debates. He has never tried to explain and defend his viewpoints either in speeches or on TV or through articles in print-media. How then to know if he has any stuff? Actually, the very fact that he avoids all these is because he is afraid he would stand exposed. He has also not allowed himself to be subjected to grilling interviews. *Times Now* interview was an exception, and he got badly mauled in it. It's doubtful if he would again take the risk.

He just makes a statement, and runs away.

### *Has good and innovative ideas?*

AK: Yes.

Modi: Yes.

RG: No. Has weird ideas. Mostly borrowed ideas? No originality seen yet. No whiff of freshness. Mouths bad-old, Nehru-Indira period stale, failed ideas that can only doom India.

### *Good administrator and good in execution?*

AK: Time will tell. Has been CM for only a few months. But, likely to do well, judging by the performance so far.

Modi: Yes.

RG: Has run away from responsibilities in the past. Has not given occasion to test his abilities.

### *Good leader?*

AK: Yes.

Modi: Yes.

RG: No. The Congress has failed under him.

### *Inspiring leadership?*

AK: Yes.

Modi: Yes.

RG: No. Not at all. You can't inspire unless you have practically proved through your deeds that you can deliver.

### *Can carry party-persons along?*

AK: Yes and no. Has succeeded with many, and has failed with many.

**Modi**: Reasonably. But, not always.

**RG**: Congress party-persons are slaves of the Dynasty. So, the question of carrying them along democratically does not arise. While all are expected to only reverentially bend, many ambitious ones prefer to crawl before the Dynasty. A few who periodically rebel or protest are either thrown out or are line-attached till they come around and agree to be lap-dogs.

***Can manage well even with the opposition parties and groups?***

**AK**: Doubtful.

**Modi**: Perhaps. To be tested.

**RG**: Can manage with anyone, honest or dishonest, scoundrel or otherwise, as long as direct or indirect support to the Dynasty is assured.

***Capable of delivering goods for the nation?***

**AK**: Yes, provided does not descend into socialistic clap-trap.

**Modi**: Yes.

**RG**: No. Idea-wise: defective. Execution-wise: incompetent.

### Can Rahul Measure up as a PM?

*The only problem with politicians taking 2 week [or 8 week] vacations every year is it's about 50 weeks [or 44 weeks] too short.*

—Jarod Kintz

*Suppose you were an idiot, and suppose you were a member of Congress; but I repeat myself.*

—Mark Twain

*I am often wrong, but never in doubt.*

If Rahul Gandhi is indeed honest and sincere, he must ask himself the following questions, and also share the answers with the general public. Does he realise that the Congress Party—the shape that it is in: full of chamchas; corrupt netas; ambitious, incompetent, arrogant ex-bureaucrats; self-seeking lawyers—is incapable of delivering goods for the country? What has he done for all these years—when he was not in the government, and has only been doing party work—to stem the rot? Is the Congress significantly better, and significantly less corrupt, as a body compared to what it was when he got involved with the Congress? In short, what has been his concrete contribution in terms of practical results on the ground? If he has utterly failed in this task, what hope is there that he would do better when in the government?

*Politics is perhaps the only profession for which no preparation is thought necessary.*

—Robert Louis Stevenson

What is his track record? Has he headed a panchayat or a municipal corporation and achieved significant results? Has he worked as a junior or a senior minister in any state and done some work? Has he worked as a junior or a senior minister at the Centre and achieved results? Has he made a single speech that has impressed people? Has he given a single interview that has shown him to be sharp and intelligent? If he has done none of these, why should any reasonable person believe he can do anything worthwhile as the PM?

*He knows nothing; and he thinks he knows everything.*
*That points clearly to a political career.*

—George Bernard Shaw, Major Barbara

Is he aware how complex India is, how difficult are its problems, and how difficult is the job of a PM? What makes him feel he is experienced and qualified for the job? As a patriot, does he not think it would be disastrous for India to be managed by people not competent for the job? Would he ask an unskilled and inexperienced driver to drive him? All those who are promoting him to be the future PM must re-examine their act and re-evaluate it to make sure it is not inappropriate, irresponsible and unpatriotic.

When sycophants shout about his fitness to be the next prime minister, the Indian public has a right to know the basis of such claims. His views and comments have always been very simplistic, and show neither intellectual spark, nor wide reading, nor the ability to think deeply and analyse, nor experience, nor wisdom; and his leadership has not been proved in practice. So far, his track record has been less than mediocre. Congress would be doing a tremendous disservice to India by imposing him on the nation.

If you look at the sequence from the beginning to hopefully the end—Nehru, Indira, Rajiv, Sonia and Rahul—you find a steep deterioration. Nehru himself did not measure up to what our first PM should have been—if you go by the facts, the concrete results of his reign, his many blunders whose consequences we are still suffering, and not the fiction trotted out by the fawners. However, his successors have been progressively worse. The general trend in most families, which are well-to-do and can afford education, is that each generation is better than the previous. Nehru dynasty is an exception. Each generation is worse than the previous: the degradation has been in geometric progression.

It is important to realise that managing a country as large and as complex as India requires deep knowledge of India's different regions and people, its politics, its administration, its economy, its culture, its history, its strengths, its weaknesses and its international relations; intelligence to absorb them, experience to manage, competence to deal with complexities, and wisdom to take right decisions. Do Rahul-Sonia-Priyanka measure up? Certainly not.

In the interest of the nation, an iron law should be laid down: First prove your leadership competence in a public or private or political organisation or an NGO; then as a minister in a state or at the Centre or as a chief minister of a state for at least five years; and then only a candidate should be allowed to put himself or herself up as a prime minister.

Of course, the Nehru Dynasty would never like to follow such a rule. They know they would badly flunk in the first two stages, depriving them a chance at the top slot. They want to fail only at the top-slot!

We study, analyse and implement risk-mitigation in all walks of life: finance, banking, management, software, health, transport, security and so on. Practically, no segment is left untouched by it. However, when it comes to the biggest risk of all—that of the position of the prime minister—we seem to be casual, rather criminally callous.

## Can Kejriwal Measure up as a PM?

Arvind Kejriwal has a long way to go before laying claim to the top post. He has got a wonderful opportunity as the Chief Minister of Delhi. He must prove himself over the next five years. If he delivers, his stature would grow. He and his party should then try and spread across India. He can then take a shot at the post of the prime minister in the 2024 Lok Sabha elections.

He and his party should have patience and should build themselves. The party also needs to articulate in detail their economic and other policies. If they wish to become a pan-India party and come up on the national front, they cannot limit their political pronouncements to anti-corruption and homilies on participative governance.

Of all policies, the economic philosophy and the economic policies that they would implement are the most critical. If they mouth the same stale, populist, socialistic, leftist nonsense that the Congress, communist and other opposition parties have been mouthing, they would be one among the many competing parties fighting for a share of votes from the same constituency. That cannot bring them to power. Even if they manage to get into power by outdoing the competing parties, by being more left that the other leftists or by being deeper red than the other hues of red and pink, or by getting into cahoots with them, they would not be able to deliver anything tangible for the nation. If those poverty-perpetuating and prosperity-preventing socialistic policies of the Congress and their leftist allies have taken India to dogs over the last six decades, there is no reason to think that more-of-the-same would result in anything better.

If the AAP is indeed different than all the other parties as it claims to be, and if it really wishes to pull India out of its poverty and wretchedness and take it on the path of happiness and prosperity, it stands to reason that it has to have economic policies other than the ones that have been tried and have failed. No socialist or communist country anywhere in the world has ever prospered. China moved to prosperity at a blazing speed after it junked all its socialistic-communistic economic policies and adopted capitalist, free-market norms. This aspect has been detailed elsewhere in this book.

It is, therefore, necessary that the AAP adopts free-market economic policies if it really wishes to deliver for India.

Would Kejriwal and group do so? Going by the past, they have been more into the populist stunts that they feel would fetch them votes. A number of leaders among the AAP are of leftist bend. Having ejected the duo of Prashant Bhushan and Yogendra Yadav, and several others of similar thinking, the AAP must NOT plunge back into effete leftism and socialism.

Would Kejriwal be able to lead the AAP on to the right economic path? That would be his litmus test. If he fails, it may not be worth having him as a national leader. If he passes the test, then coupled with his established honesty, integrity and incorruptibility and that of many of his colleagues, India can look forward to good days ahead.

One looks forward to the AAP as an alternate party of the pragmatic right.

## Is Modi a Good PM?

*Perseverance is the hard work you do after you get tired of doing the hard work you already did.*

—Newt Gingrich

*Men of integrity, by their very existence, rekindle the belief that as a people we can live above the level of moral squalor. We need that belief; a cynical community is a corrupt community.*

—John W. Gardner

(The quotes above fittingly describe some of the qualities of Modi.)

Within about a year in power, the achievements of the Modi government are the following (a partial list):

**Foreign Affairs.** Narendra Modi and his government have surprised everyone by showing themselves to be unexpectedly comfortable, quick off the mark, and highly adept in conducting foreign affairs. His foreign tours have been resoundingly successful, and his welcome abroad has been so grand that its pales all earlier tours by India's earlier PMs. His popularity with PIO has brought together Indians worldwide, and the politicians abroad have realised the electoral benefit in associating themselves with Modi and the PIOs. This has added a new dimension to the Indian foreign policy.

Only a person as hard-working, as adept at planning and as disciplined as Modi could have squeezed in so many vital foreign tours within a year of being in office, despite his intensely busy domestic schedule. Thanks to Modi's foreign tour blitzkrieg, India's global profile has gone up considerably, and India now has a high standing in world capitals.

India under Modi has accorded due respect to its neighbours Bhutan and Nepal, which were among the first nations Modi paid visit to.

India's expeditious help to Nepal during the recent earthquake was lauded by all nations. India also acted with alacrity in rescuing Indians and people of other nationality too from Yemen under very difficult circumstances. This gained immense respect for India globally. While numerous nations praised and lauded India for its work in Nepal and Yemen, in India, a section of the MSM chose to give it a spin and run it down—there is something terribly sick about a section of our news-media.

**Dismantling of the Planning Commission.** It was appropriate that the fossilised relic of the Nehru-Indira-Dynasty socialism was given an unceremonious burial.

*Niti Ayog* that has replaced it is NOT Planning Commission by another name. Its purpose and agenda are different. It is fittingly headed by Professor Arvind Panagariya, with Professor Bibek Debroy as a member.

**Greater Economic Federalism and Democratisation, rather than Centralism and Dictatorship.** The Modi government has entrusted much larger economic resources to the states allowing them a much greater say in how they spend money in their states. This is a welcome move towards greater economic federalism. Earlier, by keeping major resources with itself, the Central government and the party in power at the Centre used to dictate its terms to the states—that amounted to economic dictatorship.

That the MSM which has been unfairly accusing Modi of dictatorship did not adequately highlight this bold, generous, democratic, federal and courageous move of Modi in delegating more power to the states and in reposing more faith in them is yet another proof of the bias of the MSM, its lack of integrity, and its continuing kowtowing to the disastrous dictatorial Dynasty.

**Indian Railways: At last, on the Right, New Track.** Dramatically breaking away from the irresponsible and harmful Dynastic tradition of the Congress and its allies of being populist and primarily playing to the gallery for the sake of votes, the Rail reforms and the Rail budget proposed by the Railway Minister Suresh Prabhu is the most sincere and wide ranging attempt yet to transform the Indian Railways into a magnificent centrepiece of a transport network, and to transform the Indian economy in the process. If things do pan out as planned by Suresh Prabhu and the Modi government, the railways transformation over the next four years of the Modi government would perhaps be the single most important legacy of NDA-Modi-I.

**Digital India.** Modi articulated his dream of a "*Digital India*" by 2019 in his first Independence Day speech on 15 August 2014. "*Digital India*" would encompass e-governance for efficient government, delivery of online and corruption-free government services through a unified portal, broadband for all, IT-enabled education, telemedicine, aadhaar-based digital life certificates called *Jeevan Pramaan* for pensioners, simplification of pension payments, and so on.

**Smart Cities.** This long-term plan envisages building of 100 smart cities in India on a flexible PPP (public-private partnership) model that would be well-designed, well-planned, environment-friendly, and technologically integrated. Many developed countries, including the US, Japan and Singapore, have committed to play a role in setting up such smart cities.

**Swachh Bharat.** Modi is the first PM who is attempting to turn the cleanliness drive into a mass movement through "Swachh Bharat". Certainly a noble cause. It would be a great achievement if implemented properly all through India on the ground. However, there is a long way to go in its implementation. Currently, "Swachh Bharat" is more of sloganeering and advertisement and an occasion for photo-op than anything substantial, except in some isolated pockets. Much, much more needs to be done to expedite it and make it all-encompassing.

**Clean Ganga Project**

*The activist is not the man who says the river is dirty.*

*The activist is the man who cleans up the river.*

—Ross Perot

The NDA government launched the 'Namami Gange' project in 2014 to divest river Ganga of its pollution and bring it back into its past glory. The Modi government has devised a three phase plan spanning 18 years at ₹ 51,000 crore to clean the river. The first phase includes stopping open drains from falling into the river, plugging industrial and chemical discharge into the river, and so on. For the purpose "Clean Ganga Fund" has been created. Website nmcg.nic.in of the "National Mission for Clean Ganga" provides relevant details.

**Make in India.** The Modi government's innovative "*Make in India*" campaign signals its commitment to transforming India into a manufacturing hub of the world. Its main benefit is in job creation for the increasing army of young coming into the job market every year both from the rural and the urban areas.

The success of "*Make in India*" is dependent upon the degree to which the government can provide an enabling environment by improving the ease of doing business in India; and that process, given India's abysmal babudom, is slow in unfolding.

**2G Spectrum Auction.** The massive 2G Spectrum Scam under the Congress-led UPA had resulted in an estimated loss of about 1.76 lakh crores, as per the CAG. That was thanks to its crony-capitalist, corporate-enriching unfair policies, which ironically Rahul has been accusing the Modi government of! The Modi government has put in place a just and robust mechanism of spectrum auction. Thanks to the same, in the auction held in March 2015 for sale of 418.05 MHz of spectrum, the government managed to raise ₹ 1,09,874 crores, after 19 days and 115 rounds of bidding by the telecom corporates.

**Coal Blocks Auction.** Allocation of 204 coal mines/blocks made by the UPA was cancelled by the Supreme Court holding it as arbitrary and illegal. CAG Vinod Rai had computed the overall loss as ₹ 1,86,000 crores—a figure that had seemed fantastic, and was ridiculed by the Congress.

The Modi government instituted a fair and just procedure for auction of the coal blocks. Out of 204 blocks, 18 operational blocks and 13 about-to-open blocks were put up for auction during February-March 2015. The revenue that is likely to accrue to the government over the next 30 years from these 31 blocks is of the order of ₹ 2,07,000 crores. The net present value (NPV) of these ₹ 2,07,000 crores would be much less, but then the figure given by Vinod Rai of ₹ 1,86,000 crores was also an overall figure, and not a computed NPV.

If all the 204 blocks are put up for auction, the aggregate income is likely to be a mind-boggling ₹ 10,00,000 crores (a million crores) over the next 30 years.

In other words, while the Congress was ridiculing a figure of ₹ 1,86,000 crores for 204 blocks, the actual amount, thanks to the auction by the Modi-BJP-led NDA, is a massive ₹ 2,07,000 crores for just 31 blocks, and could be ₹ 10,00,000 crores for all the 204 blocks!

Honesty and integrity pays!!

Rahul Gandhi has been yelling Modi-government is a *suit-boot sarkar*, that is pro-corporate and pro-rich. That's a case of "*ulta chor kotwal ko dante*"! Who unjustly favoured the corporates with what now turns out to be a bounty of ₹ 10,00,000 crores (because, the Congress gave away the blocks for free)! So, it was the Sonia-Rahul Congress that caused a massive loss of ₹ 10,00,000 crores to the exchequer.

As per an article by R. Jagannathan in the *Firstpost.com*: "*If we assume a discount rate of 10 per cent, compounded annually, a 30-year income inflow period, a ₹ 10 lakh crores total bid for all 204 blocks (which works out to cash inflows of around ₹ 34,000 crores annually for government on zero investment), we would get an NPV of over ₹ 3,20,515 crores. If the actual bids reach ₹ 15 lakh crores (₹ 50,000 crores inflows a year for 30 years), the NPV would be even higher at ₹ 4,71,345 crores.*"

**Economy**. The economy is gradually looking up. The International Monetary Fund (IMF) has projected that India will overtake China as the fastest growing emerging economy in 2015-16 by clocking a growth rate of 7.5 per cent, helped by its recent policy initiatives, pick-up in investments and lower oil prices. World Bank too has similar GDP growth forecast for India for the current fiscal year.

Low inflation has enabled the Reserve Bank of India to marginally cut interest rates. Fiscal deficit is down to 4.1%. Forex reserves have climbed to an all-time high of over 350 billion USD. The industrial growth which was down to 1.1% in 2012-13 and 0.1% in 2013-14 has now climbed up to 2.1%.

**2015 Land Amendment Bill**. Its purpose and benefits are detailed in a separate chapter in this book.

**Black Money**. The first act of the Modi government after assuming power was to setup an SIT for black money, something which the UPA government was stalling for many years despite the instructions of the Supreme Court. The government has also brought in strict laws on black money.

**Mudra Bank**. To promote finance to small business units, *Micro Units Development and Refinance Agency Ltd* (MUDRA) Bank was launched on 8 April 2015 with a corpus of ₹ 20,000 crores and a credit guarantee corpus of ₹ 3,000 crores for refinancing micro-finance institutions (MFI) in the business of lending to small entities.

**Jan-Dhan Yojana.** *Pradhan Mantri Jan-Dhan Yojana* (PMJDY) is a National Mission for Financial Inclusion of the deprived section for access to banking, financial services, credit, insurance, pension, etc. in an affordable manner. PMJDY bank accounts can be opened with zero balance. Accident insurance cover of rupees one lakh is provided with the account. The account would be linked to Aadhaar-number to enable *Direct Benefit Transfer*, credit of pension, and other facilities. A record 125 million PMJDY accounts have been opened.

**Other Schemes for the Poor.** *Pradhan Mantri Jeevan Jyoti Beema Yojana* for life insurance cover of ₹ 2 lakhs at an annual premium of only ₹ 330; *Pradhan Mantri Suraksha Beema Yojana* for accident insurance cover of ₹ 2 lakhs at an annual premium of only ₹ 12; and *Atal Pension Yojana* for pension of up to ₹ 5000 for senior citizens have been launched by the Modi government.

**Law.** Modi's cabinet has approved amendments to the Juvenile Justice Act that will treat minors above 16 years as adults for heinous crimes like rape, acid attack and murder.

**Ensuring Foreign and Indian NGOs comply with Law.** There is reported rampant misuse and diversion of money received by the Indian and Foreign NGOs in India. The illegal activities include helping or defaming political parties, derailing critical development projects, causing communal tensions, and funding and encouraging illegal proselytization.

The Modi government has since tightened control over them and is examining their compliance to the laws of the land.

*The above are only a partial listing of achievements of the Modi government; yet the achievements are phenomenal. Yet another notable factor is this*:

**Scandal-free, Scam-free Year.** Unlike the previous Congress-led UPA government notorious for scams and scandals, and for at least one mega-scam a quarter, the Modi-government has thankfully been singularly free from scams and scandals so far. Central government corruption too seems to have come down, given Modi's strict administration and his well-articulated principle, "*Na khaunga, na khane dunga* (Will neither take grease money, nor allow others to take it)!" That is in sharp contrast to "*loot and let loot*" of the Congress.

*On the other hand, what is it that the Modi government has so far failed to achieve or has not come good on?*

The government is lagging on the economic and financial reforms, which are affecting FDI and growth. There is a huge amount of work to be done and reforms to be undertaken in the HRD area, but the pace is lethargic. There have been little movements on banking, administrative, police and judicial reforms. It is a long list—mainly because the expectations from the Modi government, unlike from any previous government since independence, were sky high.

Modi's ministries are starving of talent and experts. He has to remedy the situation to deliver. Modi can't depend upon the rusted babudom to deliver. There are scores of critical things in various fields, neglected for decades, crying for attention, and unless Modi inducts talents and experts from within and from outside and hands each a mission to accomplish those things by a targeted date, we would continue to remain laggards and would just plod along. That requires spotting, selection and appointment of talent; delegation of responsibilities to them; provision of resources; and their empowerment. *The usual, normal ministries with their stale, deficit-in-talent, short-of-ideas, cautious, conservative, look-back-and-move-forward, precedent-digging bureaucratic babudom can't accomplish those important tasks.* There is enough talent in India. Give them a chance and a challenge. Encourage and empower them. Shun the bureaucracy. Let the babudom handle run-of-the-mill, routine, precedent-driven administration. Deploy experts and talent from within, other than from the babudom, and from outside.

If Modi's BJP has to be a much better national alternative, it has to rise much above and far beyond the current Left, Centre, Right, the Far Right, and the populist sops and doles and nonsense. It has to be a modern, non-dogmatic, daring, pragmatic, problem-solving, forward-looking innovative force with fresh ideas. It must steer India onwards on competitive capitalism and free enterprise economy.

Commented Shekhar Gupta in his article 'National Interest: Left, Right or Standstill' of 18 January 2014 in *The Indian Express*: "...Narendra Modi can look at this as a challenge or an opportunity. Challenge, because his own party, in its utter bankruptcy of imagination, has also chosen socialism as its economic philosophy. Years ago, confused and short of ideas, and inspired by the Neanderthals of Nagpur, it proposed the concept of Gandhian Socialism (1980),.... Socialism is the most persistent virus in Indian politics and the party has never even tried to get rid of it. Atal Behari Vajpayee's reforms, particularly disinvestment, were blocked more by his own party's pinkos than the Congress's or the Left's.... The fuel growth needs, is entrepreneurship. Which, in turn, needs lesser, cleaner government, fair and clear regulation and a market-friendly environment. The Congress, and now the AAP, have fully vacated this space for him. He doesn't have to make the BJP the new Swatantra Party. But he can certainly benefit from moulding his party's economics more to the ideas of Vajpayee...."

Going forward, the BJP would have to curb an influential section of their conservative, narrow-minded ideologues, with their inward looking, jingoistic cultural, religious and economic nonsense. Also, the jokers from the fringe groups, owing allegiance to them and deriving clout through that association, who rampage as moral police telling women what to wear and what not to do. If Modi wants support from young women, he must promise he would firmly deal with such obnoxious characters.

Let us hope and pray that the Modi government would come good on many parameters over the next two years. However, it cannot be doubted that the Modi government is incomparably better than the UPA-I and UPA-II. If one could be patient with the hopeless UPA-I and UPA-II for a long period of a decade, can we not be patient with the Modi-government till the end of its legitimate term of five years till 2019?

Modi is about the best thing that has happened to India in a long time. Let us hope he would take India to promised heights by the end of his five-year tenure in 2019. If he does that, he would deserve a second term, and the people of India would gladly grant him that.

## Aspects of Rahul that Puzzle You

There are far too many aspects of Rahul that would puzzle anyone who has some expectations from him.

Why after over a decade in active politics, Rahul has so little to show for his political achievements, despite the massive unfair advantage he has been so unfairly equipped with? Why is he unable to articulate cogent, consistent reasoning for any of his stands? Why does he restrict himself to only a set of (apparently pre-coached) statements? With nothing to back them up! Why is he so casual with facts? Why does he often rely on sheer lies to make his point? Is it deliberate? Or, is he unaware of the actual facts? Over a decade in politics, and not a single wise or interesting or worthwhile remark or quote or statement from him! Is he really so dumb? Why Amethi and Raebareli continue to be so backward despite decades of association of the Nehru-Gandhi Dynasty with them? Can a Dynasty which has failed even in Amethi-Raebareli deliver anything in a far larger and complex scenario of the nation? Does a Dynasty that was repeatedly granted a chance during the last six decades and that repeatedly failed the people after each chance deserve yet another? Do Rahul-Sonia-Congis deserve another chance even though the two chances of 2004 and 2009 to Sonia-Rahul have proved a betrayal; and the 2004-14 decade of Sonia-Rahul-MMS rule has been the worst in India's post-independence history?

Such questions are too many. Only a sold-out section of the MSM (Main Stream Media), the commentariat and the intellectuals may directly or indirectly or shamelessly promote him. However, a reasonable person is not likely to have any expectations from Rahul of delivering anything worthwhile. Hence, none of his negative aspects—and there are many—would puzzle him. A reasonable, patriotic person having good of the country at his heart and an empathy for the poor would only hope that he and his dynasty disappear from India's political scene.

### Aspects of Kejriwal that Puzzle You

It is unfortunate that not too seldom Kejriwal disappoints even his well-wishers.

Having regained power at Delhi with an unprecedented, historic majority, and with everything going in his favour, why did he and the AAP had to make news headlines for all the wrong reasons, and on their own initiative? Is it necessary they remain in the news—if not for the right and positive reasons, then at least for the wrong ones? That Delhi is not a full state like other states is well known, then why unnecessarily pick-up a fight with the LG? If you want the status to be changed, then follow the constitutional route, rather than being abusive towards the LG and the BJP? And, what low-level language you use! Does it behove an educated person, an IITian, a chief minister? Even if you wish to be severely critical, choose your words carefully. Clean politics is not merely corruption-free politics, it needs to have many other positive attributes, including decorum in dealing with others, be it officials or employees or public or colleagues or opposition. And, how can you publicly deride an official, and not follow due process?

If you do have ambition to continue with your high office, and man even higher positions, you need to not only project an image of a serious, competent, sober, dependable, trustworthy leader; you need to be genuinely that. You can't be a tamasha leader—making tamasha of yourself and your party, and those of others. Kejriwal's penchant for theatrics rather than for responsible governance is disconcerting. Kejriwal's conduct make people doubt his temperamental adequacy for high office. Alarmed by his erratic behaviour, one actually feels relieved Delhi is not a full state and Kejriwal does not have full powers! He has been unnecessarily harming his own cause.

You can't talk of high moral values, point fingers at others, demand resignations of others on flimsy grounds, and yet continue with your own law minister having serious allegations against him. That's height of hypocrisy. Also, where is the political wisdom in continuing with such persons?

It is also reported that AAPians in Punjab are trying to cosy up to Khalistanis in view of the forthcoming state elections. Would a "principled" political party do anything—even aligning with anti-nationals—just to get votes?

People have been having high expectations from the AAP and Kejriwal, and they should not betray them. If they stick to principles, high moral values, shun *tamashabaji*, and deliver in Delhi, sky is the limit for them.

## Aspects of Narendra Modi that Puzzle You

It is sad and cruel on the part of Narendra Modi to ignore and disappoint many of those who had been his ardent, enthusiastic and selfless supporters, and who significantly contributed to his becoming the prime minister. They had not bargained for a leader who would forget to even acknowledge their contribution or to thank them. Not only that, who would not come good on many expectations. Granted Modi's government has proved to be far, far superior to the UPA, yet the expectations from it were not merely to be better than the UPA. UPA had set too low a standard—indeed, a negative standard in many cases! The questions that puzzle Modi's supporters are the following:

Why no effective steps have been taken to bring back black money stashed abroad? Yes, they have passed a so-called black money bill in the parliament. But, that only provides for punishment in case black money is discovered. That begs the question: how to discover and recover the black money in the first place? Little has been done on that score. People say it is unlikely anything effective would be done in that direction as long as Arun Jaitley is the Finance Minister. How true is that one doesn't know.

It is also said two of the most important portfolios have been given by Modi neither on merit nor on seniority—that of the Finance and the HRD. Finance, of course, is critical for Modi government to deliver on a large number of promises it has made and for its re-election in 2019. A lawyer in that position is a square peg in a round hole, as is an actor as in-charge of HRD. Incompetent to put life into the economy, and incapable of ground-breaking ideas, Arun Jaitley is sticking to pedestrian bureaucratic ways. People have been patiently and tolerantly giving time to the incumbent government and have been hoping something good would come out on the economic front in at least the second year. But, waiting alone doesn't lead to anything good. There have to be good actions. And, given Jaitley, it appears increasingly foolish to expect something grand might be in the offing. Modi needs to do course correction, and replace the incumbent FM. The same applies for the HRD. The concerned ministers may be a very competent persons for an appropriate portfolio, but certainly not for the HRD or Finance.

Further, it is not a question of just a few competent ministers. There are so many things crying to be done that each ministry requires a large set of experts who could independently take charge of their segments and make a success of it—it is beyond one minister to competently handle diverse requirements of her/his ministry. And, by and large, babus are unfit to handle those tasks—they can only look behind for alibi and handle routine stuff. Modi needs to identify and induct a large number of experts from outside the babudom. Sadly, that's not happening. Predominant reliance is on babus who have failed this country since independence.

The recently released book of Pradip Baijal titled *The Complete Story of Indian Reforms: 2G, Power, and Private Enterprise—A Practitioner's Diary* reconfirms the considerable competence and genius of Arun Shourie. As it is, Modi's cabinet is short of talent. Given such a pathetic situation, it is surprising that an available talent, so close to the BJP ideology, and with proven credentials, has been ignored. There are many other available talents who have been given no opportunity to contribute their might to the nation building. A real leader and statesman is one who can build a large, strong, competent team, because he alone can't do much.

Modi, well-known for his articulation and communication, has miserably failed to manage the media, and his government has been unable to effectively put its points across. What is Arun Jaitley doing as an I&B Minister? He seems to have failed here too! He seems to be maintaining only his personal rapport with the media, and not that of the government. Why not have a competent person as a minister for I&B too? Why does Modi fight shy of an open, televised press conference? In fact, he ought to have a press conference on a monthly basis. He is quite capable of handling the press. Press conferences and interviews would help clarify many matters, and would provide the right exposure. While one-way communications like speeches and "Man ki Baat" are good, two-way communications like press conferences and interviews are also a must. As the elected chief of a government of a democratic country, he ought not to avoid press conferences or interviews.

There is too much talk, and not enough action. It affects the credibility of the government.

One of Modi's pre-election, and even post-election, mantras has been "Minimum Government, Maximum Governance". That, of course, can't mean the simplistic lesser or bigger ministry. You actually need many more experts to handle scores of long pending urgent tasks. What are required for "Minimum Government, Maximum Governance" are Administrative Reforms, Police Reforms and Judicial Reforms. Where are we on that?

Another of Modi's mantras has been "It's not the business of the government to be in business". What have been the Modi government's efforts to get out of business? Atal Behari Vajpayee, thanks to his highly competent and honest disinvestment minister, Arun Shourie, had done wonders on the front. UPA had slept and scammed through its decade of misgovernance doing nothing further about it. But, what has the Modi government and his lawyer FM done in the matter? Precious little!

During his pre-election rallies, Modi had slammed the UPA for its plethora of mega scams and corruption. But, how many of the culprits have been brought to book during the last one year? The cases filed during the UPA tenure are dragging on, there being little progress. As for NDA, has it filed any fresh cases? Hardly any! Not only is the Centre controlled by the BJP lax in this regard, even the states run by the BJP have done little to bring the culprits to book. What's the point of shouting against the corrupt, while doing nothing about it, when you have the power to do so? That's being irresponsible. It's a betrayal of the trust reposed by the people in you. When people voted for you, they not only desired you run a corruption-free government (which Modi has done to a considerable extent at the upper levels at the Centre), but you also bring to book the persons who have looted India, and also recover that loot. Who is protecting the culprits?

Modi and the BJP had talked of transparency during their Lok Sabha election campaigns. What of their promise to declassify documents on Netaji Bose disappearance mystery? What about the full disclosure of the Henderson-Brooks report on the 1962 India-China war debacle?

There are many questions that genuinely puzzle a Modi well-wisher. Hopefully, he would provide adequate answers to them in the times to come.

# 19

# PROFILES (IN ALPHABETIC ORDER)

## Anna Hazare

*The country did not get actual freedom even after 64 years of independence and the only change was that the whites have been replaced by the blacks.*

—Anna Hazare

*Life-long selfless service to the society.*

Kisan Bapat Baburao 'Anna' Hazare was born on 15 June 1937 in Bhingar, near Ahmednagar in Maharashtra.

### *Family*

Among seven siblings of two sisters and five brothers, he was the eldest son of Baburao Hazare and Laxmi Bai. His father struggled to support the family, being a low-paid unskilled labourer in an ayurvedic pharmacy. The family owned a small plot of agricultural land in their ancestral village of Ralegan Siddhi, to which they later moved. Hazare is unmarried.

### *Early Life*

There being no primary school in the village, a relative took Anna to Mumbai for education. As the relative was himself not well-off financially, Anna's schooling had to be terminated in the seventh grade.

Anna then started selling flowers at Dadar railway station in Mumbai. Gradually, he became owner of two flower shops.

### *Military Service*

Hazare joined the Indian Army in April 1960, where he initially worked as an army truck driver.

He was fortunate to be the sole survivor of an enemy attack while driving a truck in the border-area in the Khem Karan sector during the Indo-Pak War of 1965. The truck attack "*sent me thinking. I felt that God wanted me to stay alive for some reason. I was reborn in the battlefield of Khem Karan. And I decided to dedicate my new life to serving people.*" Later, he came across Swami Vivekananda's booklet "*Call to the youth for nation building*" at a book-stall at New Delhi railway station. That inspired him to action. He then also read Gandhi, Vinoba Bhave and other works of Swami Vivekananda.

During his various postings while in the army, Hazare survived a road crash and an underground Naga attack.

He was honourably discharged from the army in 1975 after completing 12 years of service.

#### *Simple Living*

After retirement from military service in 1975, Hazare has been living in a small room attached to the Sant Yadavbaba temple in Ralegan Siddhi. His meagre landholding of 0.07 hectares is being used by his brothers. He has re-donated to his village pieces of land donated to him.

### *Social/Public-Causes Activities*

Anna Hazare has spearheaded movements for transparency and honesty in governance and for rural development. He has often resorted to hunger strikes, *a la*` Mahatma Gandhi, to further his causes.

#### *Ralegan Siddhi*

Through his unstinted efforts, Hazare changed the face of his village Ralegan Siddhi in Ahmednagar district of Maharashtra. Ralegan Siddhi was previously plagued by acute poverty, deprivation, neglect and hopelessness, besides being mired in illegal manufacture and sale of alcohol.

He made the village and villagers alcohol-free. Through his efforts, Hazare managed to force the government of Maharashtra amend the Bombay Prohibition Act, 1949 whereby prohibition would come into force in a village if 25% of the women in the village demanded it.

Through the co-operation of the villagers, he managed to ban the sale of tobacco, cigarettes, and beedies in the village.

Hazare introduced many innovative schemes in the village. Looking to the farmers' distress during drought or crop failures, he launched a *Grain Bank* at the temple with grain donations from the rich to provide food security to the needy, who could borrow grain during difficult times, but had to return the quantum of grain borrowed plus some additional as interest during better times. This ensured that nobody in the village ever went hungry or resorted to distress sale of assets.

Under Hazare's initiative, Ralegan Siddhi undertook watershed embankment and associated works to help recharge ground water level and improve irrigation. That solved the problem of water scarcity in the village and immensely helped agricultural production. Irrigated land of merely 70 acres, when Hazare came to Ralegan Siddhi in 1975 after his military stint, expanded to a huge 2500 acres with his efforts.

At the instance of Hazare, villagers shunned cultivation of water-intensive crops like sugarcane, changed cropping pattern and took to high-yield varieties of crops with low water requirements such as pulses and oilseeds.

Based on his success in Ralegan Siddhi, Hazare has helped farmers in many more villages in the drought-prone regions in the state of Maharashtra.

Anna Hazare started a high school in Ralegan Siddhi in 1979.

Hazare's moral leadership inspired villagers to shun caste discrimination and untouchability, and integrate Dalits into the social and economic life of the village. Community marriage programmes include marriages of Dalits. The villagers have also helped build houses for the Dalits.

He was awarded the third-highest civilian award *Padma Bhushan* in 1992 by the Government of India for turning Ralegan Siddhi into a model village worthy of emulation by others.

### *Anti-Corruption Movements*

Hazare launched BVJA (*Bhrashtachar Virodhi Jan Andolan: People's Movement against Corruption*) in 1991. His protest against the collusion of 40 forest officials with timber merchants led to their transfer and suspension. Hazare led many protest-movements against corruption in Maharashtra and managed to bring many culprits to book.

### *RTI Movement*

Hazare's movement in the early 2000s forced the Maharashtra state government to enact a revised *Maharashtra Right to Information Act*. That formed the basis for the Central *Right to Information Act, 2005 (RTI)*. The Union Cabinet tried to dilute the RTI on 20 July 2006 by excluding the file notings by government officials from its purview. Hazare protested against it and began his fast-unto-death on 9 August 2006 in Alandi. Finally, the government caved in.

### *Regulation of Transfers and Prevention of Delay in Discharge of Official Duties Act*

Thanks to Anna's relentless campaign, Maharashtra government was compelled to enact the *Prevention of Delay in Discharge of Official Duties Act, 2006* that provided for disciplinary action against officials who move files slowly; enabled monitoring of officials who overstay a post; and mandated transfers of government officers and employees no sooner and no later than three years, except in emergency or exceptional circumstances.

### *Jan Lokpal Movement*

Hazare led the anti-corruption *Jan Lokpal Movement* during 2011-12. Details are in the first chapter in this book.

*Film*

*Mala Anna Vhaychay* (I want to become Anna), a Marathi film, is based on Hazare's work.

*Awards*

Anna Hazare has received numerous Indian and international awards. He received Indira Priyadarshini Vrikshamitra Award of Government of India in 1986; Krushi Bhushana Award of Government of Maharashtra in 1989; Padma Shri in 1990; Padma Bhushan in 1992; CARE International Award in 1998; Leading Social Contributor Award of Government of India in 1999; Integrity Award of Transparency International in 2003; Jit Gill Memorial Award of the World Bank in 2008; NDTV Indian of the Year Award with Arvind Kejriwal in 2011; and Allard Prize for International Integrity of University of British Columbia in 2013.

## Arvind Kejriwal

*An IIT-graduate, rising from a revenue officer to a civil-activist to founder of a political party to a chief minister within 14 years!*

Arvind Kejriwal, aged 47, was born on 16 August 1968 on the day of Janmashtami in Siwani in district Bhiwani of Haryana.

### *Family*

His father, Gobind Ram Kejriwal, graduated in electrical engineering from the Birla Institute of Technology. Arvind was the eldest of the three children. He has a younger brother and a younger sister. In 1995, he married his Indian Revenue Services (IRS) batch-mate Sunita. The couple have two children: daughter Harshita and son Pulkit.

### *Education*

Kejriwal did schooling from Campus School in Hisar and from Christian missionary school at Sonipat. He graduated in mechanical engineering from the Indian Institute of Technology, Kharagpur in 1989.

### *Employment*

His first employer was Tata Steel which he joined in Jamshedpur in 1989. He quit the job in 1992 and spent time at the Ramakrishna Mission in Kolkata, and in assorted activities, and in preparing for the Civil Services Examination.

After qualifying in the Civil Services Examination, he joined the Indian Revenue Services (IRS) as an Assistant Commissioner of Income Tax in 1995. After leave of about five years for various purposes between 2000 and 2005, Kejriwal resigned in 2006 from his position as a Joint Commissioner of Income Tax in New Delhi. He was known to be honest and upright, something rare in revenue services.

Reportedly, on his first day in the IRS, Kejriwal's boss had advised him: "In the first few years of your service you should make sufficient money for yourself so that you can appear to be honest for the rest of your life.... But now I am honest because I have made sufficient money for myself, and I have made several investments." Kejriwal was astounded.

### *Social/Public Causes Activities*

During his leave between 2000 and 2005, Kejriwal involved himself with various social activities and NGOs.

#### *Parivartan*

While still in service, Kejriwal, along with Manish Sisodia and others, founded *Parivartan*, a movement for 'change'; and took a sabbatical in January 2000 to carry forward its work of addressing citizens' grievances on income-tax, electricity, public works, PDS (Public Distribution System), and so on, and corruption in those areas.

Parivartan used the Right To Information (RTI) Act enacted in Delhi in 2001 to access government records and help people get their work done without paying a bribe, and expose scams and misappropriation of funds in PDS and other government schemes.

Kejriwal received the *Ramon Magsaysay Award* for *Emergent Leadership* in 2006 in recognition of his RTI-based campaign against corruption in *Parivartan*.

### *Kabir*

Kejriwal and Sisodia launched a registered NGO *Kabir* in 2005 that also worked on RTI and participatory governance.

### *Public Cause Research Foundation*

Kejriwal, Sisodia and Abhinandan Sekhri established the *Public Cause Research Foundation* in December 2006 in which they also inducted Prashant Bhushan and Kiran Bedi as trustees. Kejriwal donated his *Ramon Magsaysay Award* prize money as a seed fund for the *Foundation*. The body used the RTI Act in corruption cases in many government departments.

### *Protest against CWG Corruption and Demand for Lokpal*

Kejriwal and group protested against corruption in the *Commonwealth Games* (CWG). They demanded establishment of *Lokpal* (public ombudsman) at the Centre and *Lokayuktas* in the states in view of the fact that the existing agencies were incapable of acting against the guilty government ministers and officials who controlled them.

### *IAC*

The *India Against Corruption* (IAC) group was formed in 2011 by a group comprising Anna Hazare, Kiran Bedi, Kejriwal and others. It demanded enactment of the *Jan Lokpal Bill.*

### *Jan Lokpal Movement*

Kejriwal associated himself with the prominent social activist Anna Hazare in early 2010s for the Jan Lokpal Bill. This made him popular.

Anna Hazare disassociated with him after he formed a political party.

## ***AAP***

Rather than favourably considering the reasonable demand for *Jan Lokpal Bill* looking to the spate of mind-boggling scams, the political parties, particularly the ruling Congress, arrogantly challenged the Jan Lokpal activists to first get elected and then pass the laws they desired, rather than dictating terms to them, that is, the elected representatives of the people.

Left with little alternative, Kejriwal and other activists decided to take up the challenge, enter politics and contest elections. In November 2012, they formally launched a political party—the *Aam Aadmi Party* (AAP). *Aam Aadmi* means "common man".

AAP fought Delhi Legislative Assembly election in 2013, and triumphed in the first attempt itself! AAP won 28 of the 70 seats, finishing in second place after the BJP. Kejriwal defeated the incumbent Congress Chief Minister Sheila Dikshit in her constituency of New Delhi by a margin of over 25,000 votes.

Kejriwal assumed the office of the Chief Minister of Delhi on 28 December 2013. The swearing-in ceremony was held at the Ramlila Maidan. He, however, resigned on 14 February 2014 after a brief stint of 49 days on the pretext of the inability to pass AAP's proposed anti-corruption legislation because of being in minority. In the re-elections held in January 2015, AAP got an overwhelming majority, winning 67 out of the 70 assembly seats, and Kejriwal became the Chief Minister for a second term on 14 February 2015. He is also the national convener of the AAP.

Kejriwal published a book, *Swaraj*, in 2012.

### *Awards/Recognitions*

Kejriwal got Ashoka Fellow, Civic Engagement in 2004; Satyendra Dubey Memorial Award, IIT Kanpur for campaign for transparency in Governance in 2005; Ramon Magsaysay Award for Emergent Leadership in 2006; CNN-IBN Indian of the Year Award in Public Service in 2006; Distinguished Alumnus Award from IIT Kharagpur in 2009; Economic Times Award for Policy Change Agent of the Year 2010 along with Aruna Roy; NDTV Indian of the Year Award 2011 along with Anna Hazare; CNN-IBN Award for the Indian of the Year 2013 in Politics. Kejriwal was featured in Time's '*Time 100 List*' of 2014 of the most influential people in the world.

### *Help from Friends*

His IIT friends helped him raise money to pay his way out of the government service. Reportedly, his college friends pitched in with funds for his monthly expenditure to enable him to focus on his political work.

## Ashutosh

*Entered the AAP after its success.*

Ashutosh (Gupta) was born on 1 January 1965 in Mirzapur, UP. His father was an income tax officer.

### *Education*

He graduated in science from Allahabad University. He earned an M.Phil. in Soviet Studies and an MA in Philosophy & International Studies from Jawaharlal Nehru University (JNU), New Delhi.

### *Professional Career*

He worked with Hindustan, the leading Hindi daily. Later, he joined the Hindi news TV channel *Aaj Tak*, where he worked as a correspondent and an anchor and rose to become its Executive Producer. He subsequently shifted to IBN7 of TV18 group as Managing Editor.

### *Political Career*

Ashutosh joined AAP in January 2014, after its dramatic success in 2013 Delhi Assembly Elections. He contested the 2014 Lok Sabha elections on the AAP ticket from Chandni Chowk, Delhi; but lost to Dr Harsh Vardhan of the BJP.

His response to the media after Gajendra Singh's unfortunate death was insensitive and unbecoming; and his subsequent crying on TV in the same context was pretentious.

*The only vice that cannot be forgiven is hypocrisy. The repentance of a hypocrite is itself hypocrisy.*

—William Hazlitt

His joining the AAP after its success indicates opportunism; and his cosying up to the power that be in the AAP is akin to what Congressmen do *vis-à-vis* the Dynasty. His opinions and comments smack of immaturity, and belie his having been a senior journalist.

### *Books*

On Anna Hazare's agitation, Ashutosh wrote the book *Anna: 13 Days That Awakened India*. His Hindi book *Mukhote Ka Rajdharm* was released in February 2015. His latest book released in April 2015 is *The Crown Prince, The Gladiator & The Hope*.

## Gopal Rai

*Credited with building the AAP's volunteer base.*

Gopal Rai was born on 10 May 1975 in Mau, UP.

He is a post-graduate in sociology from Lucknow University.

He began his political career with the All India Students Association, the student wing of the Communist Party of India (Marxist-Leninist), in Lucknow University in 1992.

He is a founder-member of AAP; and is a member of its Political Affairs Committee (PAC) and the National Executive (NE).

He was elected an MLA from Babarpur constituency in the 2015 Delhi Legislative election; and is currently the Transport and Rural Development Minister of Delhi.

His uncalled-for intervention in Gen. V.K. Singh's speech during Anna Hazare's indefinite hunger strike for passage of Jan Lokpal Bill in Ralegan Siddhi in December 2013 forced Anna to ask him to leave Ralegan.

## Kumar Vishwas

*A poet and a non-stop speaker.*

Dr Kumar Vishwas was born on 10 February 1970 in Pilkhuwa, Ghaziabad.

### *Family*

He is the youngest among four brothers and a sister. His father Dr Chandra Pal Sharma was a lecturer in a college. His wife, Dr Manju Sharma, is a lecturer of Hindi literature.

### *Education*

He has done MA and Ph.D in Hindi Literature.

### *Poet/Profession*

Kumar Vishwas has been teaching Hindi Literature in a college.

He is a Hindi poet who has written several anthologies of poems. He performs regularly at *Kavi sammelans* in India and abroad.

### *Civil Activist/Political Career*

Vishwas actively participated in Anna Hazare's *Jan Lokpal Movement*, and was a key member of the team.

He is the founder-member of the Aam Aadmi Party (AAP), and is a member of its National Executive (NE). He had contested the 2014 Lok Sabha election from Amethi, and had campaigned vigorously, but had lost, coming at the fourth place and losing his deposit.

Several attempts have been made to defame him, but all the allegations have proved to be false.

Unfortunately, it is not uncommon among the stand-up comedians, poets and performers in the subcontinent to be derogatory towards women at times, and to crack unseemly jokes or make comments at their expense. Kumar is also guilty of having done so on some occasions.

## Manish Sisodia

*From a journalist, a writer, a radio anchor, a news producer for a television channel to a social and political activist to joint-founder of a political party to a Deputy Chief Minister at a young age of 43!*

Manish Sisodia, aged 43, was born on born 5 January 1972 in village Faugata in Hapur district in UP. His father was a teacher.

### *Education*

Diploma in journalism from Bhartiya Vidya Bhawan.

### *Profession*

Manish is a journalist by profession. He was a news producer and a news reader at *Zee News* between 1997 and 2005. He was also associated with the All India Radio.

### *Social/Public Causes Activities*

Sisodia founded NGO *Kabir* in 2005 along with Kejriwal. They later founded *Public Cause Research Foundation* in 2006 jointly with Abhinandan Sekhri.

He was associated as a key-member with Anna's *Jan Lokpal Movement* of 2010-2012 all through. He was the joint-drafter of the *Jan Lokpal Bill*. He had sat on a fast of 10 days along with others demanding setting up of an SIT to probe cases against corrupt ministers. He was jailed with Anna Hazare and others during the anti-graft agitation.

### *AAP*

Sisodia is founder-member of AAP.

In the Delhi state assembly elections of 2013 Sisodia defeated Nakul Bhardwaj of BJP from the Patparganj constituency of East Delhi.

During the first term of the AAP in power in Delhi during December-February 2014, Sisodia was a cabinet minister holding the charge of Education, PWD, Urban Development, Local Bodies, and Land & Building.

In the 2015 Delhi Legislative Assembly election he was re-elected from Patparganj defeating Vinod Kumar Binny of the BJP by over 28,000 votes.

In the current term since February 2015, Sisodia is Deputy Chief Minister of Delhi government holding the charge of Finance & Planning, Revenue, Services, Power, Education, Higher Education, Information Technology, Technical Education, and Administrative Reforms.

Sisodia is a member of the Political Affairs Committee (PAC) and the National Executive (NE) of the AAP. He has stood by Arvind Kejriwal like a rock.

## Pankaj Gupta

*An innovative technology, finance and organisational brain, he has done wonders for the AAP, while being a sincere, silent, devoted worker and a sharp strategist.*

Pankaj Gupta is a 48-year-old software professional who is now full time into the AAP.

### *Education*

Pankaj graduated from Motilal Nehru Regional Engineering College in Allahabad.

### *Employment*

Pankaj worked for over 25 years in senior positions in various software companies before he switched to social work. He had worked at TCS in the US. His last job was with a US-based software outsourcing company KMG Infotech at Gurgaon where he was heading a team of 250.

### *Social Work/Activist*

He devoted himself to social work after resigning from service. He also taught children from economically backward sections of society.

Much before the TAA and the AAP, he had worked with Arvind Kejriwal at Parivartan, a non-profit organisation. He was associated with Anna's *Jan Lokpal Movement* on a full time basis.

In 2011, he had formed an organisation, Saksham, to help candidates fight the municipal elections in Gurgaon.

### *AAP*

He is AAP's founder-member, and is currently its general secretary and a member of the National Executive. His IT prowess has greatly helped AAP. He also manages funds and establishment of branches of the party.

## Prashant Bhushan

*The purpose of life is a life of purpose.*

—Robert Byrne

*An upright, committed, gutsy and real-life Dabangg lawyer, famous for his PILs, social and political activism, and selfless service to the society—Prashant's stale socialism is his undoing.*

Prashant Bhushan was born on 20 June 1956 in Delhi.

### *Family*

Prashant Bhushan is the oldest of the four children of Shanti Bhushan (please see separate sub-section on him) and Kumud Bhushan. Prashant was inspired by his father for public activism. Prashant is married to Deepa, a former lawyer. They have three sons. They live with Shanti Bhushan in Noida.

### *Education*

Prashant earned his law degree from Allahabad University.

He initially went to study mechanical engineering at IIT-Madras in 1973 but quit after one semester: was very homesick, as per a report!

### *Books*

Prashant, while still a student, wrote a book on the case (fought by his father Shanti Bhushan) that set aside Indira Gandhi's election in 1974: *The Case that Shook India.*

In 1990, Prashant wrote *Bofors, the Selling of a Nation.*

### *Associated with*

He is associated with CPIL (Centre for Public Interest Litigation), PUCL (People's Union for Civil Liberties), TI (Transparency International—India), and with the *Campaign for Judicial Accountability and Judicial Reforms.*

### *PILs*

Prashant has used PIL (Public Interest Litigation) for a number of public causes: against corruption, for environmental protection and for human rights.

### *Upright, Committed, Gutsy and Dabangg Lawyer*

Prashant devotes his major time to cases for public causes, and he does not charge any fee for them. Even for other cases, he charges a fraction of what other lawyers charge, and takes up only those cases where he is convinced the client is indeed right. Prashant is known to have turned down fees worth millions for defending the guilty. "*If he has taken up your case, then it means he is convinced of your innocence and will fight tooth and nail to prove it*", says a lawyer.

Prashant has stated that he looks forward to a time where the legal system would be so honest and transparent that people would be able to negotiate their own cases, making lawyers redundant.

You have filmy heroes taking up cudgels against the rich and powerful. Prashant Bhushan has been a real life hero in practice fearlessly taking up scores of cases against the mighty. "*The name Bhushan is synonymous with fear for corrupt judges, politicians, bureaucrats and now corporate honchos*", said a top Supreme Court lawyer.

### *CJA/Judicial Accountability*

In 1990, Prashant founded the *Committee on Judicial Accountability* (CJA) along with his father to fight corruption in the judiciary. The Bhushans expanded CJA in 2007 to include citizens and form the *Campaign for Judicial Accountability and Reform* (CJAR).

Prashant took up active interest in judicial accountability following the Justice V. Ramaswami case. There were many charges of corruption against Justice Ramaswami of the Supreme Court, and his case came up for impeachment before the Lok Sabha in 1993. States Prashant: "*This was a case of a brazen and thoroughly corrupt judge and it was impossible to catch him. Impeachment doesn't work. You can't get even 50 to 100 MPs to sign up for an impeachment. Nobody wants to annoy the judges. It is a case of loot and let loot.*"

Prashant alleged in an interview in 2009 that about half of the 16 former Chief Justices of the Supreme Court were corrupt. He had campaigned against the Chief Justice of the Sikkim High Court P.D. Dinakaran, who was later forced to resign.

Prashant has proposed amendment to the *Contempt of Court Act* clause on the ground that some of its clauses effectively prevent exposing of corruption in the judiciary.

### *Fight Against Corruption*

In 2005, the Supreme Court directed the UP government to remove Neera Yadav as Chief Secretary of UP for corruption. That was consequent to the PIL filed by Prashant on behalf of CPIL.

In 2011, the Supreme Court struck down the appointment of P.J. Thomas as Central Vigilance Commissioner, after he had been charged in the palmolein scam, following a PIL filed by Prashant.

Prashant Bhushan acting for the CPIL took the lead in filing a suit against the Central Government for irregularities in what is now known as the *2G Spectrum Scam*. In 2012, the Supreme Court held the allocation of the spectrum as illegal.

Prashant also fought through his PIL against the *massive scam in coal block allocations* by the Central Government leading ultimately to their cancellation by the Supreme Court in 2014.

Prashant filed a PIL against illegal iron ore extraction in Goa which led to the Supreme Court halting all the mining operations in the state in 2012.

### *Fight Against Wrong-doings/Malpractices*

He took up the issues/cases of *1984-Delhi-Anti-Sikh-Attack* victims and the victims of the *Bhopal Gas Tragedy*.

In 2006, Prashant represented the CPIL in a petition alleging that Pepsico and Coca-Cola were luring people through misleading advertising, and were failing to warn the public of harmful ingredients in their beverages.

### *IAC and Jan Lokpal Movement*

Prashant was a prominent member of IAC (India Against Corruption). He was part of the main group that carried out Anna Hazare's *Jan Lokpal Movement*.

### *AAP*

He was one of the main persons who founded the AAP (Aam Aadmi Party).

Prashant was voted out of Political Affairs Committee of the AAP on 4 March 2015. He was also removed from the National Executive on 28 March 2015.

**The unfortunate negative facets of an honest, principled person of high integrity.**

### *Controversial Views on J&K*

Prashant has stated that while the government should try to persuade the people of the Kashmir valley to align with India, it should permit them to separate from India if they so wish. He had also advocated revocation of the *Armed Forces Special Powers Act* in J&K. Anna Hazare had disassociated his team from Prashant's remarks, saying that those were his personal views.

***Advocacy of Outdated Socialist/Communist Ideas that have failed in theory and in practice globally, and have benefited not a single country in the world.***

Consequent to the case fought by Prashant and Rajinder Sachar on behalf of CPIL, the Supreme Court gave a decision in 2003 restraining the Union government from privatising

Hindustan Petroleum and Bharat Petroleum without the approval of Parliament. They argued that the only way out for the government if it wished to disinvest in those companies was to repeal or amend the Acts by which they were nationalised in the 1970s.

### *Defending the Indefensible*

Prashant had criticised the Operation Green Hunt against the Maoist Naxal insurgents in the tribal-dominated areas.

In the Maoist attack in Dantewada in April 2010, 76 policemen were killed. Prashant quite disingenuously sough to deflect the blame on to the government's anti-Naxal operations that led to the retaliation!

Right since the time of the fight for Indian independence the communists-Marxists have always had their heart, and mind too, in the wrong place!!

### *Support for Wrong Causes*

Prashant spoke against the hanging of *Ajmal Kasab*, the captured terrorist in the *2008 Mumbai Terrorist Attack*. Why? He is against death penalty—even in such cases!

Prashant legally assisted the *Narmada Bachao Andolan* (please also see the first chapter) activists opposed to the Sardar Sarovar Dam. Thankfully, the Supreme court ruled to allow the massive project to recommence in October 2000 after massive delays and six years of hearings. The facts and results prove how hugely the project has benefited MP, Gujarat and Maharashtra. Shouldn't those activists, including Prashant, be charged with the crime of causing massive losses, or be publicly disgraced for what they did, or at least take the moral responsibility for their wrong stand that caused huge losses; especially considering their quickness in taking moral high ground in most matters.

Rightly, a criminal petition was filed in the Supreme Court in February 2001 accusing Medha Patkar, Prashant Bhushan and Arundhati Roy of contempt of court for having demonstrated in front of the Supreme Court in protest against the judgement on the Sardar Sarovar Dam. In March 2002, Arundhati Roy was sentenced to one day in jail for contempt of court and for publicly criticising judges in the dam hearings. Prashant had commented that the judges were "just affronted by the fact that somebody has dared to criticise them". Proof of pudding is in the eating. The right judgement of the Supreme Court (though delayed) that led to the completion of the construction of the Sardar Sarovar Dam that led to the prosperity of millions has to be seen against the arrogance of the Marxists-Maoists-Communists-Socialists-Leftists-FiveStarActivists who have, in the final analysis and as per the practical results on the ground, by and large acted against the interests of the nation and the people, and have hence been effectively anti-poor, anti-farmer, anti-peasant, anti-worker, anti-prosperity, anti-development, anti-progress, and are actually effectively pro-poverty, pro-misery, pro-backwardness and pro-wretchedness.

### *Promoting Lies*

Prashant had accused Narendra Modi of being corrupt and a "puppet" of Ambanis. Personally, Narendra Modi is perhaps the most honest politician of India; and he certainly has his own mind—far from being a puppet of anyone. He had also reportedly accused RSS of supporting terror activities. One does not expect such things from an otherwise honest person like Prashant, who is also a person of great integrity. Perhaps, it is politics.

## Sanjay Singh

*A devoted, hard-working founder-member and a prominent leader and trouble-shooter of the AAP.*

Sanjay Singh was born on 22 March 1972 in Sultanpur in Uttar Pradesh.

He did Mining Engineering from Odisha School of Mining Engineering in 1990.

He participated in the project to clean the Gomti River by *Shramdan*. He had protested against the corruption in the Clean Gomati River Project of the UP government. As a social activist, he had campaigned for the rights of street hawkers.

He was involved in Anna Hazare's *Jan Lokpal Movement*, and later became the founder-member of the Aam Aadmi Party. He is a member of the AAP's National Executive (NE) and the Political Affairs Committee (PAC).

## Shanti Bhushan

*The one who was instrumental in deposing Indira Gandhi.*

Shanti Bhushan was born on 11 November 1925 in Allahabad.

### *Family*

He has two daughters and three sons, including Prashant Bhushan.

### *Education*

He studied at Ewing Christian College in Allahabad.

### *Legal Career*

Shanti Bhushan is a very senior advocate of the Supreme Court of India.

Shanti Bhushan represented Raj Narain in the famous case that unseated the then Prime Minister of India Indira Gandhi in 1975, making her declare the infamous Emergency to save her position.

He was a senior counsel for Transparency International in the Provident Fund scandal case of Ghaziabad which allegedly involved several judges.

*Not so commendable cases*: In 1994, he appeared for two of the defendants accused of participating in the *1993 Mumbai Bomb Blasts Case*; in 2002, he appeared for Arundhati Roy in a contempt case against her in the SC; and in 2008, he represented Shaukat Hussain for an appeal against his 10-year conviction for his role in the *2001 Indian Parliament Attack*.

### *Legal Activism*

Shanti Bhushan was the joint-founder of the *Centre for Public Interest Litigation* (CPIL), an NGO that conducts litigation on matters of public interest; and of *Campaign for Judicial Accountability and Judicial Reform* (CJAR). CJAR activism resulted in the provision of declaration of assets by judges.

During a hearing on the contempt of court case for his statement, along with his son, on the corruption in higher judiciary, specifically, the former chief justices of the Supreme Court, Shanti Bhushan was bold enough to state: "*The question of apology does not arise. I am prepared to go to jail.*"

### *Political Career*

Shanti Bhushan was an active member of the Congress(O) that later merged to form the Janata Party in 1977 following the lifting of Emergency. He was a Rajya Sabha member between 1977 and 1980, and was the Union Law Minister in the Morarji Desai ministry during 1977-79. He joined the BJP in 1980, but resigned in 1986.

He took active part in Anna's *Jan Lokpal Movement* during 2011-12; and jointly founded Aam Aadmi Party (AAP) in 2012.

### *Books*

He wrote his autobiography in 2008: "*Courting Destiny: A Memoir*".

## Shazia Ilmi

*A competent and valuable leader, and a popular TV face, the AAP should have had the good sense to retain her.*

Shazia Ilmi was born in 1970 in Kanpur.

### *Family*

Shazia Ilmi's father was the founder-editor of *Siyasat Jadid*, a Kanpur-based newspaper. She is the youngest of four brothers and two sisters. Her sister is married to Arif Mohammed Khan, a former Congress politician and minister. Her husband, Sajid Mallik, is an investment banker. He is half Gujarati-Muslim and half Tamil Iyer.

### Education

Shazia was educated at St Mary's School in Kanpur and Nainital and at St Bede's College in Shimla. She did a degree course in journalism and broadcasting from the *Jamia Millia Islamia* and the *University of Wales*. She also did a *Diploma in 16mm Film Production* at New York Film Academy.

### Career in Journalism

She has been a television journalist and an anchor at *Star News*, where she hosted and produced a popular prime time news show *Desh Videsh*. She has also worked on documentary production.

### Jan Lokpal Movement

She was closely associated with Anna Hazare's *India Against Corruption* (IAC) *Movement* for Jan Lokpal; and was its spokesperson.

### Political Career

She was a founder-member of the Aam Aadmi Party, and was part of its National Executive.

When the AAP contested the Delhi Legislative Assembly elections for the first time on 4 December 2013 winning 28 seats, Shazia contested from the Rama Krishna Puram constituency, but lost narrowly by mere 326 votes. Her brother Rashid Ilmi had also fought the election from the same constituency, but he too had lost. Had he not fought, Shazia might have won.

She contested the 2014 Lok Sabha elections from Ghaziabad on the AAP ticket but lost to Gen. V.K. Singh of the BJP. Unhappy with the AAP's leadership for lack of intra-party democracy, she resigned from the AAP on 24 May 2014. She joined the BJP in January 2015, a few weeks before the 2015 Delhi Assembly elections.

## Yogendra Yadav

*A mega establishment-beneficiary out to project anti-establishment image; an over-courteous Uriah Heep with ambitions racing far ahead of talent, work and sacrifice; an articulator of stale, failed ideas and socialistic claptrap booted out from the alternate political arena of the AAP, now propagating yet another alternative to that alternate politics—in short, a unique humbug with hypocrisy unlimited!*

Yogendra Yadav was born on 5 September 1963.

### *Family*

Yogendra Yadav's father is a retired professor of economics, and his wife, Madhulika Banerjee, is an associate professor at the University of Delhi.

### *Professional Career*

He received the Malcolm Adiseshiah Award for Development Studies in 2008; and the Global South Solidarity Award by The International Political Science Association in recognition of outstanding work on the politics of the developing world in 2009.

Yadav was a professor of Political science at Punjab University, Chandigarh during 1985-1993. He was the founder-convenor of the Lokniti network during 1995-2002; and was the founder-director of the *Centre for the Study of Developing Societies* (CSDS) Lokniti research programme on comparative democracy during 1997-2003.

Since 2004 he has been a Senior Fellow at the *Centre for the Study of Developing Societies* (CSDS). He was a member of the *University Grants Commission* (UGC) and the *National Advisory Council* (NAC) on the *Right to Education Act* (RTE) appointed by the UPA government.

He has been a member of the Governing Council of the *Indian Council of Social Science Research* and of the Governing Board of the *Indian Institute of Advanced Study*, Shimla; and an Honorary Fellow, *Indian Institute of Political Economy*, Pune.

He was also a member of the Expert Group appointed by the Government of India in 2007 to examine the structure and functioning of an *Equal Opportunity Commission*. Prof. Yadav was a visiting Fellow at the Wissenschaftskolleg Zu Berlin (Institute for Advanced Study at Berlin) for a year in 2009-10.

He has also been a psephologist. He has appeared on many TV channels as a political commentator.

### Publications

He has authored/edited a number of books and articles on democracy and elections, and political and social science. He co-authored *State of Democracy in South Asia* in 2008; *Electoral Politics in Indian States* in 2009; *Democracy in Multi-national Societies* in 2010. He was joint Chief Advisor of the NCERT publication of 2006: *Democratic Politics*-1 & 2. He has co-authored/co-edited works in Hindi on social sciences.

He was the Joint Chief Advisor for the *National Council of Educational Research and Training* (NCERT) for writing of the new textbooks for Political Science for class IX, X, XI and XII.

### Political Career

It is said that he was one of the advisors to Rahul Gandhi for the 2009 elections.

He was a member of AAP's National Executive (NE) and Political Affairs Committee (PAC), but was removed from both the positions in March 2015.

He had contested from the Gurgaon Lok Sabha constituency in 2014. He came fourth and lost his deposit.

### The Seamier Side

*Politics is the art of looking for trouble, finding it everywhere, diagnosing it incorrectly and applying the wrong remedies.*

—Groucho Marx

There are many academicians far more competent than Yadav, but they are not into so many government bodies as Yadav has been. The "anti-establishment" Yadav has been a member of dozens of establishment bodies and government committees. What's the secret?

Nobody knows better that the Nehruvian academicians, leftists and socialists which side the bread is buttered. His over-courteous mannerisms and demeanour that would put Dale Carnegie to shame, and his slow, measured delivery, heavy with "wisdom"-laden words give his pretensions away.

> *Not long ago when Yogendra Yadav was one of Rahul Gandhi's political advisors Yadav told me RG brighter & astute than any other politician.*
>
> —Tweet of Madhu Kishwar; 10:59 P.M., 17 Dec. 2012

That Yadav was in NAC and had cozied up to Rahul Gandhi as an advisor reveals the true story of this "anti-establishment" figure out to reform the society and polity of this country. What he actually does is a far cry from what he pretentiously professes. Yadav left no stone unturned to say things that would please the then power that be, namely the Gandhis and the UPA. True to being a loyal courtier, he was one of the first persons to have signed a petition to the US authorities to cancel the US visa of Modi in 2005, after the UPA assumed power. He had reportedly stated that if Narendra Modi comes to power "*...aag lag jayegi*". On Modi's victory, he commented: "*Modi victory symbolises the dark side of democracy and goes against* ***Idea of India***." The idea of these "*Idea of India*"-wallas has been how to benefit personally by saying the "right" things.

True to his grandiloquent style he had proclaimed: "*We are not an anti-BJP or anti-Congress party but an anti-political establishment party.... Ours is a politics of alternatives....*" His is indeed the alternative politics of how quickly to rise up the power ladder sacrificing as little as possible, retaining all that he got during his pro-establishment UPA days. Yadav has a knack of running with the hares and hunting with the hounds.

Earlier, he had been with the foreign-funded NGOs and the so-called "people's movements" like the *World Social Forum* (WSF) and Medha Patkar's *Narmada Bachao Andolan* (please also see the first chapter, and the profile of Prashant Bhushan) that had the potential to quickly bring you into the limelight, no matter if what they did effectively damaged the country.

Yogendra and Prashant, along with Medha Patkar, Arundhati Roy, Aruna Roy, are active members of the five-star, jet-setting Anti-Globalisation Brigades (AGBs), well-funded by the western-donor agencies, whose job is to tarnish, decry and delegitimize all necessary steps of economic liberalisation and development that alone can pull India out of the perennial poverty and misery the socialist policies have condemned it into, by tagging them as anti-poor, pro-capitalist and pro-multinationals. These people suffer from very poor self-appreciation. If they analysed the effect of their actions they would realise that it is they who are the most anti-poor, anti-progress, anti-development, and pro-foreign powers and pro-western-donor agencies who want to let India remain backward and dependent.

The AAP had come up as a principled party that was above all divisive agenda, including caste and religion. That's why it had become popular among all groups in a short time. Yogendra Yadav tried to contaminate the AAP with his casteist Lohiaite worldview. Not only that, he started promoting the stale "secular" partisan agenda that began to make it indistinguishable from the Congress, SP, RJD, TMC, and such parties. His nonsensical views on the resettlement of the Kashmiri Pandits in the Kashmir valley are now public. Could the AAP have continued to associate with such people?

While one might sympathise with Yogendra Yadav for his unceremonious booting out from the top positions in the AAP, one might perhaps ponder over his insidious role in easing out the original stalwarts of the IAC that morphed into the AAP: persons such as Baba Ramdev, Sri Sri Ravi Shankar, Kiran Bedi, Madhu Bhaduri and Anna Hazare.

Although Yogendra Yadav was removed for his anti-party activities, and with reasonable factual proof, he, as expected, tried to give it a spin: that it was his principled opposition that led to his removal.

* * * * *